Southern Literary Studies

Southern Literary Studies

LOUIS D. RUBIN, JR., EDITOR

Building Poe Biography

EDGAR ALLAN POE, ABOUT 1848
The "Stella" Daguerreotype

Poe gave this daguerreotype to Mrs. Stella Lewis in 1848. At her
death in 1880, she willed it to John Henry Ingram. It is now Item 477
in the Ingram Poe Collection in the University of Virginia Library.

Building
POE
Biography

JOHN CARL MILLER

Louisiana State University Press
BATON ROUGE *and* LONDON

Copyright © 1977 by Louisiana State University Press
Manufactured in the United States of America

Designer: Dwight Agner
Type faces: VIP Fairfield Medium and Aster
Typesetter: Graphic World, Inc., St. Louis, Missouri
Printer and binder: Kingsport Press, Kingsport, Tennessee

LIBRARY OF CONGRESS CATALOGING IN PUBLICATION DATA

Miller, John Carl.
    Building Poe biography.

    (Southern literary studies)
    Bibliography: p.
    Includes index.
    1. Poe, Edgar Allan, 1809–1849—Biography—Sources.
2. Ingram, John Henry, 1842–1916. 3. Authors, Ameri-
can—19th century—Biography. 4. Biographers—England—
Correspondence. I. Title
PS2630.5.M5   818'.3'09 [B]   76–47653
ISBN 0–8071–0195–8

To my daughter and son,
Martha Marie and John Christopher

ULYSSES.   Time hath, my lord, a wallet at his back,
Wherein he puts alms for Oblivion,
A great-siz'd monster of ingratitudes.
Those scraps are good deeds past, which are devour'd
As fast as they are made, forgot as soon
As done. Perseverance, dear my lord,
Keeps honour bright; to have done is to hang
Quite out of fashion. . . . Take the instant way;
For honour travels in a strait so narrow,
Where one but goes abreast. Keep then the path;

.   .   .   .

One touch of nature makes the whole world kin,
That all, with one consent, praise new-born gawds,
Though they are made and moulded of things past,
And give to dust that is a little gilt
More laud than gilt o'er dusted.

                          Shakespeare's *Troilus and Cressida*
                          Act III, scene iii

Contents

Illustrations

.

Preface

POE BIOGRAPHY, as it has been known, was built almost single-handedly by the Englishman John Henry Ingram. Even though he was never able to visit the United States, Ingram worked in England, collecting and publishing materials about Poe's life, character, and literary career, from the late 1860s until 1916, the year he died. His efforts and publications not only laid the foundations for Poe biography but they also erected most of the superstructure, for every biographical account of Poe that has been published from 1874 to this date owes most of its contents to Ingram's discoveries and publications about Poe.

Ingram's devotion to the memory of Poe and to his work on Poe biography is literally without parallel in the annals of biography. At times he worked carefully and painstakingly; at other times he behaved ferociously even to many of the persons who were sending him almost daily new materials about Poe. By nature Ingram was both irascible and volatile, and he often worked under strong emotional pressures. Moreover, he was badly handicapped by his strong predetermined notions of what Poe had really been like and what his biographer should reveal and what he should keep hidden; therefore, if materials reached Ingram which did not fit his preconceived ideas about Poe, he was perfectly capable of slanting them to fit, or of disregarding them altogether.

John Ingram's collection of Poe materials in the University of Virginia Library contains more than one thousand letters, manuscripts, documents, photographs, and newsclippings—primary source materials sent to Ingram by various persons in response to his persistent inquiries and widespread, fervent appeals for help in writing his biographies of Poe. The wealth in these materials is by no means depleted, for most of the letters and manuscripts reproduced here are published for the first time. Those partially published by Ingram were usually so garbled by him that succeeding biographers were misled, since Ingram never allowed anyone to see his materials in toto. Most of his materials had been gathered by 1878 and they remained in his keeping until his death in 1916, after which they were purchased by the University of Virginia in 1921, where, after a while, only a very few carefully selected students and Poe biographers were permitted access to them until they were put on microfilm in 1967.

The purpose of this volume is to present with editorial commentary these letters which are among the more important primary source materials Ingram used to build his biographies of Poe. Because Ingram seldom reproduced a letter or document or manuscript exactly as he received it, this provides that the many persons interested in Poe scholarship, especially future biographers, have available the foundation stones Ingram used, as he received them from persons who had been very close to Poe: his aunt and mother-in-law, Maria Poe Clemm; his sister Rosalie; Mrs. Marie Louise Shew Houghton;* and Annie Richmond.* William Hand Browne* of Johns Hopkins University and George W. Eveleth,* whose correspondence with Ingram is presented here, are among the few represented who did not know Poe personally. At the end of this volume there are bibliographies of Ingram's many books and magazine and newspaper articles about Poe and other subjects. This is the first time anyone has ever compiled bibliographies of the almost incredible number of books and articles written by this energetic Englishman.

Volumes Two and Three are expected to follow, containing the large unpublished correspondence that passed between Ingram and Sarah Helen Whitman of Providence, Rhode Island, beginning in 1873 and ending at her death in 1878, as well as important articles about Poe and his works that Ingram wrote and published during the 1870s in magazines that are now almost inaccessible. Volume Four will pick up with Ingram's struggles, achievements, and defeats, from 1880 through 1916, when he attempted to claim and hold an indefensible position as the sole arbiter of all things concerning Poe. Many of these situations were brought about, ironically, because Ingram had succeeded in amassing the largest and most valuable collection of primary source materials for Poe biography that anyone had ever owned.

As readers watch Poe biography slowly taking shape in these pages that follow, it is important that they keep in mind that I have faithfully reproduced the contents of the holographs or copies exactly as they were sent to or made for Ingram, not as he quoted from them, directly or indirectly, in his many publications. When ellipses marks indicate omissions, they are either Ingram's or his correspondents', unless they are enclosed in brackets. Editorial comment within the letters is contained in single brackets, except in the notable case of the copies of letters sent by George W. Eveleth, who enclosed his own comments in brackets; in these letters alone editorial comment is enclosed in double brackets.

Faulty spelling, punctuation, capitalization, and other grammatical errors, as well as paragraph structure, have been allowed to stand when in my opinion they were integral to the reader's comprehension of the writers' levels of education, emotional states, or personalities. When they grew monotonous or bordered on caricature after many repetitions, I silently corrected them, but at no time did I make any substantive changes in the texts; for I believe the contents of these letters and documents to be more important to Poe students and scholars than their individual writers' slips in composition. Handwritten documents are perforce subject to interpretation, but every effort has been made to transcribe these as closely as possible, with allowance for conceding the writers the benefit of the doubt. In any cases where reproduced errors might mislead readers or be attributed to editorial carelessness, they have been indicated by *sic*. I have not attempted to reproduce in any of these letters the varieties of spacings used in the headings, salutations, and paragraph indentions, but in many cases spacing had to be used as a sort of punctuation, following the word spacing of the manuscripts.

Letters are grouped and numbered in sequence. Following the number of each letter the names of the writer and addressee are given, with addresses. After the names, I give the form in which Ingram received some letters, if they were copied for him and by whom, or if he copied excerpts and returned the holograph to its owner; otherwise, readers can assume that all letters and documents are reproduced by me from the originals. Then I state whether I know or believe the letter to be unpublished or published only in part. The numbers in brackets that follow refer to the number of the item in the Ingram Poe Collection in the University of Virginia Library and in my book *Ingram's Poe Collection*, published by the University of Virginia Press in 1960.

After each letter, the first paragraph of editorial commentary deals with the relation the letter has to Poe biography, the use Ingram made of it in his volumes and/or articles, or whether he chose to ignore it. The second paragraph of editorial commentary identifies the persons, places, and situations mentioned. In order to avoid repetition, many of these names are identified in the Appendix, as indicated by asterisks following the first mention.

My gratitude for being able to work with the Ingram Poe Collection actually begins with librarian John S. Patton, who was partially responsible for bringing Ingram's papers to the Alderman Library, and it continues down the list of his successors: the courtly Harry Clemons, the learned Jack Dalton, the brilliant John Cook Wyllie, and the present librarian, Ray W. Frantz, Jr. The unfailing courtesies of the curators of rare books and manuscripts, Messrs. William Runge, Francis L. Berkeley, Jr., Edmund Berkeley, Jr., and Miss Anne Freudenberg, and the ever-efficient help of their staffs, especially Messrs. Michael Plunkett and Gregory Johnson, are deeply appreciated.

I acknowledge with pleasure, too, the invaluable help given me in preparing this manuscript for the press by Mitchell Summerlin, graduate student in English at Old Dominion University, and by Dean Wadsworth, both my former students.

The gentle shade of James Southall Wilson has brooded over me and this work for a very long time, as has the seemingly acrimonious one of Armistead Churchill Gordon, Jr. Whatever the errors here, I cannot feel that these professor-mentors and friends would withhold all approval.

Acknowledgments and appreciations are due and extended to the Research Councils of Bridgewater College and the University of South Alabama for grants-in-aid which made summer traveling and research possible. Most especially am I indebted to the Research and Publications Committee and to the Research Foundation of Old Dominion University for the summer grant that freed me to complete this book.

All of the materials reproduced in this book are from the Ingram Poe Collection in the University of Virginia library except two of Maria Clemm's letters, the originals of which are in the Poe Collection at the Josiah K. Lilly Library, Indiana University, Bloomington, Indiana, and are so acknowledged in their headings. I am very grateful indeed to Saundra Taylor, curator of manuscripts, for allowing me to print these revealing letters.

Rosalie Poe's letters and some of the material in Chapter III herein appeared first in my article "Poe's Sister Rosalie," printed in *Tennessee Studies in Literature*, VIII, 1963, 107–117, edited by Richard Beale Davis, and are here reprinted by permission of the University of Tennessee Press, copyright © 1963 by the University of Tennessee Press, Knoxville.

John C. Miller

Old Dominion University
November, 1976

Building Poe Biography

I
Poe's English Biographer

JOHN HENRY INGRAM was a product of lower middle-class English society. He was born on November 16, 1842, at 29 City Road, Finnsbury, Middlesex, and he grew up in Stoke Newington, the London suburb where young Edgar Poe had lived and gone to school, a fact always construed by Ingram to be a tangible link between his life and Poe's. As a child, Ingram read Poe's poems and tales many times over, and his early fascination with Poe's writings developed into a feeling of mystic rapport with the personality of the dead Poe; and from that feeling grew Ingram's determination to cleanse Poe's name and reputation of the scurrilous allegations Rufus W. Griswold had made against them in the obituary and *Memoir* of Poe he had published shortly after the poet's death. At this point, Ingram had no more to go on than an intense instinctive feeling that Griswold had lied about Poe.

Educated in youth by private tutors and in private schools, Ingram entered the City of London College when he was eighteen, but his college career was cut short by his father's death and he had to withdraw and find employment to support himself, his mother, and two sisters. On January 13, 1868, he received a commission in the Civil Service, with an appointment to a clerkship in the savings bank department of the London General Post Office. By this time he had served a literary apprenticeship of sorts, which will be described later, and having done so, he was ready to turn to his life's work: finding out everything possible about Edgar Poe and writing a biography of him that would be both redemptive of Poe's name and reputation and would also be recognized everywhere as definitive.

Ingram began by searching out Poe's friends in America, and when they gave him names of other persons who had known and been friendly to Poe, he immediately wrote strongly worded, persuasive appeals to them. The letter that follows is quite characteristic. It was sent to George W. Eveleth, whose name had been relayed to Ingram by Sarah Helen Whitman. Eveleth had corresponded with Poe during the last few years of his life, and, though they never met, Eveleth's deep interest in Poe and in all efforts to defend him never flagged. Eveleth forwarded Ingram's letter to William Hand Browne, who was, in addition to being a professor of English literature at Johns Hopkins University, also the editor of the *Southern Magazine*, and Eveleth added an appeal of his own to Ingram's for help in finding trustworthy materials about Poe. Browne not only published the two requests in "The Green Table" section of his magazine for October, 1874, but added still another request of his own for all who could to help.

> England, London
> General Post-Office
> Engineer-In-Chief's Office
> 10th March 1874

Dear Sir:

Your name has been given me as that of a gentleman able and willing to assist me in my researches into the life of E. A. Poe. The enclosed cutting will give you some idea of how I am going to work; but it necessarily represents but a very small portion of my discoveries. Assisted by American correspondents, I am able to refute nearly every one of Griswold's filthy lies. To disgust Poe's friends, he seems to have stopped at nothing.

In the biography which I am writing, I of course utterly discard all Griswold's "Memoir." I have correlated many dates, and have already obtained much correspondence, but shall be very thankful still for the slightest scrap of information, or any *reminiscence* of Poe or of his family. I am told that you are a Marylander; you may, therefore, know something of the family. He is stated to have been engaged to a Southern lady of fortune, after his engagement with Mrs. Whitman was broken off—do you know her name, or anything of the circumstances? Do you know who "Helen S———" was?—said to have been mother of a school-fellow of Poe while he was at the Richmond Academy. Do you know *anything* whatever of Poe's brother, Wm. Henry L.—what he was, etc.? Can you procure me copies of what John Neal and Geo. R. Graham wrote about Griswold's character of Poe? I would willingly pay for them, or for any copies of letters written by Poe, or anything useful about him. Can you give me a few lines of reminiscence? I believe you knew him personally. Can you refer me to any one in Baltimore, or in Richmond, Virginia, who knew him, or anything about him? The *slightest* information or clue will be acceptable.

His sister Rosalie is alive, but old and very poor. I am raising a sum of money for her. I am afraid *she* is not able to give me much reliable information.

I shall be glad to purchase any paper or publication containing anything not included in the 4 vol. collection of his works (New York, Widdleton, 1864). Anything he wrote before 1834 would be acceptable, or *any* information as to *where he was* and *what he did* between March, 1831, and the autumn of 1833.

In hopes of your kindly aid toward furnishing the world with the true story of this great man's life,

I remain yours truly,
John H. Ingram
F. R. His. Society

This letter contains, in brief, a summary of Ingram's personality and his approach to Poe biography: it is abruptly to the point, perfunctorily and somewhat brusquely courteous, slightly pompous, but obviously sincere and forceful.

This kind of plea was most effective. William Hand Browne became Ingram's loyal and valuable ally from the time of its receipt, and as a result of his printing it in the *Southern Magazine* a number of correspondents unknown to either Browne or Ingram responded very quickly. It took Eveleth four years to answer the letter, but when he did answer he enclosed forty-four closely copied pages, on both sides of thin paper, containing copies of six of the seven letters he had received from Poe (later, he added the seventh), and copies of many other letters he had received from persons who had known Poe. All of these letters are reproduced in Chapter VII.

In accord with this response, Ingram shaped his life into a pattern of work and study and writing and answering letters, and he followed that pattern doggedly for his remaining forty-eight years. He spent almost every waking hour away from his Civil Service job in searching out new facts for his proposed biography of Poe; he read indefatigably and he wrote letters to hundreds of persons in England, France, America, and Ireland who had known Poe or who were interested in him and who could possibly help him write a true account of Poe's life. As he grew surer of himself and his materials, he began to write and publish articles revealing the discoveries he had made, the "new facts" he had brought to light. (See Bibliography I for a list of these articles.)

Ingram's master stroke in collecting Poe materials was in getting to know, either personally or through frequent letters, a number of the women who had known Poe better, perhaps, than had anyone else. He discovered that Stella Lewis* and Mary Gove Nichols* had moved from America to London, and he sought them out. He wrote to Sarah Helen

Whitman, Annie Richmond, and Marie Louise Shew Houghton in America and told them at length of his own passionate loyalty to Poe's memory and of his plans to restore Poe's good reputation. Without fail, these letters evoked, almost inexplicably, these ladies' immediate and militant devotion to his work and to him personally. They either gave or sent to him Poe's autograph letters or copies of them, first editions of Poe's books, magazine articles by and about Poe, and newspaper clippings; they wrote out at great length their recollections for Ingram's use; and some even gave or sent to him many precious keepsakes that Poe had given to them himself.

With this kind of support, Ingram brought to his biographical work on Poe an unprecedented power and passion that have not since been approximated, and perhaps desirably so. Measured by modern standards, Ingram was not a good scholar; he was emotionally involved with his subject, to the point that he would deliberately suppress testimonies that were as valid as were many he printed, if they showed Poe to be petty or spiteful, as Poe sometimes was. He grew unreasonably possessive about his subject, resenting anyone else who tried to write about Poe, especially if that person were an American. As his collection of Poe materials grew, his publications increased in number and value, giving him an enviable reputation as a Poe scholar. It was at this point that he began attacking in print, sometimes sarcastically, sometimes more viciously, almost every article and book printed about Poe, accusing each author of having stolen materials from his own previous publications, which circumstance was in many cases actually true. Ingram had still to learn that he could not copyright facts.

With all of these serious faults, John Ingram made indelible marks in early Poe scholarship: he edited and published the first reliable four-volume edition of Poe's works since Griswold's in 1850; he prefaced that edition with a memoir of his own that had in it much new and important information; in 1880, he brought out a two-volume biography of Poe that contained much of its new information from the letters in this volume and which is still indispensable to any serious study of Poe. In addition to these important pioneering efforts, he edited and published eight separate editions of Poe's tales, essays, and poems, and he wrote and published nearly fifty articles on Poe affairs in the most important periodicals of the day.

Ingram achieved a truly remarkable number of Poe "firsts." It was he who first openly called Griswold a liar and a forger—and proved both charges. It was he who, as late as 1874, settled once and for all the true date of Poe's birth. It was Ingram who discovered the first known volume of Poe's *Tamerlane*, in the British Museum Library in 1876; and with this priceless find, it was Ingram who was able to assemble for the first time all four of Poe's voiumes of poems and write the first bibliographical description of them. Then too, it was Ingram who was able to "discover" that Poe had written "The Journal of Julius Rodman" and add it to the Poe canon. Finally, it was Ingram to whom more Poe autograph letters were entrusted than to any other Poe biographer.

Ingram's edition of Poe's works, his two-volume biography, and his separate editions of the poems, tales, and critical essays were widely circulated and of course went through many editions for at least twenty or more years, and some of them are still actually available in second-hand bookstores. His discoveries about Poe were immediately copied and republished by other writers, more often than not without acknowledgment, which served to embitter Ingram for the rest of his life. The writers and editors who copied Ingram's published facts and Poe letters did not attempt to check either the accuracy or validity of his sources or his editorial methods, and their own publications have been recopied ever since, with minor variations designed to ward off possible copyright infringement lawsuits. Thus, Ingram's approaches to biography and his editorial practices have established facts and created attitudes, even myths, for much that has never been questioned in Poe biography. Many of these facts, attitudes, and myths should be questioned, as this volume will show.

During his lifetime John Ingram would never have permitted any rival Poe biographer to examine his entire collection of source materials, even though now and again he made halfhearted offers to a very few persons to share with them. But Ingram has been dead for more than sixty years and his collection of papers about Poe has been in the Manuscript Department of the University of Virginia Library for more than fifty. The author of that much-desired and still-to-be-written definitive biography of Poe will have to examine all of this collection closely indeed.

In this volume, and in the volumes to come, Ingram and his correspondents at last speak out. They all have much to say, and they speak joyfully, or angrily, or sorrowfully, each according to his bent and his reaction to Edgar Poe. Sometimes it is apparent that they are revealing more than they are aware, but they always speak with emotion, for none was indifferent to Poe, and each deserves to be heard.

Remarkably enough, Ingram interspersed his writings on Poe—especially after 1880, when he thought his work on Poe was done—with numerous magazine articles about other persons and subjects, and he wrote and published at least five other volumes of biography, including lives of Oliver Mádox-Brown, Elizabeth Barrett Browning, Robert Burns, Christopher Marlowe, and Thomas Chatterton. It is wryly true, and perhaps has significance of a sort, that almost without exception Ingram chose for biographical treatment an author who had in some way been associated with Poe, or who had been a child-prodigy poet, who had died at an early age and left a reputation that needed to be redeemed from slander.

Ingram was retired in 1903 after thirty-five years spent at his job in the English Civil Service, but he remained living in London for another nine years. As Poe's centenary year drew close, he became especially active. He prepared most of the materials included in the London *Bookman's* memorial edition for Poe in January, 1909, and he edited and published still another edition of Poe's poems to be brought out that year. Moreover, he answered every request from numerous other British and American magazines with contributions to their sections honoring Poe's hundredth birthday. These numerous calls on him certainly were satisfying, and he must have been very happy as he answered them.

When the centenary celebrations were over, Ingram began writing steadily on his last biography of Poe. He believed that he alone controlled all of the important materials about Poe's life, and now that all of his correspondents who had sent him personal information were dead, he felt free to use the materials in his files in any way he chose. And so he set to work, believing that his last biography, to be called "The True Story of Edgar Allan Poe," would establish forever his reputation as the final authority on Poe.

In 1912, with his sister Laura, he moved his household from London to Brighton, where he so much enjoyed the sea bathing, and he continued work on his last biography of Poe. And there, four years later, after finishing his work, he died, on February 12, 1916. For various reasons, among them the disruption of printing caused by World War I, this last biography remained unpublished.

Immediately after her brother's death, Laura Ingram put her brother's various biographical collections up for sale; but it was not until late 1921 that the two huge packing cases containing John Ingram's Poe collection actually reached the University of Virginia Library. The rich materials were examined by the young professor just come from William and Mary and who was to become a great Poe specialist, as well as the Edgar Allan Poe Professor of American Literature in the university, James Southall Wilson. An agreement in price was reached and the sum paid, and for years thereafter Miss Ingram continued to send to the university library package after package of things overlooked that really belonged in her brother's Poe collection. Finally, in the 1930s, feeling that her death was close, she sent as a final gift the manuscript of his last unpublished biography of Poe. [1]

Even had this manuscript reached publication, it would not have given John Ingram the position he coveted. It contains little that is really new and important and its whole tone is one of unrelenting bitterness aimed at Poe's detractors and Ingram's rival American Poe biographers. At the last, Ingram's spleen had completely overridden his editorial and critical judgments. The manuscript is interesting to the Poe student, but it is not a definitive biography of Edgar Poe.

Ingram's abilities to ferret out facts, to work long, hard hours, coupled with a reasonable amount of luck and an inordinate amount of love for his subject, have made for him a unique and undeniable place of importance among all Poe biographers. But this would not have been enough for John Ingram.

Actually, his unparalleled contributions to Poe biography resulted from his fortunate timing in reaching Poe's closest friends before they died and succeeding in garnering from them most of their memories and keepsakes and materials about Poe. By maneuvering when he did, he was able to amass and partially use a collection of Poe source materials that has been the puzzle and envy of Poe scholars everywhere for over a century.

This volume, with its many reproduced autograph letters and with its commentaries, is designed to show how John Ingram built Poe biography, and to remove some of the puzzles.

Apprenticeship

As a youth John Ingram wrote bushels of verses, as he termed them, which were rejected without exception until he learned the mysteries of

---

1. This entire collection of Ingram's Poe papers has been catalogued in book form: John Carl Miller, *John Henry Ingram's Poe Collection at the University of Virginia* (Charlottesville: University of Virginia Press, 1960).

metrical lines; after that he published a great many of them in cheap magazines in London. By 1863 he gathered about one hundred of these verses and published them in a little book, using a nom de plume, as *Poems by Dalton Stone*. Obviously he had learned something about scansion, for one of the poems in this volume was written professedly in the meter Edgar Poe had used in his "Ulalume." This poem, called "Hope: An Allegory," was reprinted in Walter Hamilton's *Parodies* (London: Reeves and Turner, 1885), II, 66, with the following explanation: "This imitation of 'Ulalume' written by Mr. John H. Ingram, was published in 1863, when its author was in his teens. The little volume which contained it, entitled 'Poems by Dalton Stone,' has been suppressed, and is now very scarce."

Ingram was not in his teens; he was actually twenty-one years old when he published this little volume. By this time, apparently, he had already decided to alter his birth date from November 16, 1842, to November 16, 1849, to coincide with Poe's death year. The date 1849 is still carried by standard reference books, in error, as his birth year. [2]

Ingram was educated in private schools and by private tutors until he entered first Lyonsdown and then the City of London College. In 1867, when he was twenty-five years old, he was a fellow of the Royal Historical Society; he spoke and wrote, in addition to his own language, French, German, Spanish, and Italian; and later he added a working knowledge of Portuguese and Hungarian. He contributed articles on literary and historical subjects to leading reviews in England, France, and America, and he was a frequent lecturer on contemporary literature in London.

But John Ingram was no poet, as even he had to realize, and by 1864 he had bid adieu to the dearest hope of his life—that of becoming a great poet. Actually, he continued to write rather bad verse intermittently until as late as 1912.

Having published and suppressed his first volume of verse, Ingram then turned to a more ambitious publication, a book on flowers, *Flora Symbolica: Or the Language and Sentiment of Flowers*. This history of floriography examines the meanings and symbolisms of more than one hundred separate flowers, garlands, and bouquets; there are long essays on each flower, and the volume is elaborately gotten up with great detail, clearly printed, and beautifully illustrated in many colors.

2. See my article "The Birthdate of John Henry Ingram," *Poe Studies*, VII (June, 1974), 24.

Ingram's methods as an author and compiler are clear in this volume: he has ransacked every previous publication on flowers, and sifted, condensed, and augmented whatever his predecessors have had to say on each subject. He tells his readers bluntly, "Although I dare not boast that I have exhausted the subject, I may certainly affirm that followers will find little left to glean in the paths that I have traversed." He was probably right.

The significance of the 1868 publication is that Ingram's methods and habits of bookmaking were exercised and found good, by him at least, before he began his important work on Poe biography; for he altered his procedures scarcely at all, no matter what his subject was, in the next forty-eight years. Such was John Ingram's cast of mind, such was his training, when he began the great task of his life, that of destroying Griswold's *Memoir* of Poe and replacing it with a vindicatory one of his own.

The Case Against Poe

By 1870 there was a growing interest on both sides of the Atlantic in Poe's genius. The power and beauty of Poe's writings, available only in Griswold's edition, caused enough interest to call out a number of editions and to produce varied reactions to the discrepancy between Poe's personal character, as Griswold had pictured it, and the purity of Poe's artistic achievements. Griswold's *Memoir* was generally accepted as regrettable but true, for its position prefacing the authorized edition of Poe's works gave it final authority. A number of "complete" editions of Poe's writings had appeared in Europe and America, but none of these had added any poems to the Poe canon established by Griswold, and no new tales or essays were discovered and printed. In Europe, no biographical account of Poe was published, sympathetic or hostile, that was not based on Griswold's.

Griswold had said, both in the obituary of Poe he had published in the New York *Tribune* on October 9, 1849 (the infamous "Ludwig Article,") and in his *Memoir* prefacing his 1850 edition of Poe's works,[3] that Poe did possess great powers of imagination, but that as a man he had few or no friends and that his harsh experiences in life had deprived him of all faith in humanity. Then Griswold had quoted, in the *Tribune*

---

3. The *Memoir* was originally placed as a preface to the third volume but was later moved in succeeding editions to the first volume, where it remained.

obituary, almost verbatim, an ugly paragraph taken from Bulwer-Lytton's novel *The Caxtons*, which describes Francis Vivian as being "without moral susceptibility and having within himself little or nothing of the true point of honor." By quoting these terrible judgments in Poe's obituary, Griswold intended to imply that they were applicable to Poe's personality. Even worse, when Griswold reprinted the same paragraph in his *Memoir* of Poe, he omitted the quotation marks. Thus, Bulwer-Lytton's damnation of his fictional character was read and accepted as Griswold's own judgment of Poe, and incalculable damage was done to Poe's reputation.

In addition to this, Griswold's *Memoir* was even more savage and bitterly denunciatory, repeating the old charges of Poe's arrogance, envy, misanthropy, and debased sense of honor, and adding a list of new charges:

That while Poe was a student at the University of Virginia he had "led a very dissipated life," and that he had been expelled in consequence of his excesses there.

That after leaving West Point, Poe had enlisted in the United States Army, but had presumably deserted.

That he had been guilty of a still darker crime in his relations with the second Mrs. Allan.

That in certain of his publications—among them his *The Conchologist's First Book*—he had been guilty of plagiarisms that were "scarcely paralleled for their audacity in all literary history."

That his "unsupported assertions and opinions were so apt to be influenced by friendship or enmity . . . that they should be received in all cases with distrust of their fairness."

That Poe exhibited "scarcely any virtue in either his life or his writings," and that both his life and his writings were without "a recognition or a manifestation of conscience." [4]

The Case for Poe

Evert Duyckinck, editor of the New York *Literary World*, was the first to voice a suspicion about the validity of Griswold's *Memoir* of Poe by

---

4. These condensations of Griswold's major charges against Poe are taken largely from Killis Campbell's *The Mind of Poe and Other Studies* (Cambridge: Harvard University Press, 1933), 76–77.

inquiring whether Griswold, in publishing Poe's "Literati" papers had not tampered with the text.[5]

Mrs. Clemm was much distressed and very indignant over the *Memoir*. Heretofore, she had praised Griswold for his "labor of love," but now and forever after, she was to refer to him as "that villain." But she could not escape the facts that she had made Griswold Poe's literary executor and had turned over to him all of Poe's papers, expecting, of course, to receive in return thousands of dollars from the sales of her beloved Eddie's writings.

George Graham* wrote to Mrs. Clemm to remain quiet, that he had a "host of Poe's friends prepared to do him justice," and that he intended to devote nearly half of the December number of his magazine to the memory and defense of Poe. But Graham was not ready with his defense of Poe in December of that year of 1850, and actually did not publish it until February of 1854; but when it finally did appear, it was a long, detailed, well-documented article which refuted several of Griswold's charges against Poe with undeniable evidence.

Three years later, in November, 1857, James Wood Davidson,* editor of the Columbia, South Carolina, *Register*, published a strong defense of Poe's character in *Russell's Magazine*. Also John Neal* of Portland, Maine, published a strong dissent against Griswold's estimate of Poe. N. P. Willis* republished in 1851, in his *Hurrygraphs*, a reply he had made to Griswold's obituary of Poe. He also republished in the *Home Journal* for March 16, 1850, Graham's first article on Poe, which was the sole instance of anyone republishing anything in Poe's defense.

These protests and defenses were sincerely and earnestly meant to vindicate Poe's name from Griswold's calumnies, but the forms in which they were presented to the reading public defeated their ends. They reflected honest indignation and were even passionate at times, but they were not sustained and were shortly forgotten; furthermore, none of them attempted to come to grips with the whole problem. Twenty-five years after he had published his fiery denunciation of Griswold, John Neal did not have a copy of it, nor could he remember what he had said in it, or even in what year it was published. Seventeen years after his publication, James Wood Davidson, after a long search, did manage to find a copy of his article in defense of Poe to send to John Ingram. But George Graham's articles, the most important defenses of Poe published by anyone, had, in twenty years, disappeared so com-

---

5. In the Boston *Literary World*, September 21, 1850, pp. 228–29.

pletely that it took the able and energetic Sarah Helen Whitman four months to locate them and make copies by hand for Ingram.

Such was the state of Poe biography when John Ingram began his efforts to plunge into the entire background of all that had been written about Poe, sift it, determine its value, keep or discard, and in addition, discover or uncover materials that would let him fulfill his purpose of writing the true story of Poe's entire life.

Making a Beginning

After serving his literary apprenticeship in the 1860s by publishing his small volume of verse and the large volume on flowers, John Ingram was occupied in the 1870s with very few literary activities that did not directly contribute to his planned biography of Edgar Poe, the biography that would prove that Griswold had deliberately lied in his 1850 *Memoir* of Poe and that would establish Ingram as the world's authority on the American poet, since he and he alone had been able to uncover facts that had redeemed Poe's reputation from the slanders that had been heaped upon it and had presented him to the world as a greatly misunderstood but fine human being and as one of the world's truly great poets and storytellers.

The first article that Ingram published in defense of Poe had of necessity to be thin; but it was thick with rage and invective against Griswold. The article was called "New Facts About Edgar Poe," and it was published in the London *Mirror* on January 24, 1874. Unfortunately, the files of that magazine were in that section of the British Museum Library which was bombed and destroyed during World War II, and copies, if any are extant, have not been located. [6]

Having exhausted the resources at hand in gathering information about Poe, Ingram turned to America in the hope of finding there friends of Poe who still resented the injustice done enough to help clear his name.

It was Mrs. Whitman who wrote Ingram that William J. Pabodie * had published a letter in the New York *Tribune* on June 7, 1852, in direct and specific denial of the account published by Griswold of Poe's committing outrages in the house of a New England lady to whom he

6. A second article, "More New Facts About Edgar Allan Poe," was printed in the London *Mirror* for February 21, 1874. A single copy has survived and is in the Ingram Poe Collection, Item 570.

was engaged to be married, resulting in the police having to be brought into that house on the evening appointed for the marriage. Mrs. Whitman also told Ingram about the letters from the University of Virginia authorities which denied Griswold's charge that Poe had been expelled from that institution for leading a drunken, dissolute life.

With these facts plus a few others Ingram rushed into print with an article called "More New Facts About Edgar Allan Poe," in the London *Mirror*, on February 21, 1874. In this article, Ingram for the first time had concrete evidence to prove that Griswold had been wrong in many of his statements, and he made the most of it, as follows:

He challenged Griswold's statement that Poe had been born in 1811 by offering the matriculation record at the University of Virginia showing that 1809 was Poe's birth date.

He clarified the issue of Poe's reputation at the University of Virginia. Griswold had said "that Poe had returned to the United States from England in 1822, spent a few months at an academy in Richmond, then entered the University at Charlottesville, where he led such a very dissipated life . . . [that] he was known as the wildest and most reckless student of his class . . . [and that] his gambling, intemperance, and other vices, induced his expulsion from the university." Ingram pointed out that if Griswold's date for Poe's birth was accepted as true, then at the time of his dissipation and expulsion from the University of Virginia Poe could have been only eleven years old. Then Ingram quoted from letters written by Socrates Maupin, chairman of the faculty, and William Wertenbaker, librarian—both certainly responsible officers of the university—in which both denied that Poe was addicted to drink when he was a student, or that he had ever been expelled from the University of Virginia.

He debunked a story about Poe in trouble in Russia. Griswold had written in his *Memoir* that on Poe's 1828 trip to St. Petersburg "our minister was summoned one morning to save him from penalties incurred in a drunken debauch." Ingram countered this by pointing out that James Russell Lowell's version of the incident showed that Poe's difficulties in Russia stemmed from the lack of a passport. (It had not been established at this time that Poe never was in Russia.)

Ingram caught Griswold in a contradiction about the 1827 edition of Poe's poems. Griswold, in his *Memoir*, had professed to doubt that Poe had published a volume of poems in 1827. Ingram promptly referred to

Griswold's obituary of Poe, in which Griswold himself gave the year 1827 as the date of Poe's first publication.

Ingram demolished Griswold's statement that Poe had won the prizes offered by the *Saturday Visiter* in 1833 for both poetry and prose "by virtue of his beautiful handwriting," by quoting letters from the judges of that committee awarding the prizes, J. H. B. Latrobe* and John P. Kennedy.*

These and other revelations of Griswold's malice made this an important publication for John Ingram. His frontal assault on Griswold's *Memoir* had succeeded; he had proved that Griswold's charges against Poe were biased, and he had also proved that Griswold had fabricated at least some of his evidence against Poe.

Ingram's next public attack on Griswold's *Memoir* appeared in *Temple Bar*, June, 1874, entitled simply "Edgar Poe." As was his custom, he opened this article with a statement of his purpose of destroying Griswold's account of Poe's life; he then proceeded to sketch Poe's life himself, drawing heavily on Mrs. Whitman's little book and other authorities; juxtaposing Griswold's statements and his own refutations, he here repeated many of his important points already made in the *Mirror* article for February. His object in repeating his publications was to reach as many readers as possible, and since this particular article was reprinted in *The Gentleman's Magazine*, *Every Saturday*, and the *Eclectic Magazine*, he was successful.

Ingram's Memoir of Poe and His Edition of Poe's Works

The tempo of Ingram's work and correspondence increased mightily in early 1874, as he began preparing his memoir of Poe to preface the four-volume edition of Poe's works which he had promised to the press for fall publication. He continued his rapid correspondence with Mrs. Whitman, receiving from her at least thirty-seven long letters between January and mid-August, 1874; he had in his files letters from John Neal, to whom Poe had dedicated *Tamerlane*, from James Wood Davidson, from N. H. Morison* of the Peabody Institute in Baltimore, and from Rosalie Poe, as well as correspondence with West Point Military Academy authorities and the American Legation in St. Petersburg, Russia, plus countless magazine articles, newsclippings, and books about Poe. (And he had learned a valuable but unpleasant truth by midsummer of 1874: not all of his correspondents could be trusted to tell the whole truths when they wrote about their conversations and experiences with Edgar Poe.)

Volume I, with Ingram's ninety-page memoir of Poe, was off the press in October, 1874; Volumes II, III, and IV followed almost monthly until the whole edition was completed in February, 1875.[7] Ingram's articles in defense of Poe had been composed and based almost entirely on his belief that Griswold's *Memoir* was untrustworthy; and now he was offering the world convincing *proof* that it was: the unarguable refutations, the new information about Poe, the number of "firsts" contained in these volumes testify eloquently to Ingram's energy, devotion, and anger. Here are some of the accomplishments of this publication:

Presented as the frontispiece of the first volume a new photograph of Poe, made from a daguerreotype which Poe had sat for in Providence and had given to Mrs. Whitman.

Reproduced in full for the first time a facsimile of Poe's letter of December 4, 1848, thanking William J. Pabodie for his hospitality when Poe had visited Mrs. Whitman in Providence. This was a first printing of this letter, and it was one of the few times Poe signed his name in full, "Edgar Allan Poe," because Pabodie had requested that he do so.[8]

Printed for the first time a letter from Poe to Stella Lewis, November 27, 1848.

Printed for the first time excerpts from two letters Poe had written to Mrs. Whitman, October 18, 1848, and November 24, 1848.

Told portions of the true story of Poe's engagement to Mrs. Whitman; this account is far from complete, but it differs radically from the one told by Griswold and from the ones handed around by the literati. Mrs. Whitman had written out the whole story for Ingram, but had forbidden

7. John H. Ingram (ed.), *The Works of Edgar Allan Poe* (4 vols.; Edinburgh: Adam & Charles Black, 1874/75; New York: W. J. Widdleton, 1876).

8. William J. Pabodie was a neighbor, close friend, and possibly an admirer of Mrs. Whitman's. He was very courteous to Poe, but he did not approve of their marriage plans. He committed suicide in 1870, leaving this letter as a gift in his will to Mrs. Whitman. She later gave it as a present to Thomas C. Latto, who had from time to time helped her gather information about Poe; she borrowed it back from Latto, and with his permission sent it to Ingram to have copied for his book. Ingram returned the letter directly to Latto, but the original was subsequently lost, and this facsimile remains the source of the text.

him to use it until after her death. She was not pleased that he told even this much of it.

Proved the falseness of Griswold's story of Poe's having been held in detention in St. Petersburg, Russia. Ingram had written to the American Legation in that city and the secretary, Eugene Schuyler, had the records searched. That search showed that Poe had never been detained in St. Petersburg, and Ingram was with this evidence able to scotch Griswold's story of Poe's drunken debauch there, as well as raise serious doubts that Poe had ever revisited Europe at all, after his childhood trip with the Allan family.

Presented for the first time the story of Poe's career at West Point. Correspondence with the authorities showed that Poe was admitted as a cadet on July 1, 1830, that he was tried by a general court-martial the following January, and on the sixth of March, 1831, he was dismissed. Ingram had brushed off as totally unreliable Griswold's statement that Poe had enlisted and presumably had deserted from the United States Army in 1827; now it was his painful duty to add and confirm an equally ignominious chapter in Poe's personal history. But in doing it, Ingram managed to convey the impression that everyone at the academy was out of step but Poe.

Tries to explain away Poe's questionable action in publishing *The Conchologist's First Book* and signing his name to it as the author. Ingram defiantly says that poverty forced Poe to turn his pen to any project that offered pay, and besides, Poe's knowledge of science was so comprehensive and exact and he made such large contributions to the book the publishers were justified in using his popular name on the title page. It was a fairly good try, but, even so, it couldn't make that cat jump.

Published the suppressed final stanza of "Ulalume," which had been dropped at Mrs. Whitman's suggestion when Poe was courting her in 1848.

Reprinted full and authenticated letters from the University of Virginia testifying to Poe's good behavior while there. By doing this in his memoir, Ingram gave the letters final form and wider circulation than the previously published but garbled versions ever had, and he established once and for all certain facts about Poe's career at the university: he was born on January 19, 1809; he entered the university on February 14, 1826; he was neither disciplined by the faculty nor was he expelled or graduated with highest honors; he simply left the university after a single session, sometime between December 15 and 22, 1826. With these letters, Ingram was able to print, too, for the first time in full, an authoritative account of Poe's ordinary behavior at the university, written by a fellow student, William Wertenbaker, who later became librarian of the university.

Presented William Gowans' "Recollections of Poe." This account of Poe's gentlemanly behavior and sobriety, written by a respectable, well-to-do bookseller who had lived with the Poes for six months at 113½ Carmine Street, New York City, had appeared once before in the New York *Evening Mail*, December 10, 1870. With this printed account and with portions of Mrs. Whitman's letters from Thomas C. Latto, to whom Gowans had recounted in conversations his recollections of Poe and his family, Ingram was able to reconstruct a story of Poe's uniform quietness and sobriety as it was remembered by a man who had known Poe and his family intimately by living with them.

Reprinted in full George Graham's letter to N. P. Willis, a fine account of Poe which had been printed in *Graham's Magazine* for March, 1850. After much searching, Mrs. Whitman located a copy of the long-sought volume, which had seemingly disappeared from the face of the earth, but the friend who owned it would neither sell it to her nor allow her to cut out the three pages; Mrs. Whitman therefore copied them by hand for Ingram, omitting "one or two trifling" repetitions or irrelevant "reflections." In the meantime, James Wood Davidson had found another complete volume of *Graham's* for 1850 and had forwarded it to Ingram.

In the four volumes themselves, Ingram made many valuable additions to the Poe canons in prose, poetry, and criticism. By a stroke of great luck, Ingram had found the first known copy of Poe's *Tamerlane*, which had been sold to the British Museum for one shilling; he was therefore able to include in his edition the eight poems Poe had published in 1827, 1829, and 1831, which had not been included in Griswold's edition or in any other later edition. He added Poe's "Pinikidia," "Some Secrets of the Magazine Printing House," "Anastatic Printing," and "Cryptography," none of which had been included in Griswold's edition. Poe's papers on judging the characters of his contemporaries by their handwriting had appeared in the *Southern Literary Messenger* for February and August, 1836, under the title "A

Chapter on Autographs." A further paper, styled "An Appendix on Autographs," had appeared in *Graham's* for January, 1842. Ingram published these papers on handwriting for the first time in a collected edition of Poe's works, in his fourth volume, and there he named them "Autography."

The immediate reviews of Ingram's edition were mixed but generally favorable. Almost everywhere it was conceded that Ingram had destroyed Griswold's *Memoir* and had exposed that author for the liar and fraud he was. Ingram's volumes were brought out in America in 1876 by W. J. Widdleton; they were translated into French and German, and for at least twenty years were considered to be the standard edition of Poe's writings.

But in America, Ingram's scornful remarks about Poe's countrymen neglecting their great poet and his volumes themselves were considered something of a national insult: an English author had appropriated one of their major literary figures and was now triumphantly posing as his discoverer and redeemer, or so it seemed.

The impulsive William Fearing Gill* rushed into premature publication with what he termed a complete *Life of Edgar Allan Poe*. Richard Henry Stoddard,* an able writer and critic, but no friend of Poe, bestirred himself and began publishing on Poe. Eugene L. Didier* of Baltimore, a rather inept but angry writer on the scene of Poe's last activities, began publishing articles of scant value, but filled with invective against the "presumptuous Englishman." A new day was dawning in Poe writing and scholarship, especially in America.

In England, John Ingram complacently felt that he had destroyed for the world the Griswoldian concept of Poe, and having done so, his next step was to produce a full-scale biography. And he set to work at it, already with bulging files of Poe materials no one else had; and with many friends in America, England, and France adding to his knowledge and materials daily, he was more than a few lengths ahead of his nearest competitors.

II
Maria Poe Clemm Mourns Her Lost "Eddie"

EDGAR POE apotheosized his mother-in-law Maria Clemm in his sonnet, "To My Mother," addressed to her and published in 1849, the last year of his life. After Poe had died, N. P. Willis added to this glorious image of her by characterizing her as "one of those angels upon earth that women in adversity can be." And for years thereafter she was extolled by almost everyone concerned as the saintly guardian of Edgar and Virginia Poe, the spirit incarnate of motherhood, one who had selflessly devoted herself to strengthening the frail hold her children had on life. After Virginia's death in 1847, the phrase most often used to describe her was, "Edgar's sole ministering angel."

There is certainly no reason to doubt that Edgar Poe deeply loved Maria Clemm and that he depended on her to serve as refuge or bulwark, as situations demanded. His unfailing courtesy to her and his often-expressed affection for her are matters of record. There is only one instance known of his having lost patience with her, and that was when she borrowed money, without his permission or knowledge, from Rufus Griswold. We know, too, that Poe cried out to her in his last agony.

Nor is there any more reason to doubt that Maria Clemm loved Poe during his lifetime and sincerely mourned him for the nearly twenty-two years she survived after his death. It is well, however, to remember, as one reads her letters below, that she was by nature selfish and lugubrious, that she was a true daughter of her times, which was an era that literally hugged the symbols of death to itself, placing great emphasis on a code of dress, manners, and attitudes. But these things are not the whole story.

John Ingram was the first Poe biographer to suggest even obliquely that Maria Clemm's influences on Virginia and Edgar were other than an unmixed blessing.[1] As he read many of her letters addressed to persons who had become his reliable correspondents in America, as well as gathered reports about her attitudes and actions while visiting in their homes, he became convinced, and said so, that she had not always been good for Edgar and Virginia, even in actions that surely seemed to her to have been dictated by mother love. Many of the letters Ingram received that were written by Mrs. Clemm and her hosts are here printed for the first time, and the readers may judge for themselves.

Maria Poe Clemm was the daughter of David and Elizabeth Cairnes Poe and sister to David, Jr., Edgar's father. Maria was born on March 17, 1790. When she married William Clemm on July 12, 1817, she inherited a ready-made family, for William's first wife, Harriet, had died in 1815, leaving him with five small children. Three additional children were born to Maria and William Clemm: Henry, born in 1818, grew up to work in a Baltimore brickyard, and while still in his teens, to go to sea at least twice, and to die unmarried sometime after 1836; Virginia Marie was born in 1820 and died in 1822; Virginia Eliza, Poe's wife-to-be, was born in 1822 and died on January 30, 1847. William Clemm had died in Baltimore, on February 8, 1826, in his forty-seventh year.

Married for less than ten years, left the sole support of her own two surviving children, plus several left over from her husband's first marriage, burdened with the care of her invalid mother and her invalid nephew, Edgar's brother William Henry Leonard, Maria Clemm was rather early cast in the role of the sorrowing widow with orphaned children plus far more family responsibilities than she could well bear alone.

Edgar Poe himself came to live for some time in this Baltimore household that was already crowded and was being held together precariously enough by Mrs. Clemm. Several years later, after Edgar had married Virginia, the invalids were dead, the children from William Clemm's first marriage had dispersed, Henry Clemm had gone away, either to sea or to the West, and Maria Clemm was, remarkably and strangely for her, free of dependents. It was only natural, from her viewpoint at least, that she should take charge of Edgar's new household, and take charge she did, until that household was no more.

1. Possibly from gallantry, no Poe biographer except Ingram has ever dealt truthfully with the extent of Mrs. Clemm's undeniably strong influence on Poe, in matters good and bad.

Again, after Virginia's death in 1847, and Edgar's in 1849, Mrs. Clemm was once more alone. She had no home of her own, no really close relative left. For the next twenty years, she moved from place to place, living for various periods of time with persons or families who had either known Poe personally or had become fascinated with his writings, and who welcomed her warmly, at first anyway. She did manage to stay in one or two households for periods up to three years. But she could not have been an easy person to shelter, for she had so long been accustomed to directing the activities of the persons around her, and even though her situations kept changing, her habits did not. She criticized the behavior, the dress, and even the manners of those around her, and she was given to incessant crying and deploring her desolate condition. Given any audience that would listen, she would talk of nothing but her beloved lost children. Then too, in one particular household where she was considered a permanent guest, she was unwise enough to take the husband's part against the wife; when Sylvanus D. Lewis lost that particular quarrel, Mrs. Lewis permanently ejected Mrs. Clemm from the household.

No matter with whom she was living or where, Maria Clemm wrote a steady stream of letters to other persons asking for help to relieve this ill or that one, or for help to make a trip here or there. She appeared to be always in dire need of one thing or another.

Edgar Poe's facility in writing ingratiating letters solely for the purpose of borrowing money is widely known; and when Mrs. Clemm continued her practice so diligently after his death, much of the blame for her reprehensible practice was added to the attack on Poe's character. But almost from the beginning, John Ingram suspected Mrs. Clemm's influence in the matter on Poe, rather than his on her. He had no proof that his suspicions were valid until very late in his career of building Poe biography, when William Hand Browne, his loyal ally in Baltimore, sent him in December, 1909, a copy of a characteristic letter which Maria Clemm had written *before* Edgar Poe had come to be closely associated with her. The letter was addressed to a prominent judge in Baltimore whose grandson allowed Browne to copy the letter for Ingram but had absolutely refused to allow his grandfather's name to be used in connection with it. Browne withheld the addressee's name, but Ingram did not especially care; for with this copy in hand he at last had his absolute *proof* that Maria Clemm was adroit and well practiced at writing begging letters long before Edgar Poe came to live with her:

[*ca.* 1831]

Dear Sir:—

I am not myself personally known to you, but you were well acquainted with my late husband, Mr. Wm. Clemm, and also I believe, with many of my connexions. For their sakes as well as my own I venture to solicit a little assistance at your hands. For a long time now I have been prevented by continual ill health from making the exertions necessary for the support of myself and children, and we are now consequently enduring every privation. Under these circumstances I feel a hope that you will be inclined to give me some little aid. I do not ask for any material assistance, but the merest trifle to relieve my most immediate distress.

Very respy.
Maria Clemm [2]

Mrs. Clemm wrote innumerable similar letters over a period of not less than forty years; yet no matter how much she received, there never appears to have been a time when her needs were actually alleviated. It remained for Ingram to make the hard-headed point, in his unpublished biography of Poe, that it was indeed remarkable for people who borrowed or begged as much money as did Poe and Mrs. Clemm, never to have had any!

The letters and portions of letters written by Mrs. Clemm that follow reached Ingram at various times, but they are here presented chronologically; thus it is possible for the reader to follow her career from early in 1847 until just a few weeks before she died in the Episcopal Church Home infirmary in Baltimore on February 16, 1871. It is possible, too, to see in her letters the facts Ingram learned that would help to contribute to one or the other of his double purposes, refuting Griswold or adding to his own proposed true life of the poet.

Letter 1. **Maria Clemm, Fordham, to Marie Louise Shew, New York.** Copied by Mrs. Houghton and forwarded to Ingram in 1875. Printed in Ingram's *Edgar Allan Poe: His Life, Letters & Opinions* (2 vols.; London: John Hogg, 1880), II,

---

2. This letter was later printed in the *Maryland Historical Magazine*, VI (March, 1911), 44, as having been addressed to "a former member of the Judiciary." Item 436 in the Ingram Poe Collection, University of Virginia. Materials in that collection are hereafter referred to simply by the item numbers enclosed in brackets.

111–12. All subsequent references are to this two-volume biography published in 1880 and will hereinafter be cited as *Life*. [Item 34, Ingram Poe Collection, University of Virginia Library]

[*ca*. February, 1847]

My dear sweet friend

I write to say that the medicines arrived the next train after you left today, and a kind friend brought them up to us, that same hour—The cooling application was very grateful to my poor Eddie's head, and the flowers were lovely, not "frozen" as you feared they would be. I very much fear this illness will be a serious one. The fever came on at the same time today as you said and I am giving the "sedative mixture". He did not rouse to talk to Mr. C. as he would naturally do to so kind a friend—Eddie made me promise to write you a note about the wine (which I neglected to tell you about this morning.) He desires me to return the last box of wine you sent my sweet Virginia, (there being some left of the first package, which I will put away for any emergency)—The wine was a great blessing to us while *she needed it*, and by its cheering and tonic influence we were enabled to keep her a few days longer with us. The little darling always took it smiling, even when difficult to get it down. But for your timely aid my dear Mrs. S. we should have had no last words, no loving messages, *no sweet farewells*, for she had ceased to speak (from weakness) but with her beautiful eyes! —Eddie has quite set his heart upon the wine going *back to you*, thinking and hoping you may find it useful for the *sick artist* you mentioned "as convalescent and in need of delicacies." God bless you my sweet child and come soon to your sorrowing and desolate friend.

Maria Clemm

P.S. We look for you a train earlier tomorrow (in an early train), and hope you will stay as long as possible, what we should do without you is fearful to think of. Eddie says you promised Virginia to come every *other* day, for a long time, or until he was able to go to work again. I hope and believe *you will not fail him*, and I pray that every blessing may be yours & may follow you in life, as your angelic tenderness and compassion deserve.

Mr. C. will tell you of our condition, as he is going to call for this note in an hour's time, and until we see you farewell,

M.C.

Mrs. Clemm wrote this letter shortly after Virginia Poe's death in Fordham on January 30, 1847. When Ingram received a copy of it in 1875, he realized immediately its great value as firsthand support for his refutations of some of the specific charges Rufus Griswold had made about Poe's life and character. Griswold had opened his obituary of Poe by saying that Poe had few or no friends; with this letter, Ingram could prove that Poe and his family did indeed have friends, and devoted ones at that. Griswold had labeled Poe extremely selfish; with this letter, Ingram could offer evidence that, on the contrary, Poe, even in sickness, was much concerned about another sick person's welfare. Griswold had said that Poe was an irresponsible drunk; now Ingram could cite an instance of Poe's undeniable control and unselfishness in a matter involving at least several bottles of wine.

In addition, this letter revealed facets of Mrs. Clemm's personality and letter-writing habits that Ingram had already begun to watch for: she overwhelmed her benefactors with expressions of gratitude for past favors and insured future ones with emotional reminders of their promises to the dead. The recipients of her letters were left with small choice.

This was indeed a valuable letter for Ingram's purposes, and he filed it for future use, for whenever it would do the most good. One such time came when he prepared his full-scale biography of Poe in 1880; another came, nearly thirty years later, when he chose to use it again in an article in the New York *Bookman* (January, 1909), called "Edgar Allan Poe's Lost Poem 'The Beautiful Physician.'"

The person to whom this letter was addressed as "dear sweet friend" and "Mrs. S." was Marie Louise Shew (later Mrs. Roland Houghton) of New York City, who had been introduced into the Poe household by Mary Sargeant Neal Gove Nichols, a water-cure physician of sorts, who had firsthand knowledge of the Poes' distressed condition. Mrs. Shew's practical medical training and nursing experience made her especially valuable to Mrs. Clemm during Virginia's last sickness and Edgar's collapse after Virginia's death and funeral. "Mr. C." was Mr. H. D. Chapin,* a very close friend of Mrs. Shew's.

Letter 2.   Maria Clemm, Fordham, to Annie Richmond,

Lowell, Mass. Fragment sent by Mrs. Richmond to Ingram on October 3, 1876. First printing. [Item 52]

[*ca*. November–December, 1848]

But I so much fear *she* is not calculated to make him happy. I fear I will not love her. I *know* I shall never love her as I do *you*, my own darling. I hope at all events they will not marry for some time. (Thank you a thousand times, *dearest*, for inducing Eddy to make that promise to you, and which I feel so sure he will *never* violate. He says he will *die* before he will deceive you or break his word with you[)] Give my dearest love to Sarah—tell her I love her for her kindness to my dear Eddy—remember me affectionately to your kind mother [page cut].

[on left margin, in Mrs. Richmond's handwriting] It is the letter containing this promise she borrowed and never returned!

[on verso]

Mother and sincere friend,
M. Clemm

Did you see the lines addressed to *our* Eddy in the "Home Journal" week before last? I forget the beginning, but the concluding line is—"And knowing this alone knows too much." Mrs. W.* says they were written by Grace Greenwood! They were sent to Eddy in *manuscript*, and Mrs. W. says she *knows* it to be Grace Greenwood's.

Ingram did not choose to print this letter. When he received it he was working very closely with Mrs. Whitman, to whom Poe was engaged to be married when Mrs. Clemm wrote this letter to Mrs. Richmond, and he could understand Mrs. Whitman's personal embarrassment and hurt if she learned of Mrs. Clemm's attitude toward the proposed nuptials.

But the greatest importance of this letter to Poe biography is in the intensity of feeling evident in Mrs. Richmond's marginal note. No biographer of Poe has even hinted about how disillusioned, how angry, Annie Richmond became with Mrs. Clemm over the loss of Poe's letters which Mrs. Clemm repeatedly borrowed and some of which she never returned, despite her insistence that she had.

Poe was indeed planning to marry Mrs. Whitman when this letter was written, but he had met Mrs. Richmond after he had proposed marriage to Mrs. Whitman, and he was more emotionally involved with Mrs. Richmond than he was with Mrs. Whitman. Mrs. Richmond urged Poe to go on with his plans to marry Mrs. Whitman, for she certainly had no intention of divorcing her husband and marrying Poe herself, flattered as she was by his genius and person.

Mrs. Clemm and Mrs. Whitman never did personally meet, although after Poe's death Mrs. Clemm initiated a correspondence between them that continued for twenty years, during which Mrs. Clemm expressed her deep affection and repeatedly hinted for an invitation to come and live with Mrs. Whitman for the rest of her life. Mrs. Whitman was already burdened with an elderly mother who still disliked everything and everybody associated with Edgar Poe, as well as with a mentally affected sister to care for, and she had, in addition, learned enough about Mrs. Clemm's personality and attitudes to understand that she would be an extremely disturbing influence in their home. She skillfully sidestepped Mrs. Clemm's hints for shelter, which finally became open requests, and she sent to Mrs. Clemm untold amounts of money through the years to avoid taking her in as a permanent guest.

The "promise" Poe made to Mrs. Richmond in the lost letter was almost certainly to the effect that he would not again try to kill himself, as he had recently done with an overdose of laudanum.

"Sarah" was Miss Sarah H. Heywood, Mrs. Richmond's younger sister, of nearby Westford, Massachusetts, who spent much of her time in the Richmonds' home in Lowell. On various occasions and for many months at the time after Poe's death, Mrs. Clemm lived in the Richmonds' home, and she alone had access to Poe's letters to Annie Richmond. Later, Mrs. Richmond was to write Ingram that Mrs. Clemm not only did not return this borrowed letter containing Poe's promise, but that several others were missing, after Mrs. Clemm's departure.

"Grace Greenwood" was Sara Jane Clark Lippincott (1823–1904), author of *Greenwood Leaves* (1850), and one of the earliest female newspaper correspondents in America. She wrote popular Washington columns for the New York *Times*, travel sketches, and poetry in a very light vein. Mrs. Clemm appears to have found her reported notice of Edgar Poe a signal honor.

Letter 3. **Maria Clemm, New York, to Annie Richmond, Lowell.** Excerpts copied before Ingram returned the letter to Mrs. Richmond. First accurate printing. [Item 59]

July 30 [Tuesday]—[18]49

My dearest Annie,

    I have this moment rec'd your of 27th . . . This day week received a letter from my own sweet Eddy. He writes he is better in health and rather better in spirits. He assures me he never did anything while he was so deranged that was in the *least disgraceful*. He fancied he was pursued by the police but it was not so. I have gained all the particulars from several gentlemen to whom I wrote when I found I could not go to him.

    . . . Dear Eddy wrote me in his last that he was going from Richmond in a few days, to stay with a friend in the country for a short time. I hope that is the reason I did not hear from him today.

Ingram handled this letter in the characteristic way he treated materials about Poe that even hinted of unsavory matters: he condensed the letter, quoted inaccurately from the text of it, and summed the matter up by remarking, "There is no need to repeat the details of this episode." (See *Life*, II, 223–24. George E. Woodberry* and A. H. Quinn* saw the need—see Woodberry, II, 311–13; Quinn, 616–18 for complete details.)

    Poe's letter received "this day week" was written to Mrs. Clemm from Richmond, on Thursday, July 19, 1849. (See Ostrom,* 455–56.) Poe's derangement took place in Philadelphia, on his stopover there after leaving Mrs. Clemm in New York on June 29, 1849. The "several gentlemen" to whom Mrs. Clemm wrote very likely were C. Chauncey Burr, George Lippard, and John Sartain, for these were the persons who had helped Poe to recover and had given him money to continue on his trip to Richmond.

Letter 4. **Maria Clemm, New York, to Annie Richmond, Annisquam, Mass.** First complete printing. [Item 60]

August 4th Saturday [1849]

My own dear Annie,

    I wrote to you on teusday [*sic*] last, and promised to write to you again the next day,   But when I came home I was so sick

New York. August 4th. 49.
? Sunday
Monday?

My own dear Annie.
            I wrote to you on tuesday last, and
promised to write to you again the next day. But when I came
home I was so sick and wretched, that I could not hold a pen.
It is nearly two weeks since I have heard from my poor Eddy.
I fancy every thing in the world. This I am perfectly sure of, if he
were living and in his senses he would write. Annie I cannot bear
it much longer I must sink! Yesterday was five weeks since he
left, and the misery I have endured since I cannot tell you.
When I parted with him aboard of the steam boat, he was so dejected
but still tried to cheer me. He said "God bless my own darling
muddy do not fear for your Eddy see how good I will be while
I am away from you, and will come back to love and comfort
you" But I did fear my Annie! Oh that I could have gone with
him! I could have saved him all this suffering, But I could
not get the means. Even now I cannot succeed in getting enough
to go to him were he dying. I sold every thing I could to get
him the means to go with and a few articles that he could not
do without. The day after he left I received yours with one to him
enclosed, oh! if it had only come one day sooner. He had waited
for a week in hopes to hear from you. Poor dear Eddy how
grieved he was. I have explained it all to him. Oh darling
Annie never for one moment think he will love you less.
I know he loves you more than any thing on this earth. Mrs
Lewis promised him to see me often and see that I did not
suffer. For a whole fortnight I heard nothing from her.
at last I went there, and would you believe it she had

Maria Clemm to Annie Richmond, August 4, 1849
Letter 4

and wretched, that I could not hold a pen. It is nearly two weeks since I have heard from my poor Eddy. I fancy every thing in the world. This I am perfectly sure of, if he were living and *in his senses*, he would write. Annie I cannot bear it much longer. I *must* sink! Yesterday was five weeks since he left, and the misery I have endured since I cannot tell you. When I parted with him aboard of the steam boat, he was so dejected but still tried to cheer me. He said "God bless my own darling muddy do not fear for your Eddy see how good I will be while I am away from you, and will come back to love and comfort you." But I did fear my Annie! Oh that I could have gone with him! I could have saved him all this suffering. But I could not get the means. Even now I cannot succeed in getting enough to go to him *were he dying.* I sold every thing I could to get him the means to go with and a few articles that he could not do without. The day after he left I received yours with one to him enclosed. Oh! if it had only come one day sooner. He had waited a week in hopes to hear from you. Poor dear Eddy how grieved he was. I have explained it all to him. Oh darling Annie never for one moment think he will love you less. I know he loves you more than any thing on this earth. Mrs. Lewis* promised him to see me often and see that I did not suffer. For a whole fortnight I heard nothing from her, at last I went there, and would you believe it? She had a letter from Eddy to me begging her for Gods sake to send it to me without a moment's delay. It was enclosed in a one to her, of two lines, saying, it was of vital importance that I should receive it immediately. Annie if I had received it I would have gone on to Philadelphia, if I had to have *begged* my way, and then how much misery my darling Eddy would have been saved. I wrote to dear Eddy and have told him that I have wanted for nothing, have told him that Mrs. L. has been *very kind* to me and did not breathe about the detention of the letter. It takes all I can get to take me in and out of New York. But oh how freely would I do without bread to hear from my precious Eddy. You say you will come on here. Oh Annie if I could only see you, how much I could explain to you which must look to you so strange. When I commence writing I think I have so much to tell you, but in a few moments my mind becomes confused. I enclose to you the last letter I got from *our* dear Eddy, take care of it for if I should lose *him* I would never forgive myself for parting with it for an instant. You had better write to him darling, at Richmond but don't sign your name for fear he does not get it—I have confided so much to you dearest Annie, of our troubles. But I need not ask you never to betray them. If you write him, do not say that I told you the *cause* of his illness. But oh Annie tell him your fears and intreat him for all our sakes to refrain altogether. He will thank you for urging him for he will know it is your love for him that induces you to do so—You will see in Eddy's letter to me what he says of Mrs. L. it is gratitude to her for what *he thinks* her kindness to his poor deserted Muddy—He cares nothing about her indeed less than about any one I know—He would devotedly love any one that is kind to me—But oh Annie if I had been her, how soon I would have relieved some of our misery, how unlike you dearest—She says she knows Eddie does not *like her*. Oh my Annie how few there are in this world, that we can love.

I am going to the city today, and if I do not get a letter from him my senses will certainly leave me. If I hear, be it good or ill, I will write that moment to you—write soon dear Annie, your letters comfort me so much, for I always feel in reading them, that I have one friend left—And now dearest Annie Goodbye God Bless and when you pray for your self and your dear ones, remember *our* dear wanderer, and your afflicted but sincerely affectionate Mother and friend,

M. Clemm

From this very revealing letter Ingram printed only a few sentences, Poe's parting words to Mrs. Clemm (*Life*, II, 220–21). He enclosed these words in quotes, but he changed "Muddy" to "mother," and he added information from another letter from Mrs. Clemm to make it appear that Mrs. Clemm had written it in this one.

Poe had left New York on Friday, June 29, 1849, en route to Richmond via Philadelphia on a combination lecture tour and campaign to solicit subscriptions to raise money enough to start publishing his long-dreamed-of magazine, the *Stylus*. He and Mrs. Clemm had dined the day of his departure with Mr. and Mrs. Lewis and had left from the Lewis home about five o'clock to go aboard the steamboat. Mrs. Lewis had promised Poe that she would take care of Mrs. Clemm in his absence, for she was exceedingly anxious for more of his flattering reviews of her published poems.

Poe's frantic, almost incoherent letter telling Mrs. Clemm of his sickness and begging her to come to him in Philadelphia was enclosed in a three-line letter addressed to Mrs. Lewis, dated July 7, 1849. (See Ostrom, II, 452–53, for texts of both letters.)

Poe did dislike Mrs. Lewis, but he was much obligated to her for past loans she had made to Mrs. Clemm; Mrs. Lewis considered flattering reviews of herself and her verses from the great critic Edgar Poe sufficient payment, and she got them.

Mrs. Clemm's strong, pitiful attempt to get Annie to urge Poe to refrain from drinking altogether shows how ever-present and intense this worry must have been to her.

Letter 5. **Maria Clemm, New York, to Annie Richmond, Lowell.** First printing. [Item 61]

Sept. 3, 1849

Dearest Annie,

I received your dear kind letter of the 27th on Thursday last, but would not write to you in hopes I would have something pleasant to tell you. But alas! alas! darling, what have I to tell you, only that I have heard nothing from our poor dear Eddie since I last wrote you. It is three weeks since I have had one line from him—the letter I received from Mrs. Nye was the last I heard from him. I think perhaps she told him she had written for me, and he is constantly expecting me, this I think is the most likely reason. Or else he is entirely bereft of *his senses*. Oh God support me in this deep deep affliction, or enable me to bow submissive to it. I have written to Mr. R.* to ask him to loan me enough to go to him, if he *does* I will go the moment I get it, if he *does not*, all that I can do will be to pray for *him*, and give *myself* up to despair. Oh, Annie, I have prayed to our merciful God to put it in his heart to aid me. Before applying to Mr. R. I made several attempts to get it elsewhere, but without success. I have told him as much as I could, but do you dearest Annie tell him *all*. I have requested him to keep sacred the confidences I have reposed in him, and I feel sure he will do so—darling Annie I will not trouble you again with my troubles, it is indeed selfish—But never never can I cease to love you—next to my *Eddy*, you are the dearest object of my poor *widowed childless* heart—Oh! what a privilege to love you and confide in you—The instant I hear of my Eddie I will write to you God bless you My dear Annie.

M.C.

Ingram neither reproduced this letter, nor quoted from it; consequently it has not made its way into Poe biography. Perhaps no other letter reveals Mrs. Clemm's distress so acutely, or indicates so clearly her limited finances. As deep as was her agony when she wrote this letter, even greater pain was in store for her; but when that came to her, she at least knew with what she had to deal.

The Nye family in Richmond were friends of long standing, and Mrs. Nye had written Mrs. Clemm in July that she would "make" Edgar stay at her house while he was in Richmond and that she "would take every care of him." W. A. R. Nye was connected with the newspaper, the Richmond *Whig*. "Mr. R." was C. B. Richmond, Annie's husband, who, up to this point, had been spared details of the many troubles and infirmities that continually beset Mrs. Clemm and Edgar Poe. As a diminutive for Edgar, Mrs. Clemm used "Eddy" and "Eddie" interchangeably.

Letter 6. **Maria Clemm, New York to Annie Richmond, Lowell.** First complete printing. [Item 62]

Sept. 15, 1849

My dearest Annie,

I am only able to write you a very few words. I have had a severe attack of nervous fever, and am now only able to be up long enough to write this—this will account to you for my not answering Mr. R's kind letter and enclosure of 5 dollars—it found me ill, and if he had sent me sufficient to have gone to Eddy, I could not have done so until now. The anxiety I felt about him brought on my sickness. But my Annie the dark dark clouds I think are beginning to break. I send you his letter, the only one I received for nearly four weeks. I yesterday received a very short one with the slip of paper I enclose. God of his great mercy grant he may keep this pledge. I have written to him telling him of *all* your kindness since he left—what should I have done without my Annie— But I hope I will soon be able to return it all a thousand fold—you see how he loves you, darling. Thank Mr. R. for me, and write to me as soon as possible. Oh, Annie you have been ill too! Are you better? Do write and let me know. I was too ill to write to you and was so much distressed I could not hear from you. If you cannot write get dear Sarah* to do so for you.

Yours devotedly,
M.C.

[on left margin] Gen. Morris*—& Mr. Duyckinck both say he only wanted that—I mean to be temperate—to be the *greatest man living*!!

This is a first printing of this letter, with the exception of a single sentence, that one dealing with Poe's temperance pledge. Ingram enclosed the sentence in quotes (*Life*, II, 230), but, as was usual with him, he made some slight alterations in the wording.

Poe's letter to Mrs. Clemm, dated September 12 or 13, 1849, has not survived. The "slip of paper" Mrs. Clemm enclosed to Annie was the copy of the temperance pledge Poe had taken in Richmond shortly before he wrote the now missing letter to Mrs. Clemm. William J. Glenn was at that time the presiding officer of the Shockoe Hill Division, No. 54, of the Sons of Temperance, and he remembered initiating Poe into that body.[3]

"Gen. Morris" was George P. Morris, coeditor with N. P. Willis of the New York *Mirror* and *Home Journal*. Evert A. Duyckinck, editor of the *Literary World*, was at one time a good and helpful friend to Poe.

Letter 7. **Maria Clemm, Lowell, to Sarah Helen Whitman, Providence, R.I.** Copy made by Ingram before he

3. See William J. Glenn's letter to E. V. Valentine, June 29, 1899, now in the Valentine Museum in Richmond. The Richmond *Times* reprinted portions of it in an article, "Poe and His Pledge," by Robert C. Hiden, March 10, 1895. [Item 888]

returned the letter to Mrs. Whitman, *ca*. 1874. First printing. [Item 66]

Oct. 26, 1849

Dear Mrs. Whitman,

Since my arrival here, I have heard that Mrs. Locke has a letter sent to her through you—said to be written by my dear darling Eddie a few hours before his death, & which she *says* was written to her. As this so entirely contradicts the statement made by my friends in Baltimore, & who never left him for one moment, I wish to hear from *you* the truth. You loved him once. Do justice to his memory. Mrs. L[ocke] would have been the last woman in the world he would have written to. I know he———*her*. She will have to be more cautious how she speaks of *him*, or *I will have to speak* as she will not wish. Will you not reply directly?

Your afflicted friend,
Maria Clemm

Ingram did not print any portion of this letter, not has anyone else, for in it Mrs. Clemm reveals a facet of her personality that belies the general conception, fostered by biographers, that her nature was barely short of angelic. Here she brings direct pressure to bear, makes an open threat, and issues peremptory commands to get what she wants.

Sarah Helen Whitman was the brilliant and charming, if sometimes eccentric, poetess who had entered briefly in 1848 into a conditional engagement with Poe. Her reply to this singular letter from Mrs. Clemm has remained unpublished, too, until now. It is here reproduced from a copy, made by Charlotte F. Dailey, in Mrs. Whitman's papers in the Brown University Library:

My dear Mrs. Clemm—

Every day since I received the heart-rending intelligence of Edgar's death I have been wishing to address you. Not knowing whether a letter directed to Fordham would reach you, I, this morning, commenced a letter to Mr. Griswold requesting him to assure you of my sympathy in your deep sorrow and of my unutterable affection for one whose memory is still most dear to me. I had not finished my long letter to him when I received your note. Its contents greatly surprised me because I have written to *no one* since your son's death, nor have I forwarded or *received* any communication of the kind to which you allude. I cannot but think there has been some misapprehension in relation to this affair. If I am well enough to write you again while you remain at Lowell I will do so. If *not*, my letter to Mr. Griswold will inform you of much that I have been long wishing to communicate to you. In the meantime, believe me, dear Madame, respectfully & affectionately your friend,

Saturday evening   Sarah H. Whitman
Oct. 28th [1849]

How seriously and how long Mrs. Clemm took advantage of Mrs. Whitman's respect and affection will be seen clearly in the letters ahead. She had moved into the Richmonds' home shortly after Poe's death. "Mrs. Locke" was Mrs. Jane Ermina Starkweather Locke of Wamesit Cottage, Lowell. See the introduction to Chapter VI for an account of Mrs. Locke's enmity to Poe. Poe had been dead less than twenty days when Mrs. Clemm wrote her threatening letter to Mrs. Whitman, and the "coil" about his personality and reputation was beginning to be woven.

Letter 8. **Maria Clemm, Lowell, to Neilson Poe, Baltimore.** Copied by William Hand Browne and forwarded to Ingram on March 17, 1876. First printing. [Item 68]

Nov. 1, 1849

Dear Neilson,

I last evening received a letter from Mr. Willis enclosing your very kind one. God bless you for the interest you have taken in my beloved Eddie—my *poor, poor* Eddie! And to think if I had been with him I should not have lost him! Will you have the kindness to send my darling's trunk by express? It contains papers of great importance to the publishers of his work, particularly the lectures. Mr. Richmond (at whose house I shall spend the winter) thinks it will come direct and safely. I inclose you two of my dear son's letters, and you can judge who has the *better right* to anything of his, Rose or myself. God knows how freely I would have sacrificed my life *for his*. Dear, *dear* Eddy, will your heart-broken mother never see you more? Oh! Neilson, when my precious Virginia left us to dwell with the angels, I had my Eddie to comfort and console me. But now *I am alone*. I have the *kindest, best* friends of anyone in the world, but that is not my dear Eddie—What right has Rose to anything belonging to *him*— he has not even written to her for more than two years, and she never has done anything for *him* except to speak ill of him, my friends are all most indignant at her request—I received a kind letter from my friend yesterday (Gen. Morris*) who advises me to pay no attention to her, I mean her request to be included in the profits of the works about to be issued. I am with the kindest friends who do all in their power to comfort me—When you send the trunk which I hope will be as soon as you can make it convenient, please direct to me, care of Charles B. Richmond, Lowell, Mass., and let me know how and when you *may* send it. Mr. Longfellow has been to see me and has made me promise to spend part of my time at his house in Cambridge. Oh! how kindly he spoke of my dear lost Eddie. He said he considered him the greatest man living only so short a time since, and now mourns for him *so sincerely*. Give my dearest love to Josephine, ask her to write to me and let me *love her*. God bless you and all who are dear to you. Please return the enclosed letters to me, for they are *most precious*.

> Your sincere and
> heart-broken friend—
> Maria Clemm

Poe's trunk *was* sent to Mrs. Clemm at Lowell. Sarah Heywood,* writing for her sister Annie, informed Ingram on December 25, 1876, that a package was being forwarded to him containing "an early edition of Mr. Poe's works" that had been found in the trunk sent to Mrs. Clemm soon after Poe's death. Mrs. Clemm detested Rosalie Poe and feared her claim on Edgar's estate so much that she secured the free services of a lawyer, Sylvanus D. Lewis, to contest Rosalie's claim. Rosalie herself got John Reuben Thompson of Richmond to act as her lawyer, free of cost, for what turned out apparently to be a nonexistent estate anyway, for no one knows if there really were profits made from the sales of Poe's works, or, if there were, who got them.

There is no record whatsoever of Mrs. Clemm and Rosalie meeting again after Edgar's death, nor was there any correspondence between them. It is not to be believed that Mrs. Clemm, feeling as she did about Rosalie, would have relinquished Poe's trunk or anything else belonging to him to Rosalie.

Longfellow certainly had little reason to mourn Poe or to visit or entertain Mrs. Clemm in his home, considering Poe's violent and sustained attacks on him; but one has to keep remembering that Mrs. Clemm loved to drop important names and deal in hyperbole. It is of course possible that there was more than magnanimity in Longfellow's bland remark about Poe's slashing attacks: "The harshness of his criticisms, I have never attributed to anything but the irritation of a sensitive nature, chafed by some indefinite sense of wrong." "Josephine" was Neilson Poe's wife, Josephine Emily, daughter of William and Harriet Clemm, and, therefore, Mrs. Clemm's stepdaughter.

Letter 9. **Maria Clemm, Lowell, to George W. Eveleth.** Copied (with the omission here indicated) from the autograph letter by Eveleth and forwarded to Ingram on October 1, 1878. First printing. [Item 72]

May 20, 1850

Although an entire stranger to you myself, but from your kind letters to my beloved and much lamented son (E. A. Poe) I feel that I am not writing to one unknown. Your last letter to him was sent to me from Richmond, after *he* had gone to dwell with the angels. Oh! did you know the desolation of my heart, you *could* not refuse to grant the request I make in asking you the great favor of disposing for me a few copies of his works. I have not received one dollar yet from the sale of them . . .

If you will write me a few lines and let me consider you *my* friend, as you were *his*, I will indeed be most grateful. If you *do* write me, I will then tell you all about my *noble, generous* Eddie. Oh, do not, I implore you, believe all the evil things said of him; only look at the *bright* side of his character. They who speak thus of him, knew him not. Have you seen the *Graham* for March? There the truth is told of him. May God put it into your heart to listen to the request of a heartbroken and childless mother!

George W. Eveleth's relationship with Poe and the very important contributions be made to Poe biography are related in Chapter VII.

Volumes I and II of Griswold's edition of Poe's works were off the press about January 10, 1850; Griswold gave a number of the sets to Mrs. Clemm to sell wherever she chose. She spent many years later trying to get Poe's friends to buy them from her and resell them to their friends. It is not known how much she actually received from these sales, but it was not inconsiderable; at least Dora Houghton* wrote Ingram in 1875 that Mrs. Clemm had lived with her family until "she was able to support herself" with the income from the sales of Poe's works. Even if this statement is not entirely accurate, it is certainly strong evidence that Mrs. Clemm did receive some money from the books.

George Graham wrote "The Late Edgar Allan Poe" and published it in his own magazine for March, 1850 (Vol. 36, No. 3, pp. 224–26). This article was a direct and powerful repudiation of Griswold's infamous "Ludwig Article" that had appeared as Poe's obituary in the New York *Herald Tribune* on October 9, 1849, two days after Poe's death. Eveleth's ellipsis after Mrs. Clemm's remark that she had "not received one dollar yet" almost certainly was made to eliminate her request to him for money. In this letter one can feel the depth and sincerity of Mrs. Clemm's terrible grief for Poe.

Letter 10.   Maria Clemm, Lowell, to George W. Eveleth.
Fragment copied by Eveleth and forwarded to Ingram on October 1, 1878. First printing. [Item 73]

May 30, 1850

I received your kind letter a few days ago, and am most grateful for your kindness in saying you will try to dispose of some of my books for me . . . I wish to write you a long letter, and tell you many things of my own darling Eddie. Oh! how much I thank you for saying you do not believe all you have heard against him—so few understood him. But *now* he will be appreciated—God, who he is now with, understands him.

Again, Eveleth omitted a portion of Mrs. Clemm's letter; the strong probability is that the part he cut had to do with her gratitude for money he had sent to her. Eveleth remained a staunch believer in Poe's essential good character and he became a knowing and valuable ally of Ingram's in defending Poe's reputation.

Letter 11. **Maria Clemm, Lowell, to George W. Eveleth.** Fragment copied by Eveleth and forwarded to Ingram on October 1, 1878. First printing. [Item 74]

June 8, 1850

I yesterday evening received your kind letter . . . I hope I will soon be equal to writing you a long letter concerning my own lost Eddie. At present, my health is inadequate to the task. Eight long, long months since he left me to dwell with the angels, and I feel every hour more *desolate*.

The "long letter" about Poe, frequently promised by Mrs. Clemm, never reached Eveleth. Her reiterations of her feelings of desolation were to continue for nearly twenty-one years.

Letter 12. **Maria Clemm, Lowell, to George W. Eveleth.** Fragment copied by Eveleth and forwarded to Ingram on October 1, 1878. First printing. [Item 75]

Sept. 24, 1850

I have taken the liberty to send you by express the third volume of my poor, *injured* Eddie's works. I beg you will suspend your opinion until you have heard *the other* side, which will appear in the Dec. number of *Graham*. He [George R. Graham], noble fellow, wrote to me the moment of seeing the book, urging me not to grieve, for he had a very *host* of noble souls prepared to refute many of those base *exagerations* [*sic*] and vile *misrepresentations*, and which would soon make the *Right Reverend* hide his head and fly the field. There were *occasional* times that my poor Eddie was not conscious of *what he wrote* or what he said, and of this Mr. Griswold has taken undue advantage.

Angered at the attacks made on him by the friends he had denied Poe, Griswold prefaced the third volume of Poe's works, off the press by mid-September, 1850, with the biographical *Memoir* that was a virulent expansion of his infamous obituary of Poe. Vehement objections appeared in print immediately, but they were unorganized, ephemeral articles in newspapers and magazines. It was not until after Griswold's death in 1857 that a well-organized and well-written protest was published in permanent book form: Sarah Helen Whitman's *Edgar Poe and his Critics* was brought out by Rudd & Carleton in New York, in 1860 (the book was actually on the market by December, 1859). The "Right Reverend" alludes to the fact that Griswold was a Baptist minister. Mrs. Clemm did realize to a degree that her frantic efforts to sell the books given to her by Griswold were, ironically, simply spreading the damage Griswold intended against Poe, but she persisted.

Letter 13.   Maria Clemm, Milford, Conn., to Sarah Helen Whitman, Providence, R.I. Copied for Ingram by Mrs. Whitman. Original letter in the Lilly Library, Indiana University.

Nov. 7, 1852

Dear friend,

I cannot express to you how much I was disappointed, when I had to pass so near Providence and not to see you. I have had it in contemplation to go south, where I have warm friends, and *know* I would have a happy home. But I have been obliged to relinquish this truly delightful prospect for want of means. Oh if I could see you for a short time, I know for *his* sake you would advise me what to do. How often do I wish I could go to my beloved children! And oh how I regret my dear Fordham home. I have many kind friends, but I cannot open my heart to them, as I could to my beloved lost ones. I sometimes feel *so* desolate, and think if I had but *one* left. I know it is very selfish to trouble you with my feelings, but I think you will sympathise with me. Do write me a long letter, I am always so happy to hear from you. Please direct to me, care of Wm. Strong, Milford, *Conn.* I do hope I will be able to make you a short visit some time this winter. Do you ever hear from Mrs. Locke? As soon as I went to Lowell (three years ago) I was told she had said so many unkind and *untruthful* things of my dear Eddie, that I was induced to write her a cruel letter. I have often regretted it since, but I could not *live* and hear such falsehoods about *him*, without resenting them. Believe me to be your sincere friend.

Maria Clemm

Mrs. Clemm's lugubrious nature forbids any supposition on our parts that she could possibly intentionally make a pun about the temperature of her friends in relation to their geographic location. Her wishes for death and references to her lonely, desolate condition had been, were, and would continue to be familiar notes, and her references to her "want of means" was a not-so-subtle hint to Mrs. Whitman to furnish her with them. Mrs. Whitman did indeed send her many sums of money on many occasions through the more than twenty years they corresponded, as letters ahead will make clear.

Letter 14. Maria Clemm, Alexandria, Va., to Sarah Helen Whitman, Providence, R.I. Copied for Ingram by Mrs. Whitman. Original letter in the Lilly Library, Indiana University. First complete printing.

April 14, 1859

My dear friend,

I received yours the day before yesterday, and hasten to express to you my sincere gratitude. God only knows what a relief it is to me, to be able *now* to procure medicines and other necessaries, in the state of my health at this time. I trust it may be returned to you an hundred fold. The family with whom I at present reside, are intimate with Mr. William Cassinoe, who married Judge Stannard's daughter; from him I have ascertained, that Mrs. Stannard has been dead about 26 years. She died entirely deranged, and had been so many years. Mrs. C, her daughter is hopelessly so. She is now in a lunatic asylum near this city. The Judge has been dead nearly 10 years. Robert married Miss Lyons of Richmond and died 4 years ago. Eddie was not in Richmond "twice." † We left there in 1837, and he never visited it again since the death of Virginia, until 1849. My father (Eddie's grandfather), was born in Ireland, but his parents left there when he was only six weeks old. My father was so patriotic he never would acknowledge he was any other than American. He lived in

Baltimore from the time of the revolution, he took my mother there, from Pennsylvania, a bride. They both lived and died there. My father was an officer in the army during the revolution, and was intimate with Washington & Lafayette. It is true dear Eddie did love Mrs. Stannard with all the affectionate devotion of a son. When he was unhappy at home, (which was very often the case) he went to her for sympathy, and she always consoled and comforted him, you are mistaken when you say that you believe he saw her but *once* in her home. He visited there for years. He only saw her once while she was ill, which grieved him greatly, he was but a boy at that time. Robert has often told me, of his, and Eddie's visits to her grave, he has pointed to her last resting place to me often, when we would visit the cemetery. It was a favorite drive of my darling Virginia's. I think now dear friend I have answered all your inquiries. Anything else I can inform you of concerning my beloved Eddie I will do with great pleasure. Alas my memory is *too* faithful, I often wish I could forget.

I am most happy to hear you look upon death as a happy change. God grant it may prove so to both of us. This is our lenten season, and we have church almost every day. There, and at my private devotion, I *do* and will always remember you.

Please return the enclosed letters when you have read them. They are most precious to me.‡

I have not heard from Mrs. Shelton for a long time, here no one knows her. I cannot ascertain if she is living or not. She has not been the friend to me that you have, and she is *rich too*, but I will not blame her, for she I suppose is entirely estranged from me. God bless you and take you into his holy keeping is the sincere prayer of your affectionate friend

Maria Clemm

[Mrs. Whitman's notes scribbled on the margins:]

† This is a mistake. He was there in 1848, also, and at that time renewed his acquaintance with Mrs. Shelton, who received him with marked favor.

S.H.W.

‡ These two letters were the *only* letters received from EAP after his engagement with Mrs. Shelton. They were the *last ever* received from him by Mrs. C[lemm].

In one letter was a message of tender & grateful remembrance to Mrs. Richmond of Lowell acknowledging all her kindness to him & to his mother & expressing his unchanging remembrance of her. In the angry letter which Griswold wrote to Pabodie after Pabodie's article appeared in the *Tribune*, among other gross calumnies, he says, "Poe wrote to his mother-in-law that if he married the woman to whom he was engaged in Richmond for her money he must still manage to live so near a creature (!) whom he loved in Lowell as to retain her as his mistress"!!! This was the interpretation which the insane hatred of G[riswold] put upon this expression of grateful remembrance!

Two letters from Mrs. Clemm

If Mrs. Clemm is right as to the date of Mrs. Stannard's death, she must have died in 1833, at which time Edgar Poe was 24 years of age.

Robert Stannard married a Miss Lyons of Richmond & died 1855.

Poe married Virginia Clemm in 1836 when he was *27*.

The "letters" which Mrs. Clemm speaks of on the 3rd page of this letter & which she says are most *precious to her* were letters written by Edgar from Richmond announcing his marriage with Mrs. Shelton. They were very, *very*, sad. They were the last he ever wrote to her, & were apparently written with a foreboding that they *would* be his last.

They were full of anxious expressions for her happiness & contained words of tender remembrance for Mrs. Richmond of Lowell, who had been *very kind to him & to Mrs. Clemm.* Mrs. C[lemm] spent a winter with that lady not long after Poe's death.

Mrs. Clemm placed these letters in my hands *voluntarily* without any request from me. I did not *ask* for them nor did I know of their existence. I did not copy them. I believe that she was influenced to do so by the spirit of one who knew how cruelly their meaning had been misrepresented by Griswold in a letter which he addressed to Pabodie after the appearance of his printed article in the *Tribune* exposing the falsehood of his (G's) statements. I send you [John Ingram] this letter—this extract—from Griswold's letter to show you *how utterly unscrupulous he was* in them that the noblest & purest need [not?] blush to have written. They express a grateful & affectionate remembrance of a Massachusetts lady who had been most kind to him & his mother. Griswold little dreamed that I should read these very letters when he wrote about them so *grossly* & so *falsely*.

S.H.W.

Biographical details of the Poe and Stanard families in this letter were in answer to Mrs. Whitman's specific questions to Mrs. Clemm. Mrs. Whitman was busy at this time gathering data for her forthcoming book, *Edgar Poe and his Critics*, by means of which she hoped to mitigate the harshness of Griswold's biography of Poe by submitting to the public "a more equitable and intelligible theory of the idiosyncrasies of his life," rather than a point-by-point refutation of what she called Griswold's "perverted facts and baseless assumptions." At this writing, Mrs. Clemm was living with the Reuben Johnston family in Alexandria, Virginia. Mrs. Clemm boasted frequently of her reliability as to facts and dates and claimed Poe had to refer to her for these things; this letter, however, displays several instances of her inaccuracies. "Mrs. Stannard" was Jane Stith Stanard, wife of Judge Robert Stanard and the inspiration for Poe's first "To Helen," or so Poe said. She was mentally unbalanced for perhaps a year before her death on April 28, 1824, nearly thirty-five years before this letter, not twenty-six, as Mrs. Clemm writes. Poe did visit Richmond "twice" after he moved his family to Philadelphia in 1837; he was there in the summer of 1848, as well as in the summer of 1849. "Robert" was the son of Judge and Mrs. Stanard, and was Poe's boyhood friend. "Mrs. Shelton" was Sarah Elmira Royster Shelton, Poe's boyhood sweetheart, perhaps. Mrs. Clemm made pressing applications to Mrs. Shelton for money after Poe's death, but with small success.

Letter 15. N. H. Morison, Peabody Institute, Baltimore, to John Ingram, London. First printing. [Item 184]

Nov. 27, 1874

Dear Sir,

I copied the enclosed letters more than a month ago, when pressing business turned my attention in another direction. I have inserted one of the two passages omitted about "literary ladies" by interlining on the last page of the 3rd sheet. As Mrs. Clemm is dead, I can see, on reflection, no harm in inserting the other sentences. On the first page of 4th sheet where the omission is marked, insert after "all letters received," "I was offered by that *base, base* man, Griswold, $500 for a certain literary lady's correspondence with Eddie. This was the reason I destroyed them, for fear I might by poverty be induced to do anything so *dishonorable*. The other letters I confided" etc.

This gives you all that is in the two letters, except what relates to some business & other personal matters in connection with Nelson Poe,* and containing nothing whatever about Edgar.

Mr. N. Poe began a letter to you, giving an account of Poe, & his (N's) recollections of him. I hope he has sent it. I have not seen him for some weeks.

Brooks is still living here—his address is N. C. Brooks, LLD. He has charge of a Young Ladies School. I have not seen him since I received your letter, I do not know anything about his *Museum*, but will endeavor to get information from him.

We shall receive with thanks a copy of your edition of Poe's works, and shall regard it as a valuable addition to our collection of books. Our London book agent is E. G. Allan, 12 Tavestock Row, Covent Garden. Anything left with him will surely reach us. Accept our thanks for your generous offer to present it to us.

I send you a copy of my last report of this Institute.

You know, of course, that E.P.'s father ran off with, & married, an actress, and was in consequence disowned by the family. This accounts for the little interest which they have apparently taken in the fame of Edgar; but I think, from talking with them, that this apparent indifference does not arise from any thought of disgrace, but from simply indolence. Edgar Poe certainly had many faults, but that is no reason for charging him with deeds he was not guilty of. Nelson says a single glass of wine would set his brain on fire, and that his only safety was in total abstinence.

Hoping that you may succeed in your laudable undertaking, and that you may obtain the information you need, and willing to aid you as I can in this respect, I am

Yours truly,
N. H. Morison

Neilson Poe was a lawyer, which probably prompted his chariness in allowing Morison to copy possible controversial matters in Poe's and Mrs. Clemm's letters for Ingram to publish.

Dr. Nathan Covington Brooks had edited, with Dr. J. E. Snodgrass, the *American Museum of Science, Literature and the Arts* in Baltimore from September, 1838, through June, 1839; Poe had contributed articles to many of the issues.

N. H. Morison was obviously on very good terms with Neilson Poe and his family, which makes his letters and reports about them and their reactions to their famous relative important indeed.

The statement that a single glass of wine set Edgar's brain on fire certainly was not original with Neilson Poe; he could have read it as far back as 1850, in N. P. Willis' essay on Poe, which followed James Russell Lowell's, prefacing Volume I of Griswold's edition of Poe's works. With so much authority behind this statement, it has become one of those myths in Poe biography that can never be proved or disproved; it simply is in every one of them, in one form or another.

Letter 16. **Maria Clemm, Alexandria, Va., to Neilson Poe, Baltimore.** Copied by N. H. Morison and forwarded to Ingram on November 27, 1874. First complete printing. [Item 93]

Aug. 19, 1860

Dear Sir,

I wrote you nearly two weeks ago, and, as I have not heard from you, I conclude that you are waiting to hear from me again relative to some information about my dear Eddie. He was born in Boston, Mass. on the 19th of January 1811. When he was 5 weeks old he was taken to Baltimore by his parents, and remained there for 6 months. They then went to Richmond, Va. His mother died there when Eddie was 2 years old. At that time Mr. Allan adopted him. He went to school until he was 7 in Richmond. Mr. & Mrs. Allan then went with him to England, and resided there in Russell Square, London. Eddie went to school 5 miles from London, to Dr. Brandeth, returning every Friday to his adopted parents, remaining with them until the following Monday. If you have read the story of William Wilson contained in his works, you will find a description of his school days. They returned to Va. when he was 14. He soon after went to college at the University of Virginia. After leaving there he went to West Point. He left West Point *voluntarily*, and was not *dismissed* as *some* of his biographers assert. He found the discipline too severe. If you will take the trouble to write to the President of Charlottesville College you will find my statement correct. He never went to Russia as has been stated in the different memoirs written about him. I can account for every hour of his life since his return to America. He was domestic in all his habits, seldom leaving home for one hour unless his darling Virginia or myself were with him. He was truly an affectionate, kind husband, and a devoted son to me. He was impulsive, generous, affectionate, and *noble*. His tastes were very simple, and his admiration for all that was good and beautiful very great. We lived for 5 years at Fordham, in the sweetest little cottage imaginable. It was there our precious Virginia left us to go dwell with the angels. I then wished to die *too*, but *had* to live to take care of our poor disconsolate Eddie. This I *know* I did do, and, if I had been with him in Baltimore, he would not have died and left me alone in this heartless world. Oh! how supremely happy we were in our dear cottage home! We three lived only for each other. Eddie rarely left his beautiful home. I attended to his literary business, for he, poor fellow, knew nothing about money transactions. How should he, brought up in luxury and extravagance! He passed the greater part of the morning in his study, &, after he had finished his task for the day, he worked in our beautiful flower garden, or read and recited poetry to us. Every one who knew him *intimately* loved him. Judges pronounced him the best conversationist [*sic*] *living*. We had very little society except among the literati, but this was exceedingly pleasant. Eddie finished Virginia's education himself, and, I assure you, she was highly cultivated. She was an excellent linguist, and a perfect musician, and she was so *very beautiful.* How often has Eddie said: I see no one so dignified and so beautiful as my sweet little wife. And oh! how pure and beautiful she was even to the last. But I would not recall them. In a short time I trust I shall go to them. A lady called on me a short time ago from Baltimore. She said she had visited my darling Eddie's grave. She said it was in the basement of the church, covered with rubbish and coal. Is this true? Please let me know. I am certain both he and I have still friends left to rescue his loved remains from degradation.

Respectfully,
Maria Clemm

N. H. Morison appended the following commentary to Ingram:

The above is her entire letter underscoring & all except one private sentence bearing no relation to Edgar Poe.

The University of Virginia is at Charlottesville, Albermarle County, Virginia. There is no truth in the report about the remains lying under heaps of rubbish beneath a church. They lie in the open yard in the family ground. Mr. Nelson * Poe, an own cousin (their fathers having been brothers) married a half-sister of Edgar Poe's wife. Who (N's wife) was also his own cousin & the cousin of Edgar. Mrs. Clemm was therefore Mrs. Nelson Poe's step-mother. Mr. Nelson Poe took care of Edgar in his last sickness, provided every comfort for him, including a nurse, and was with him a short time before he died. He had him suitably buried in the family burying lot, and ordered a simple marble slab with a suitable inscription to be erected as a head stone, to mark the grave. But the same fatality which seemed to pursue him in life balked the kind intention of his friend. The slab was completed and placed against the wall in front of the stone cutter's shop ready for removal to the grounds. A railroad runs along the street in front of the shop. A car ran off the track, passed over the stone, and broke it into a hundred pieces—almost grinding it up. Mr. N. Poe is a man of very moderate means, and he did not order another. I understand that the money has been raised by the teachers of the public schools, a monument has been ordered, & will be erected in a few months over his remains.

The fact of the destruction of the stone I have from Nelson Poe, who, by the way, was born in the same year as his cousin & brother in law.

Mrs. Clemm was always emphatic in asserting that Edgar was born in Boston, during an engagement of his mother, who was an actress, at a theatre in that city, but she afterwards wavered a little, as she grew older, between the years 1811 & 1809, as the proper date.

The story of Edgar Poe's death has never been told. Nelson Poe has all the facts, but I am afraid may not be willing to tell them. I do not see why. The actual facts are less discreditable than the common reports published. Poe came to the city in the midst of an election, and that election was the cause of his death.

Ingram used portions of this letter from Mrs. Clemm as well as parts of Morison's appended note, following his usual custom of breaking them up into paragraphs or sentences to use here and there as he told the story of Poe's life. (See *Life*, I, 146, for an ordinary example of his method.)

Mrs. Clemm's self-proclaimed accuracy as to dates and times and facts, causing Edgar to depend on her, suffers badly enough in this single letter to cause one to doubt or at least question anything else she said: Poe was born in 1809 not 1811; he was almost three years old (lacking a month and a day) when his mother died in Richmond. The John Allans never adopted Poe legally; he was simply taken into their home on a thought-to-be-temporary basis. He was six and a half years old when he went to England with the Allans, eleven and a half when he returned with them to Richmond, in June, 1820. He enrolled in the University of Virginia on February 14, 1826, when he was barely seventeen. He did not leave West Point voluntarily; he was court-martialed and dismissed early in January, 1831, actually leaving in March, 1831.

The Poe family, including Mrs. Clemm of course, moved to Fordham in the summer of 1846 and lived there until Poe's death in 1849, making the span three years and several months residence, instead of Mrs. Clemm's reported five.

Letter 17. **Maria Clemm, Alexandria, Va., to Neilson Poe, Baltimore.** Copy made by N. H. Morison and forwarded to Ingram on November 27, 1874. First complete printing. [Item 94]

Aug. 26th, 1860

Dear Sir,

I received yours yesterday, and I think it best to answer it while I can. I am strictly forbidden to use my eyes in any way, I am under the hands of a physician in Washington. If they get better, I will endeavor to give you the information relative to Eddie. Now I could not do so. This far I will tell you. He *never* was in *Greece* or *Russia*. I know Griswold said so during Eddie's life time. *Why* he asserted this I never could imagine. Eddie used to laugh heartily when he would hear it, but did not think it worth the trouble of contradiction. There never was any correspondence between Eddie and Virginia, for he was always with her—she often with him on a journey for a few days. It is utterly false—the report of his being faithless or unkind to her. He was devoted to her until the last hour of her death as all our friends can testify. After Eddie's death, I burned every letter except those relating to literature. I destroyed hundreds that were written by literary ladies. I know so well that Eddie wished me to do so. Virginia and I were cognizant of all letters he received, for he made it an invariable rule to give us to read *all* letters he received. [N. H. Morison inserted here these previously withheld sentences: "I was offered by that *base, base* man, Griswold, $500 for a certain literary lady's correspondence with Eddie. This was the reason I destroyed them, for fear I might by poverty be induced to do anything so *dishonorable.*"] The other letters I confided to Griswold, to make extracts from them. He never would return them to me, and I cannot get them from his executors. They were all from the most celebrated men living. Eddie's letters to me were many, but I have given so many away to those friends whom I know loved & appreciated him, I have not a fragment of his writing—so many have applied to me for anything that was once his. Mr. H. W. Longfellow wrote to me a few weeks ago for two of his autographs. They were the last I had. I could not refuse Mr. Longfellow, for he is one of my best friends, and constantly writes to me. I spent some time at his home in Cambridge. I enclose you two of Eddie's letters, one written at the time you generously offered to take my darling Virginia. I wrote to Eddie asking his advice, and this is his answer. Does the affection there expressed look as if he could ever cease to love her? and he never did. (private matters)

Respectfully,
M. Clemm

P. S. If there is any other information I can give you I will do so with pleasure. Painful as the subject is to me, I will sacrifice my own feelings if I can say one word to redeem *his* character. Will you get a little book written by S. Helen Whitman called Edgar Poe and his critics. She knew him *well*, and contradicts the assertion made by Griswold relative to herself. Will you have the goodness to write to me? I expect to be in Baltimore sometime next winter to superintend a monument for my dear Eddie and Virginia.

M.C.

N. H. Morison comments to Ingram on Mrs. Clemm's letter:

> The rest of the postscript merely private matter.
> The report of Poe's visit to Greece and Russia undoubtedly arose from the fact that his brother Wm. (represented by Nelson as even more of a genius than Edgar) went to both of those countries, and was sent home from Russia by the American Minister, Mr. Middleton of South Carolina. Mrs. Clemm is emphatic about Edgar's faithfulness to his wife, and I learn from Nelson that she was equally emphatic in denying the story told of his attempt to seduce the young wife of his benefactor, Mr. Allan. She asserted that he left Allan's immediately either after or before the marriage, and never saw Mrs. Allan but once again. Yet it is a fact that Mrs. Allan,

still living in Richmond, retains a bitter feeling towards him. Mr. N. Poe thinks the trouble arose from the fact, that Edgar looked upon the young wife as an intruder into the family, who was pushing him out, & that he made his feelings known very distinctly as we might expect from his impulsive nature. This conduct on his part was deeply resented, & probably never forgiven, by both Mr. and Mrs. Allan.

I have left out at the request of Mr. N. Poe two sentences which contain a serious charge against Griswold, with reference to his attempt to get possession of some of the letters afterwards burnt. [These sentences were reincorporated above, as Morison explained in his prefatory letter.]

Edgar Poe married his cousin when she was about 14. I have no doubt that exact dates can be procured. To prevent so premature a marriage, Nelson Poe offered to take the young lady, his half-sister-in-law, into his own family, educate her, & take care of her—with the understanding that, if, after a few years, the two young people should feel the same towards each other, they should be married. One of the two letters of E.P. sent by Mrs. Clemm to Mr. N. Poe, mentioned in the last letter, is an earnest, passionate protest against this arrangement, and Mr. N. Poe's offer was declined in consequence & the marriage took place in Christ's Church in this city, the ceremony being performed by Rev. now Bp. John Johns. The parties did not live together for more than a year, when they were again married in Richmond where they were to reside. This second marriage, the bride 15, took place to save all comments, because the first one had been so private. These facts are from N. Poe. Mr. N. Poe did not know why this offer had been declined till Mrs. Clemm sent him Edgar's letter in 1860, which letter he now has. He also has five or six other letters from Mrs. Clemm, most of them expressing her affection for Edgar and Virginia, but containing, I think, no facts of any importance. Mr. N. Poe, at that time, 1860, intended writing a Memoir of his cousin, made some collection of facts, but never wrote anything. He belongs, so his friends say, to the class of dilatory men, who plan and never do. I offered to copy the letters I send, lest he should omit to do so, and he had no objection. He talks very freely about his cousin. I have not found him reticent; but I do not think the Poes fully appreciate the genius of Edgar.

Poe's romantic bent probably accounts for his laughter over biographical accounts of himself having traveled in Greece, Russia, and France. Had he troubled to contradict them he could have saved his future biographers much acrimony. John Ingram accepted as true, for instance, Marie Louise Shew's transcribed notes, dictated by Poe, stating that he had traveled in France, been wounded in a duel, written two poems and a short story which were later credited to other writers, and so on. When Ingram published this story, none of which was true, he muddied Poe biography very much indeed.

There was indeed some correspondence between Poe and his wife: Mrs. Houghton sent Ingram Poe's autograph letter to Virginia dated June 12, 1846, and Ingram printed it in *Appleton's Journal*, May, 1878. Mrs. Houghton also told Ingram that Poe wrote numerous notes to Virginia.

One can only shudder at Mrs. Clemm's revelation of having burned "hundreds of letters" written by literary ladies to Poe. The "certain literary lady's correspondence" for which Griswold offered Mrs. Clemm $500 was almost certainly that of Mrs. Frances Sargent Osgood. Griswold was much attracted to her and was angrily jealous of her flirtation with Poe. Poe autographs were much in demand when this letter was written, and while it is not clear what Mrs. Clemm means when she says she sent her last two to Longfellow, it is likely that she cut Poe's signatures from his letters and forwarded them, a practice of which even Sarah Helen Whitman was guilty. It is not known when Mrs. Clemm visited Longfellow's home in Cambridge. Poe's letter begging Mrs. Clemm not to allow Virginia to be taken into Neilson Poe's home was dated August 29, 1835, and was first published in *Edgar Allan Poe: Letters and Documents*, edited by Arthur H. Quinn and Richard Hart in 1941 (Scholars' Facsimiles & Reprints, New York, pages 9–11). The second letter enclosed by Mrs. Clemm to Neilson Poe, written "a short time" before Poe's death, was dated from Richmond on September 18, 1849, and it too was first published by Quinn and Hart, 24–25.

Nothing in the verses left by Poe's brother, William Henry Leonard, supports Neilson Poe's assertion that he was "more of a genius" than Edgar; nor has it been established that W. H. L. Poe ever visited Greece and Russia.

The story of Edgar's attempt to seduce Louisa G. Allan* made the rounds for years. Elizabeth Oakes Smith, wife of Seba Smith, the American humorist, and herself a prolific writer, repeated it again in her letter to Ingram, dated April 7, 1875.[4]

Thorough examinations of all church records in Baltimore have failed to yield any evidence to support Neilson Poe's reported story that Edgar and

4. [Item 214]

Virginia were first married in Baltimore. The "glass of wine" myth, the genius of W. H. L. Poe, and the supposed marriage of Edgar and Virginia all remain in Poe biography and are still highly controversial.

Letter 18. **Maria Clemm, Putnam, Ohio, to Annie Richmond, Lowell.** Fragment sent to Ingram by Mrs. Richmond *ca.* 1876. First printing. [Item 95]

June 29th [18]61

My dear Annie

  This day eleven years I looked upon my dear Eddie for the *last* time. O how sad I. . . . from her this morning, and as she did not mention your visit I presume you did not see her. And Mr. Cudworth has gone as Chaplin to the army? If he does. . . .

At this writing, Mrs. Clemm was living in the home of Sallie E. Robins,* Putnam, Ohio, supposedly as a permanent guest. Miss Robins, masquerading in print as S. E. R., thereby hoping to be taken as a male writer, had announced her intentions of "reversing public judgment concerning Poe," and had invited Mrs. Clemm to live in her home and be a constant source of information about Poe and his friends. Miss Robins further promised Mrs. Clemm a trip to Europe, with all expenses paid, as well as a home with her for the rest of her life. Since Mrs. Clemm had worn out her welcome in many homes on the Atlantic seaboard, she embraced both invitations.

  Concluding that she would not live to return to America, and being engrossed by the subject of death anyway, Mrs. Clemm wrote another series of farewell letters to her friends, with some justification one must admit, for she was seventy years old at this time. Unfortunately, the European trip never materialized and the "permanent home" proved to be fairly short-timed. Nor did Sallie Robins finish her biography of Poe; for in 1861 she was carried, hopelessly mad, to an asylum. Mrs. Clemm was left stranded in a household on whose members she had not the slightest claim. The ensuing time was indeed long and dreary for her, for the weather was very bad and the approaching civil war made travel hazardous at best. Sallie Robins' mother kept to her room, and her brother's wife ran off with his best friend, leaving him to care for their only son. With her unable to return to the Baltimore area for a long time, Mrs. Clemm's letters at this period show her weighted down with the awkwardness of her position, the dreariness of the weather, and the sins of this world.

Ingram has corrected in pencil Mrs. Clemm's "eleven," showing that it was twelve years since she had seen Poe; for Mrs. Clemm had said goodbye to Edgar aboard the steamboat on June 29, 1849. "Mr. Cudworth" was the Reverend Warren H. Cudworth of East Boston, a good friend and former pastor of Mrs. Richmond.

Letter 19.   Maria Clemm, Baltimore, to Neilson Poe, Baltimore. Quoted in a letter dated March 27, 1912, from Miss Amelia Poe,* Baltimore, to John Ingram, London. First printing. [Item 453]

Sept. 27, 1870

"You have been a dear kind son to me. I wish you, when God calls me, to see to my burial."

Sometime in the spring of 1863 Mrs. Clemm made her way from Ohio back to Baltimore, where she immediately began soliciting her old friends for the $150 admittance fee to the Baltimore Widows' Home. Unsuccessful in this, she did gain entrance to the Episcopal Church Home, which had been the Washington Medical College Hospital on Broadway Street, where Poe had died. Apparently she was supported there until her own death eight years later, when she was buried beside Poe in the Presbyterian churchyard cemetery. It was not until 1885 that Virginia's bones were brought from Fordham—after having remained for some time in a small box in William F. Gill's possession. Gill said he had rescued the bones in the nick of time to save them from being destroyed, when the Fordham cemetery was razed in 1883, and he brought them to Baltimore where they were reburied on Poe's left. [5]

This letter of Mrs. Clemm's to Neilson Poe, dated September 27, 1870, was the only one in Ingram's collection he received too late to use, had he chosen, in his 1880 biography. Her last note to Neilson Poe was dated January 9, 1871, in the Church Home.

All of these eighteen letters written by Mrs. Clemm, with two long explanatory notes added to two of her letters by N. H. Morison, were at

5. See my article "The Exhumations and Reburials of Edgar and Virginia Poe and Mrs. Clemm," *Poe Studies*. VII (December, 1974), 46–47.

Ingram's hand when he began writing his articles and his biography of Poe. The following *facts* were now in his possession to use in combating Griswold's *Memoir*:

Poe did have friends—close, personal ones—and that he was highly regarded by such eminent personages as General Morris, Evert Duyckinck, and George R. Graham.

Poe could and did have some real regard for many of his fellow men.

Poe could be temperate, even unselfish, in the matter of wine sent to his house for use during his wife's last sickness.

Poe had actually taken and signed a temperance pledge in Richmond.

George R. Graham, Poe's former employer, had written and published a strong attack on the spirit and veracity of Griswold's *Memoir*, and he had written and published an equally strong defense of Poe's personal and professional character.

From these letters Ingram had added many facts and stories that most certainly colored his opinions of many persons closely associated with Poe and which were inevitably reflected in his writings about them. These things he had not known before receiving the letters:

That Mrs. Clemm was always deeply concerned, deeply fearful, about Poe's drinking.

That Annie Richmond's feelings about Mrs. Clemm had changed from love and pity to distrust and suspicion.

That, even before Poe came to live with her, Mrs. Clemm was a mistress in the art of writing begging letters, and that she could be, when she chose, both vindictive and capable of making threats.

That Mrs. Stella Lewis' word, oral or written, was not to be trusted.

That Poe's trunk had indeed been sent from Richmond after his death to Mrs. Clemm in Lowell, Massachusetts.

That Poe's boyhood sweetheart in Richmond had been Sarah Elmira Royster, later Mrs. Shelton.

That Poe was devoted to the memory of Mrs. Jane Stith Stanard, mother of his boyhood chum, Robert Stanard.

That Neilson Poe believed "a single glass of wine" would destroy Edgar's mental and physical equilibrium.

That the first headstone prepared for Poe's grave had been destroyed by an unfortunate railroad accident.

Finally, from the copies of Mrs. Clemm's letters made by Morison, with Neilson Poe's permission, Ingram learned much about Edgar Poe's early life, some of these facts reliable, some otherwise; he learned too that Edgar never had been to Greece or Russia; and he learned more about Virginia Poe and of Edgar's expressed and especial love for her.

III
Rosalie Poe Begs for Help

WITHIN TWO DAYS after Elizabeth Poe died in Richmond on December 8,1811, Mrs. John Allan took three-year-old Edgar into her home and Mrs. William MacKenzie took one-year-old Rosalie into hers. These arrangements were expected to be temporary, but Edgar was to remain in the Allans' care, after a fashion, for the next fourteen years, and Rosalie was to stay with the MacKenzies for more than fifty. Something apparently happened to Rosalie's mental processes when she was ten or eleven, for she went the rest of her long life a simple, childlike person, who always looked older than she actually was. Dull, tiresome, uninterested and uninteresting, she was able to contribute only slightly to the life around her. Her oddities of behavior and dress repelled Edgar, but she adored him and followed after him, uninvited and unwanted, when he revisited Richmond in the 1840s. To Sarah Helen Whitman Poe quietly explained this awkward relationship in that decade as "a coolness or estrangement of long standing."

Publication and widespread sale of the first edition of Poe's works, which included Griswold's infamous biography, brought fame not unmixed with slander to Poe's name. Rosalie, however, began early in the 1850s proudly trying to sell postcard pictures of her famous brother on the streets of Richmond.

When the Civil War was over, Rosalie was homeless. Some members of the MacKenzie family had gone to England; others were scattered in the countryside around Richmond. They were poor and they had to learn for the first time how to work for a living. Rosalie Poe was unfitted for the work or life on a small farm and she was terribly unhappy in the country. Dreaming and talking constantly of "the old times," she soon returned to the city, where she became a pitifully familiar figure tramping the streets trying to sell her postcard pictures of Edgar. After a while she betook herself to Baltimore where her cousins lived, but her wretched appearance and poor mentality made her less than welcome to the Baltimore Poes. Before long she was reenacting her Richmond role, haunting the streets of Baltimore, begging passersby to buy her brother's picture or to contribute to the welfare of the poor sister of Edgar Allan Poe.

A committee of kind ladies in Baltimore succeeded in getting Rosalie Poe admitted, around March 1, 1870, to the Epiphany Church Home in Washington, D.C., a refuge for the poor of that parish. When admitted, she was approaching sixty years old, and her health was failing.

Small paragraphs began appearing in newspapers along the Eastern Seaboard asking readers to contribute clothing and money to Poe's poor, sick sister. One of these was forwarded to Ingram in London by an American correspondent. Avid for any new source of information about Poe, Ingram addressed a letter to Rosalie at Hicks Landing, on the James River in Virginia, the address given in the newsclipping. Receiving no reply, Ingram asked the British consul in Baltimore to help him find Rosalie. That official referred him to the Reverend George Powell, a Baltimore minister who had known Rosalie for a long while and who had delivered public lectures on Poe's works during the winter of 1873/74, raising by this means some sixty dollars for Rosalie's benefit. Powell was at this time corresponding about Rosalie with James Wood Davidson, the South Carolina editor and writer who was an ardent admirer of Poe's works. Davidson was one of Ingram's helpful correspondents too, and he forwarded Powell's letter very quickly. From the letter to Davidson, Ingram learned that Powell thought Rosalie "a good old lady, but simple," and although she badly needed financial help, Powell would not recommend that a large sum of money be sent to her, he thought too much money at one time might have "an intoxicating effect" on her.

Ingram wrote immediately to Powell and told him of his efforts to raise money for Rosalie among his and Poe's friends in London. And he wrote to Rosalie at the Epiphany Church Home. She replied rather quickly.

Letter 20. **Rosalie Poe, Washington, D.C., to John Ingram, London.** Second printing. [Item 148]

April 28, 1874

Dr. Ingram

Kind Sir Several months you kindly wrote to me that you had some idea of publishing my Brothers life over again Edgar Allan Poe contradicting things that had been said about him that was not correct and asking me if I could give you any information concerning his life not been living with my Brother until a few years before his death I did not know I had a Brother or Brothers, I may say until I was a good size girl I took your letter as I was advised to my cousin Nilson [*sic*] Poe who is a lawyer in Baltimore I asked him to read it he replied after he read, and with my permission he would answer it he said at the same time there is money coming to you concerning this. After I said to him Dr. Ingram, that I wish he would as I could give you no information concerning my poor Brothers life. Not hearing from me you wrote to Mr. George W. Powell of Baltimore asking why I did not write. Mr. Poe has got my letter that you wrote to me and will not give R[ev] G. W. Powell any information concerning my Brothers life I saw Rv G. W. Powell he said not hearing from me he did not know what to do. I told Mr. Powell when he wrote to you to say the reason I did not write Mr. Poe said he would attend to it I will write to you myself telling you that if I had not known that Nelson Poe had not written I would have done so myself. I now write telling you that I am in the Charity Home in Washington in distressed circumstances I have a Home and nothing else for a support I have nothing everything I get I beg for it Now Dr. Ingram if you have a feeling heart for the destitute and distressed Sister of Edgar A. Poe will you do some thing to help me through I am in very bad health My strength is failing daily I have not many years to live 64 is my age. I am two years younger than my Brother Mr. Poe told me when I saw him last that your Books were published if they are you need no information about my Brother now Dr. Ingram I will give you information concerning myself and you will pity me if you knew my condition in life will you be so kind as to answer this letter as soon as you can. I have to furnish my clothes in this Charitable Home without a penny to my [self?] [nor?] a cent for a Stamp I have

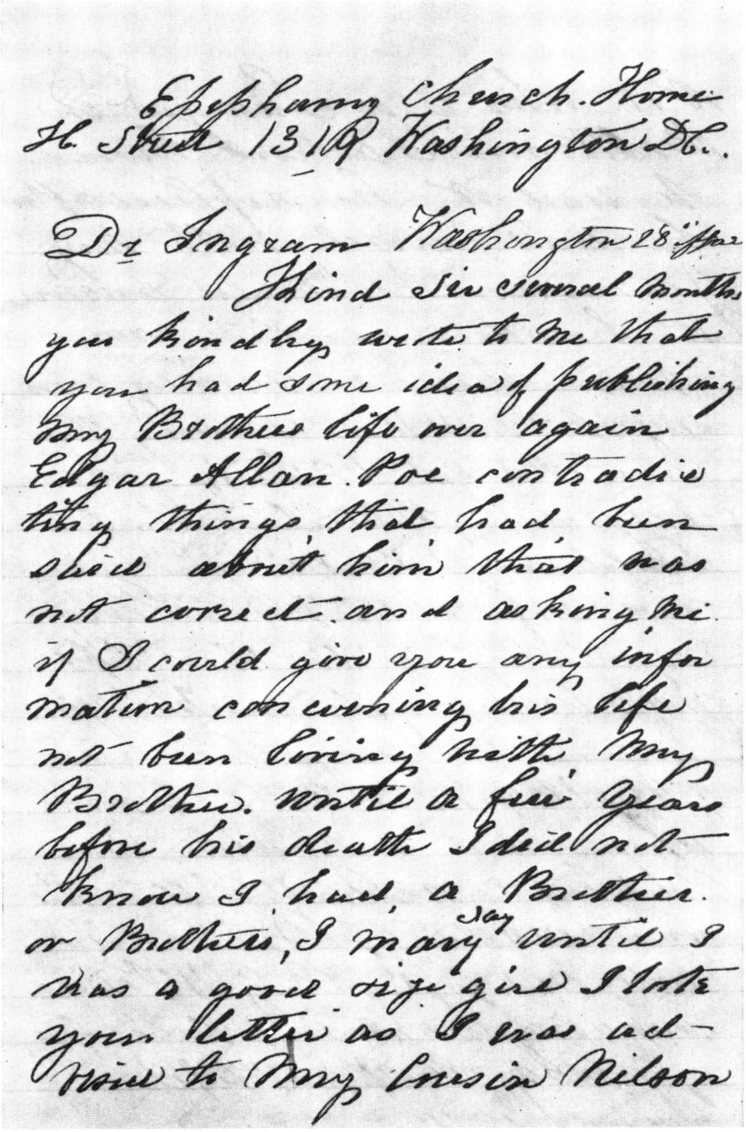

Rosalie Poe to John Ingram, April 28, 1874
Letter 20

nothing without assistance I hope you will get this letter I will give you my address

> 1319 H. Street Epiphany
> Church Home
> Washington DC
> Miss Rosalie M. Poe

This pitiful letter says much about the mental and emotional states of its writer, and it is of course filled with errors of fact, some of which are understandable, some not.

John Ingram was not "Dr." Ingram; his proudest title was "Fellow of the Royal Historical Society," granted to him in 1867.

The letter Rosalie Poe took to her cousin Neilson to read was very likely the one Ingram had addressed to her at Hicks Landing, Virginia. Neilson Poe had probably seen reprints of Ingram's articles on Poe in American magazines, which would account for his telling Rosalie that Ingram's books about Edgar were already published and that she had money coming to her from them; her letter is dated April 28, 1874, and the first volume of Ingram's edition of Poe's works actually did not come off the press until November, 1874. Neilson Poe was dilatory, to say the least, in matters concerning Edgar and Rosalie.

Several of Rosalie's statements in this letter are simply irreconcilable. Her saying that she did not know that she had a brother or brothers until she was a "good size girl" cannot be explained, for the Allan and MacKenzie families were on friendly visiting terms in Richmond when the Poe children were taken into their homes, and it is a matter of record that her older brother, William Henry Leonard, who lived with his paternal grandparents in Baltimore, did visit Edgar in Richmond at least on several occasions, and surely Rosalie was included in some of their activities.

Rosalie's statement that she had not been living with her brother "until a few years before his death" has some element of fact in it. There are good reasons to believe that she did indeed visit Edgar, Virginia, and Mrs. Clemm in Fordham in the summer of 1846, but her visit, which in those days was expected to last a week or even a month, was surely ill-timed: Virginia was sick; Edgar was away in feverish pursuit of Mrs. Frances Sargent Osgood;* and Mrs. Clemm heartily detested Rosalie.

The Epiphany Church Home in Washington furnished food and shelter, but the inmates were expected to supply their own clothes and other necessities of life.

Letter 21.   **Rosalie Poe, Washington, D.C., to John Ingram, London.** Second printing. [Item 158]

Epiphany Church Home
June 9, 1874

Dr. Ingram
   Kind Sir
   I hope you will excuse this mean piece of paper. I have no more as I have no money and no means I am in the Epiphany C. Home through kind persons I am on charity I have my food given to me. I have to find my own clothes indeed I have to find everything & nothing to do it with it [*sic*] sometime ago I wrote to you but not hearing from you I am afraid you did not get it. I got your address from Mr. George W. Powell. I will now write to you again enclose I will send you a small paragraph that will give you a good account of my situation and condition I got it from a Boston paper.   after reading it Dr. Ingram you cant fail to aid me I heard you had already raise me a little money but as yet I have heard nothing of it indeed it will be an act of charity for any one to assist me I have no one at all to call on. I have relatives but they are not willing to help me Dr. Ingram will you answer these few lines and you will oblige Miss Rosalie Poe Sister of Edgar Allan Poe

Miss Rosalie Poe

Apparently, Ingram did not reply directly to Rosalie Poe's letter of April 28, 1874, although he did write to the Rev. G. W. Powell informing him that he was raising money for a fund to be established in Rosalie's name, with small amounts to be issued to her from time to time.

There is a small, unidentified newsclipping, Item 569 in the Ingram Poe Collection, that reads, "Rosalie Poe, now poor, aged, and helpless, resides in Baltimore." This, possibly, was the clipping she had enclosed in her letter to Ingram.

The Baltimore Poes either ignored or barely tolerated Rosalie when she appeared, almost certainly unannounced, in Baltimore in the late 1860s. One may be sure, too, that her appearance and her street begging did little to endear her to them.

Death came swiftly for Rosalie Poe on Wednesday morning, July 22, 1874. Summoned downstairs to sign for a registered letter, she returned to her room seeming much exhausted. Tearing open the letter, but not reading it, apparently, she threw herself upon her bed and lapsed into unconsciousness. About nine o'clock, she died.

The letter contained a postal order for fifty dollars, sent by George W. Childs, a Philadelphia philanthropist, in reply to a request from Rosalie.

The governing board of the Episcopal Church Home met and decided to bury Rosalie Poe in the plot in Washington's Rock Creek Cemetery that had been set aside for the inmates of the home. That plot was marked by a marble shaft, one side of which was inscribed, "For Epiphany Church Home"; and on the reverse, "For the Poor of Epiphany Parish." The original stone has recently been replaced.

There was little in this correspondence with and about Rosalie Poe to help Ingram in his biography of Edgar Poe. He did mention in Volume I that she was born in 1811, some months after her father died, and that she was taken in by the MacKenzie family in Richmond. In Volume II he told of Rosalie's legal adoption by the MacKenzie family; and he retold, too, of Mrs. Clemm's bitterness over Rosalie's attempts to claim a share of her brother's estate, which would have been a share in the proceeds from the sales of Griswold's edition of Poe's works.

In addition, also in Volume II, Appendix C, 256–57, Ingram told what little there was to tell of Rosalie's life and death.

IV

William Hand Browne Becomes a Loyal Ally

INGRAM SHOULD have marked the day, March 10, 1874, with a white stone on his calendar, for that was the day he mailed his first letter to George W. Eveleth, asking his help in writing a biography of Poe. Eveleth's own remarkable and invaluable contributions followed, albeit some four years later, and the publication of the letter in the *Southern Magazine* brought to Ingram a number of replies, plus the important fact that it enlisted on Ingram's side in his war against Griswold the vigorous and intelligent help of the editor of the magazine, William Hand Browne.

Long an ardent admirer of Poe's writings, Browne had also from the first believed that Poe's reputation as a man had been cruelly wronged by Griswold, and he had hoped that one day someone would appear who was strong enough to right the wrongs done to Poe. Ingram appeared to be the man for the job. Browne promptly joined forces with him, brought other influential and knowledgeable persons into the struggle, and forwarded to Ingram many, many letters and items for Ingram to use as he saw fit. Browne was a far better educated man than was Ingram, and his temper and disposition were certainly more evenly balanced; for the times came when Ingram tried his old gambit of exercising his choler on Browne, but Browne simply turned the incidents aside with quiet reasoning and explanations and continued to help the English author. Browne's correspondence with Ingram began in mid-1874 and did not cease until 1909, an unmatched period of more than thirty-five years of almost completely amicable relations with Ingram. Ingram never had a more valuable ally than William Hand Browne proved himself to be.

Browne was a Baltimorean through and through. He was born in the city, educated there and at the University of Maryland, and he lived all of his long life in and near the city. Graduated with the degree of M.D. in 1850, he found that he did not like the practice of medicine and he never followed it. He became a translator, an author, editor, historian, lexicographer, and he founded and edited a series of magazines, among the more important being the *Southern Review* and the *New Eclectic Magazine* (later called the *Southern Magazine*, coedited with Lawrence Turnbull).

In 1879, Browne began his life-long association with Johns Hopkins University, first as librarian, then, after serving in a variety of positions, as professor of English literature, and finally as a professor emeritus until his death in 1912.

Browne was mild-mannered, learned, and humorous; his wide range in classical as well as modern literature, his broad scope of information, and his artistic skill made him of great assistance to his colleagues and much admired by the brighter of his students. His most important achievements lie, however, in the fields of colonial American and Maryland history; for at the close of his life he had edited and published thirty-two large quarto volumes of the *Archives of Maryland*, the first two parts of the "Calvert Papers," and the first five volumes of the quarterly *Maryland Historical Magazine*.

Letter 22.   **William Hand Browne, Baltimore, to John Ingram, London.** First printing. [Item 167]

Office "Southern Magazine"
Baltimore, Augt. 24, 1874

Dear Sir:

I have just received from Mr. G. W. Eveleth, a note intended for publication in the *Southern Magazine*, calling upon all persons who may be in possession of authentic information in regard to the life of Edgar A. Poe, to place themsleves in communication with you (or with this magazine) that your most praiseworthy intentions of doing justice to that extraordinary genius and most misrepresented man, may be assisted. I shall have especial pleasure in assisting you in this

"Cooping" &c

Office "Southern Magazine"
Baltimore, Augt. 24ᵗ 1874

John H. Ingram, Esq.

Dear Sir:

I have just received from Mr. G. W. Eveleth, a note intended for publication in the *Southern Magazine*, calling upon all persons who may be in possession of authentic information in regard to the life of Edgar A Poe, to place themselves in communication with you (or with this Magazine) that your most praiseworthy intentions of doing justice to that extraordinary genius and most misrepresented man, may be assisted. I shall have especial pleasure in assisting you in this matter in this or any way; for I have long been anxious to see such a work as I am confident yours will be.

I think the whole annals of literature show no baser act than the publication of Griswold's and Lowell's calumnies upon the man whom they praised when alive, often

William Hand Browne to John Ingram, August 24, 1874
Letter 22

matter in this or any way; for I have long been anxious to see such a work as I am confident yours will be.

I think the whole annals of literature show no baser act than the publication of Griswold's and Lowell's calumnies upon the man whom they feared when alive, after his death had made them secure. But especially malignant was the publication of these calumnies as a "Biographical Sketch", *attached to Poe's works*, so as to ensure that every reader of *these* should have *that* placed under his eye. We know that a little wine or spirits made Poe drunk, and that when drunk, he did wild, foolish, it may be wicked things; but never, that I know of, a single ungentlemanly act when sober; nor ever, even when drunk, anything so vile as this act of his biographers.

It may be in my power to procure you some reminiscences or unpublished poems of his. I have one called "The Vale of Nis", which originally appeared in the *Southern Literary Messenger*, which is much at your service.[1] Have you access to the files of the *S.L. Messenger*? They are in our libraries here, and I would take pleasure in searching them for you.

My friend, Paul H. Hayne, Esq. was editor of the *Messenger* for a while, and I think is in possession of interesting material in reference to Poe which I am sure he would take pleasure in communicating.[2] Indeed it was from a communication of his to *Appleton's Journal*, that I cut "The Vale of Nis."

I will send you by this mail a paper on Poe which appeared in the Augt. No. of the *Southern Magazine*.[3] One point in it, referring to the circumstances of his death, may require explanation. At that time, and for years before and after, there was an infamous custom in this and other cities, at election-time, of "cooping" voters. That is, gangs of men picked up, inveigled, or even carried off by force, men whom they found on the streets (generally the poor, friendless, or strangers) and transported them to cellars in various slums of

---

1. "The Valley Nis" originally appeared in Poe's *Poems* (New York: Elam Bliss, 1831). It was reprinted in the *Southern Literary Messenger*, February, 1836.
2. Browne is mistaken. Hayne never edited the *Southern Literary Messenger*; he did edit a short-lived magazine named the *Southern Literary Gazette*.
3. W. Baird, "Edgar Allan Poe," *Southern Magazine* (XV), 190–203.

the city, where they were kept under guard, threatened and maltreated if they attempted to escape, often robbed, and always compelled to drink whiskey (frequently drugged) until they were stupefied and helpless. At the election, these miserable wretches were brought up to the polls in carts or omnibuses, under guard, and voted the tickets placed in their hands. Death from the ill-treatment was not very uncommon. The general belief here is, that Poe was seized by one of these gangs, (his death happening just at election-time; an election for sheriff took place on Oct. 4th), "cooped", stupefied with liquor, dragged out and voted, and then turned adrift to die. He died in the Washington University Hospital.

As a corroboration of what I have said of the "cooping" process, I give an extract from Scharf's *Chronicles of Baltimore*, referring to the elections of 1858. The "Reform Association", he says, was organized "to secure quiet and fairness at the polls, which at this time were scenes of the most disgraceful violence and disorder. In addition to the ordinary acts of riot and intimidation, honest gentlemen as well as unfortunate wretches were frequently seized and 'cooped' in vile dens, drugged and stupefied with whiskey, and then carried round and 'voted' in ward after ward, the police offering no opposition, and the judges receiving the votes". (*Chron. of Balto.* p. 567).

The custom had prevailed for many years; but outrages had grown so flagrant that law-abiding citizens associated to put down ruffianism, armed themselves, and extinguished it effectually. I will add, if I can procure a copy, a paper of my own on Poe's *Eureka*, which was published in *The New Eclectic Magazine* (Baltimore) of Augt. 1869.[4]

Wishing you every success in your most worthy undertaking, and renewing my proffer of service, I am

Your very obt. servt.
Wm. Hand Browne
Editor *Southern Magazine*

---

4. William Hand Browne, "Poe's 'Eureka,' and Recent Speculation," *New Eclectic Magazine*, V (August, 1869), 190–99.

Ordinarily, Lowell's name is not linked with Griswold's as Poe's principal defamer. Lowell did, however, allow a note on Poe's life that he had written at Poe's own request and had published in *Graham's Magazine*, February, 1845, to be used as a prefatory biography of Poe in Griswold's 1850 edition of Poe's works. Griswold's own *Memoir* of Poe, published in the third volume of the edition in September, 1850, later supplanted it and took first place in succeeding editions.

The importance of this letter is in Browne's calling Ingram's attention to W. Baird's article, "Edgar Allan Poe," which had appeared in the August, 1874, edition of the *Southern Magazine*, in which Baird flatly states that Poe was almost certainly "cooped" and drugged, and that he had voted on the fourth of October in Baltimore, and died as a result of the treatment he received at the hands of the gang. The quotation from Colonel John Thomas Scharf's *Chronicles of Baltimore* authenticates the practice. Ingram repeated the whole story, as he learned it from this letter, in *Life*, II, 235–36, but he did not credit Baird, Browne, or Scharf as sources of his information.

Letter 23.   **William Hand Browne, Baltimore, to John Ingram, London.** First printing. [Item 235]

June 1875

My dear Ingram:

My letter seems to have been lucky. That frightful *Schiller* disaster produced much feeling here; but in a few days it was almost forgotten by the public.[5] We live in such an age of hurrying sensations that nothing seems to make a lasting impression: yesterday's shipwreck is lost in to-day's murder, as that will be in tomorrow's "gigantic forgery."

The review of your book was already out before I sent you the sheet (I think)—I did not suppose it could possibly reach you in time for any corrections, had I had it set up as soon as written. As Gilfillan has apologised for his atrocity, I will

5. Two hundred lives were lost on May 7, 1875, when the *Schiller*, a steamboat en route from New York to Hamburg, went aground on the Scilly Islands, southwest of England, off Land's End.

mention the fact; but I am strongly inclined to suspect that it was a pure invention of his own.[6]

Before I forget it, let me say that Dr. Maupin of Univy of Va. is named *Socrates*, not *Stephen*; and he is not President of the Univy (which has no President) but Chairman of the Faculty. I do not think he is called "Dean," as in the Univy of Maryland.

I tried to get the facts of Poe's editorship of the *Messenger* & White's letter; but could not find a copy of the lst vol. of *S.L.M.* anywhere in the city.

Beauchampe and *Greyslaer* are out of print; but I may pick up an old copy at some book-stall.[7]

I am sorry that my review seemed to strike you most by its "forebearance." I had nothing on which to exercise that quality; and the impression I meant to produce (beyond the correction of Griswold's lies and the vindication of Poe) was that of admiration for, and gratitude toward the stranger whose generous enthusiasm had led him to take so much pains, under great disadvantages, in doing what none of Poe's countrymen and even kindred, had ever done. If the tone of my review seems "forebearing," I have utterly failed in my object. By the way, it has been well received—I mean your vindication as therein contained.[8]

I saw old Dr. N. C. Brooks* some time ago. He *thinks* there were some pieces of Poe's in the *Museum* that were not included in Poe's published works, and promised to hunt over his set, and if he found any, to let me copy them for you.

---

6. George Gilfillan, a British clergyman, had asserted in the London *Critic* in 1854 that "Poe's heart was as rotten as his conduct was infamous," and that he broke his wife's heart, hurrying her to a premature grave, that "he might write 'Annabel Lee' and 'The Raven'." Gilfillan withdrew these statements when he was furnished proof that Poe had written "The Raven" two years before his wife died.

7. Poe's one drama, "Politian," was based on the "Kentucky Tragedy," which took place in Frankfort, Kentucky, in the 1820s; a number of other American writers used the same events in various ways: Charles Fenno Hoffman wrote a novel, *Greyslaer* (1840) touching upon the theme; William Gilmore Simms based his novel *Beauchampe* (1842) upon the actual deeds of the characters and used their real names. See *Quinn*, 231–32, for a brief but full treatment of this matter.

8. Browne had reviewed Ingram's memoir of Poe which prefaced Volume I of his four-volume Edinburgh edition of Poe's works in the *Southern Magazine*, XVI, 640–50, reprinting the memoir almost completely. At this time the American copyright on Poe's works prevented the Edinburgh edition from being republished or offered for sale in the United States. Ingram's edition was brought out, however, by W. J. Widdleton, New York, 1876.

I have ordered a copy of the review to be sent to Mrs. Whitman.

Valentine* is, I suspect, busy. His grand statue of Lee has been set up and unveiled with appropriate ceremonies. He is a noble fellow—a true genius, with none of the drawbacks under which genius so often labors; modest, unaffected, courteous.

The Public Schools here are going to erect Poe's monument. I hear that the design has been chosen. I will let you know about it, and send you a photo. If I can get one.

Mrs. Clemm I fancy to have been one of those gentle, childlike, somewhat weak women, whom you can not help loving and losing all patience with. But a Southerner, remembering the war, must lay his hand on his mouth when he speaks of Southern women. What they dared, and what they endured, is simply beyond belief.

John R. Thompson's* word may be implicitly relied upon in all matters within his own knowledge; though in others he may have been misinformed.

In some of his [Poe's] *Marginalia* (which I trust you have sifted over, as they were in great part mere commonplace-book notes, many of which he has worked up)—in some, I say, he says some odd things. Sophocles's giving "immortality to a sore toe," is of course an allusion to Philoktêtês; but what does he mean by "dignifying tragedy with a chorus of turkeys"? The turkey was not known in Europe until the 16th century; and I have not seen anything in Sophocles (including the Fragments) that could be twisted into an allusion to it, unless he got into some confusion about *Meleager* and Meleagris, the scientific name of the species to which the turkey belongs.[9]

I have picked up a copy of *Greyslaer* at a book-stall, and it is at your service if you want it. *Beauchampe* I may pick up any day. I think I am on the trail of the *facts* in the Beauchampe tragedy; & if I get them, will send them to you.

---

9. According to the *Oxford English Dictionary*, the American and Canadian colloquial phrase "to talk turkey" means to use high-flown language. Perhaps Poe meant no more than this.

I have not heard from Dr. Morison (of Peabody Institute) yet; but no doubt the vols. consigned to him will reach me safely.

> Very sincerely yours,
> Wm. Hand Browne

Ingram's complaint of Browne's "forebearance" in his reprint of the memoir in his magazine illustrates very well the cast of Ingram's mind; he was himself emotional, burning with indignation against Griswold, and he expected all who joined with him to be equally impetuous if not fiery. Browne's level-headed handling of this matter of getting the memoir before the American public, and the quality of his reply to Ingram about his objections gave even Ingram pause. Browne was proving to be too valuable an ally for him to lose, and the depth and breadth of his perceptions, plus his position in Baltimore and his friendships with Neilson Poe and N. H. Morison, provost of the Peabody Institute in Baltimore, made Ingram temper his future remarks when he disapproved of Browne's actions or inactions.

Dr. Nathan C. Brooks was editor of the *American Museum of Science, Literature and the Arts* in Baltimore, a magazine to which Poe contributed; "Valentine" was E. V. Valentine, the Richmond sculptor who proved to be another of Ingram's valuable helpers in searching out Poe materials, especially in Richmond, because he was on friendly terms with both Mrs. Shelton and Mrs. John Allan. John Reuben Thompson did not live up to Browne's recommendation in this letter, for he proved to be an unreliable witness and reporter of Poe's activities, after Poe had died.

From this letter Ingram did learn of the increased tempo of the Poe monument committee's actions, which were to culminate in the exhumation of Poe's and Mrs. Clemm's bodies and the reburial of them in the front of the Presbyterian churchyard cemetery with the monument over them. Unveiling ceremonies were held on November 17, 1875.

Letter 24. **William Hand Browne, Baltimore, to John Ingram, London.** First printing. [Item 243]

> Augt. 17, 1875

My dear Ingram:—

I deeply sympathise with the trouble to which your letter adverts; beyond all doubt the most terrible calamity that can befall or threaten anyone.

The committee that have the Poe monument in charge, have determined, I learn, to have no inscription beyond name, birth, and death. On the whole, I think this is in the best taste; though I thank you for your suggestion about Tennyson, of which I should certainly avail myself if any epitaph were proposed. Would he write a poem (or a few verses) do you think, to be read at the celebration, or ceremony, of placing the monument?[10]

I have, as a literary man, published various carefully-prepared papers on Tennyson's poems, but I have never taken the liberty of sending him copies, much less writing to him. The Yankee itch for writing to persons of eminence, merely because they are eminent, seems to me infinitely impertinent; and I should no more think of writing to Tennyson merely because I have been a student of his poems, than I should think of marching into his house and sitting down to dinner, uninvited. Of course, any specific business (like that of the epitaph) would justify correspondence.

I went with Valentine* the other day to Poe's grave, and he gathered some mementos for you. It is a quiet old graveyard, with many quaint old monuments, and full of shrubs and trees—mimosas, fig trees, spiraea, and especially peaches. A large peach tree, laden with fruit, partly over-hangs the poet's grave, which is a grassy mound. By his side, (the sexton said) lies his mother-in-law, Mrs. Clemm.

Neilson Poe tells me that John P[rentiss Poe] has written you a long and full letter.[11] He says (Neilson) that no man has a more thorough knowledge of Poe's merits and faults, than he has. One of the grossest scandals, he says, was that Poe was unfaithful to his wife. He avers that never was there a more

10. The plans for the inscription on Poe's monument were enlarged to include an epitaph, and a number of important American, British, and European poets were asked to suggest an appropriate one. Tennyson repaid Poe's two highly laudatory reviews of his poetry by suggesting an epitaph not exactly original: *In pace requiescat*. See Sara Sigourney Rice (ed.), *Edgar Allan Poe: A Memorial Volume*, (Baltimore: Turnbull Brothers, 1877).

11. Neilson Poe's son, John Prentiss, had written to Ingram telling him much about the genealogy of the Poe family, on May 1, 1875. J. P. Poe had also stated in his letter that Edgar's brother, William Henry Leonard, was, or gave promise of being, as great a genius as Edgar. Nothing that survives by W. H. L. Poe bears this out, but it made its way into Poe biography by way of this letter.

genuine love-match, and that Poe never swerved from his fidelity during his wife's life, though he was exposed to extraordinary temptations. His remarkable personal beauty, the fascination of his manners and conversation, and his chivalrous deference and devotion to women, gave him a dangerous power over the sex.

He told me something about Griswold which I was very glad to hear. That malignant scoundrel went to So. Carolina, and there married a lady for her wealth. Almost immediately after the marriage, he found that her property was not of the extent, or in the position, he supposed, so he applied for a divorce to a New York court. The decree was granted, and he re-married straightway. The lady appealed, the former decree was reversed, and a suit for bigamy instituted against the Rev. Rufus, who, luckily for him, died before it came to trial. This was Poe's defamer! I suppose Griswold's biographers will keep that little incident in the dark.

I shall be very glad indeed to be allowed to publish your paper on *Politian*.[12] Could I get an electro-plate of the facsimile—paying for it, of course?

I wish I knew Horne. His *Orion* is a favorite book in my library. I squeezed a slender purse and had my favorites—the books which I study—bound in full calf and Russia; and *Orion* is in calf, and stands with Shelley and Tennyson. It is a most noble poem, and in flashes of splendid imagination is unsurpassed. Poe's criticism of it was careless and had errors, unless his edition differed from mine. I shall take great pleasure in reviewing *Cosmo d. M.*, as I particularly admire Horne's poetry.[13]

I send *Greyslaer* by this mail; please accept it; also my thanks for your kind sympathy with my bereavement.

Faithfully yours,
Wm. Hand Browne

---

12. Browne printed Ingram's long paper on "Poe's 'Politian'" in the *Southern Magazine*, XVII (November, 1875), 588–94. Ingram had been able to get the entire manuscript of Poe's drama from Mrs. Stella Lewis, and this paper was one of Ingram's major additions to Poe literature.

13. Browne did review Richard Hengist Horne's *Cosmo de' Medici, an Historical Tragedy; and other Poems* (London: George Rivers, 1875) in the *Southern Magazine*, XVII (1875), 630–34. His review was in keeping with his expressed opinion of Horne's writings in this letter.

One cannot be positive as to the nature of Ingram's "trouble," which drew deep sympathy from Browne, but it is possible that he had confided to Browne, as he had to Mrs. Whitman early in 1874, that he lived under the threat of hereditary insanity, to which two of his aunts, his father, and one of his two sisters had already succumbed. Some of his rival American biographers of Poe were to be of the decided opinion that he had joined them.

Griswold's biographers could not keep his three marriages in the dark, but at least his latest biographer, Joy Bayless, in *Rufus Wilmot Griswold* (Vanderbilt University Press, 1943), tells the story somewhat differently than Browne does in this letter.

This letter added to Ingram's knowledge of Poe's burial place; and he actually had a portion of it, for the "mementos" gathered for him by E. V. Valentine were bits of grass from the grave itself. Then too, he found here material to strengthen his oft-proclaimed belief that Poe had indeed been perfectly faithful to his wife, and that theirs was a true love match. From the letter sent him by John Prentiss Poe, he quoted verbatim for nearly a half page in his Appendix A on Poe's ancestry. (See *Life*, II, 248–49.)

Letter 25.   William Hand Browne, Baltimore, to John Ingram, London. First printing. [Item 254]

Octo. 28, 1875

My dear Ingram:—

By the tenor of yours of 14th inst., I see that you had not yet received my last. "Politian" is out in our Nov. No. I have ordered the *S.M.* sent to you regularly: if it fails to reach you, drop me a card. We do not appear as early as the Northern monthlies; generally coming out from 20th to 25th.

Thanks for *Cosmo de Medici*, which I have received with, I think, just appreciation. Mr. Horne's poetical work has been very appreciatively noticed by Edmund Clarence Stedman (of N. York) in a book just out, called *The Victorian Poets*, the only *real* work of real criticism that this generation has produced, so far as I have seen—I mean on this side of the Atlantic. It is at once analytic, discriminating, and thoroughly sympathetic, with unusual breadth and catholicity, and with the most delicate appreciation of excellence, or even merit, of every kind.

Col. Scharf promises to send you a copy of his *Chronicles of Baltimore*.[14] It is a rather undigested work, but you will find matters of interest in it here and there. I have promised him, in your name, that you would notice it in some one of the London literary journals.

I am glad Valentine sent you that photo., which, however, does not do his grand work justice. It should be seen from *all* sides to make its full impression.[15] He is a noble fellow—a real prince.

I will certainly send you a photograph of the Poe monument if any are taken, as I suppose they will be. Also an account of the inauguration.

I enclose Mrs. Whitman's reply to some foolish Yankee scribbler.[16]

I see in a recent paper by Proctor—"Severrier's Balance," I think, was the title, the very ground Poe presents in *Eureka*, viz:—that induction does not lead to discovery, nor has ever done so: that all great discoveries have been made by theory—that is, deduction, helped by sudden flashes of intuition—the sudden recognition of consistency between facts and a mode of explaining the facts; or an intuition that if there be A, B, and C, there ought be, and must be D and E, though we cannot yet show them. This intuition of Poe's, I consider only a swift deduction of which the separate links pass so swiftly through the consciousness that they are not recognised as links. It is often so in guessing a riddle: the answer flashes on you, you can't tell how, yet a regular series of processes has led to it. The more science, and especially study of the laws of thought, progresses, the more clearly will the truth of Poe's views be shown; though he will get no credit—"what porridge had John Keats"?[17]

---

14. John Thomas Scharf, *Chronicles of Baltimore* (Baltimore: Turnbull Brothers, 1874).

15. There is a 7 × 9 photograph of Valentine's statue of Thomas Jefferson in the Ingram Poe Collection. [Item 484]

16. Francis Gerry Fairfield had called Poe an epileptic, among other things, in an article in *Scribner's*, October, 1875. Mrs. Whitman's "A Reply to Mr. Fairfield" was published as a long letter in the New York *Tribune*, October 13, 1875, in which she cuttingly refuted Fairfield's argument. Mrs. Whitman herself felt this article to be the sharpest she ever wrote about anyone, including Griswold.

17. The last line of a poem called "Popularity," by Robert Browning.

The unveiling of Jackson's statue at Richmond—from the hand of your Foley—was a grand affair. The Southern heart beat once more. It was a graceful gift, and draws us nearer to our noble old mother, England.[18] By the way, did I ever tell you I am of pure English blood? My mother came from Warwickshire (Wilnecote, I think); and my father's family is English, intermarried with English, for 200 years.

Trusting that we may meet next year, I am

Faithfully yours,
Wm. Hand Browne

Ingram was able to quote extensively from Colonel Scharf's *Chronicles of Baltimore*, both directly and indirectly. From these records, he could establish the facts that Poe's grandfather, David Poe, had been a staunch patriot, a wealthy man who contributed largely to help finance the American cause in the revolutionary war, thus earning for himself the title of General Poe, as well as the lasting regard of General Lafayette, who on his last visit to Baltimore in 1824 paid visits of respect to General Poe's widow and to his grave. From this same source Ingram was also able to retell the incident of Poe's grandmother's personally helping to cut out and sew five hundred garments for the patriot soldiers, in response to Lafayette's bemoaning their need on his first visit to Baltimore in 1781. (See *Life*, II, 250–51.)

Letter 26.   **William Hand Browne, Baltimore, to John Ingram, London.** First printing. [Item 268]

[December 3, 1875]

My dear Ingram:—

I have sent you a day or two ago, a copy of the N.Y. *Herald*, giving an account of Poe's last moments by Dr. Moran, at the time one of the physicians at the Washington Hospital.[19] I do

18. The inscription on this statue reads: "Presented by English Gentlemen / as a tribute of admiration for / the Soldier and Patriot / THOMAS J. JACKSON, / and gratefully accepted by Virginia / in the name of the Southern People. / Done A.D. 1875 / in the hundredth year of the Commonwealth. / "Look! there is Jackson standing like a stonewall." John Henry Foley (1818–1874), sculptor, was a member of the Royal Academy.

19. New York *Herald*, October 28, 1875. [Item 625]

not know Dr. M., nor how far his statements are [to be] received; but I should be inclined to take them with a considerable modicum of salt. His memory is by far too circumstantial; unless we should attribute a good part of the details to the imagination and dramatic gifts of the reporter. With the *Herald*, truth is but a secondary matter compared with effect. I happened to be speaking of the subject this morning with an old friend of twenty years or more (who I did not know knew anything about Poe) and he said that he knew all about the facts at the time: that Poe was undoubtedly cooped, drugged and voted, and then turned adrift to die. He gave me many details, which I will not now write. When you come over, you must see him: it is James W. Alnutt, Prest. of the Bank of Commerce of this city. W. H. Carpenter, editor of the Gazette, tells me he knew Poe intimately. They were associated in some literary work: the *Baltimore Book*, a collection of light literature (not an annual) to which Poe contributed, and another similar work.[20] C. promised to hunt them up for me; but said he thought that Poe's contributions were included in the published works. Carpenter said that the last time he met Poe, the latter, with a sort of supercilious way he sometimes assumed, stretched out one finger, and C. extended his forefinger and laid it on Poe's, upon which P. laughed and shook hands. When I was a very small boy, there was a Poe in Balto., a young fellow, famous for his vagaries and practical jokes. I never knew him, and only recollect the stories told of him. I have only quite recently learned that this was the eccentric brother of the poet. One famous joke of his was this:—At that time the Germans in Balto. who were not many in number, and rather despised, raised a volunteer company, which they called *Die Jager*, generally referred to as "the Dutch Yagers". These honest Dutchmen Poe selected as his especial butts. When they would go out parading, Poe would muster a lot of mischievous *gamins*, and march in their rear, sometimes giving orders in broken English, and sometimes chanting a doggerel canticle of his own composition, of which I remember two couplets:

20. Poe contributed "Siope: a Fable" to the *Baltimore Book* for 1838. Later, he changed the name of this prose poem to "Silence—a Fable."

"Ven you hears te great pig trum
Den you sees te Yagers come;
Ven tey turns te corner apout,
Den you shmells te sauerkraut". &c, &c.

This doggerel the boys used to sing in chorus, Poe strutting at their head like a drum-major, to the great mirth of the public.

When they reached the place of parade, Poe would halt his troop (followed by hundreds of spectators) and would burlesque the call of the roll, with the answers or excuses for absence; would inspect the company, would command manoeuvers, &c., all in the wildest burlesque, to the infinite delight of his boys and a malicious public, but to the inexpressible anguish of the poor Dutchmen. At last they could stand it no longer, and had Poe up to Court. The charge was preferred, and the Court asked Poe what he had to say. He, with the greatest gravity, said he was only indulging in a little innocent mirth that harmed nobody and did not disturb the peace; that the boys liked to see the Yagers parade, and he put himself at their head to infuse a little of the military spirit into them. That as for his song, it was quite inoffensive, as his Honor could judge for himself when he repeated it. And he then began intoning his famous chant, at which the Court fairly broke down in laughter, and dismissed the case[. . . .][21]

Balto. Dec. 3, 1875

The above letter I thought I had sent you long ago, when to my surprise I found it, unfinished, in my portfolio. A later letter from me has corrected the mistake about the eccentric Poe, who was the poet's uncle.

I have anticipated your wish, and already forwarded you, by the hands of Mr. Boyd, a good photograph of the Poe monument. I think you will like the design.

The photo. of Valentine's* grand figure of Lee, only gives half its beauty. It is intended to be viewed all round; and

---

21. It was Samuel Poe, Edgar's eccentric uncle, not his brother, who perpetrated this joke at the expense of the Baltimore Germans.

while the figure is probably best from the side shown in the photo., perhaps the face is best from the other side. It is a noble tribute to one of the most flawless types of manhood the world has ever known. Your countrymen's gift to Virginia in Foley's statue of Jackson, is another noble tribute to another hero, and a princely gift to the grand old mutilated State[. . . .]

I hate parodies in general; but I saw one the other day of "The Raven," so happy and humorous, that if I can get a copy I will send it to you.

Faithfully yours,
Wm Hand Browne

Ingram quoted a long paragraph from Dr. John J. Moran's *Herald* article about Poe's last hours and death in *Life*, II, 236–37, thus adding another myth to Poe biography; for subsequent biographers immediately picked it up from Ingram, and it has never been proved or disproved. Moran had written that the conductor of the train from Baltimore to Philadelphia had recognized Poe's desperate condition and had transferred him at either Harve de Grace, Maryland, or Wilmington, Delaware, to another train returning to Baltimore. As Dr. Moran grew older and became increasingly conscious of his role at the death of one of America's greatest writers, his imagination grew correspondingly stronger; he finally published in 1885 a whole book made up of Poe's last words, which curiously enough he entitled his *Defense of Poe*.

From this letter and from Colonel Scharf's book, Ingram reprinted the whole of this incident of the Baltimore boys, led by Samuel Poe, ridiculing the Germans in Baltimore, even including the four lines of doggerel verse. (See *Life*, II, 251–52).

The Poe monument had been unveiled in the Presbyterian churchyard cemetery on November 17, 1875, with elaborate ceremonies amounting to fanfare, and the newspapers from Boston to Mobile were filled with accounts of the ceremonies and pictures of the monument.

Ingram was to publish an entire book about "The Raven" in 1885; included therein were literary and historical commentaries and many parodies of the poem (George Redway: London).

Letter 27. **William Hand Browne, Baltimore, to John Ingram, London.** First printing. [Item 287]

March 17, 1876

My dear Ingram:—

I have lighted on a *trouvaille*. I heard of an original daguerreotype of Poe in the possession of a Virginia gentleman, so I wrote to him, and he has kindly lent it to me to have copied. I propose to use it for the frontispiece to the memorial volume which I am helping Miss Rice to prepare. This picture is incomparably superior to any of the poet that I have seen. It is not perceptibly faded, and gives the relief and solidity of the head, the texture and lines of the face, so that now for the first time I have a clear idea of Poe as a living man. The other pictures are like phantoms compared to it. I am really delighted at getting hold of this picture (which was taken from life in Richmond) and which, I think, will be one of the most telling features in the "Memorial." I need not say that you shall have a copy, besides your copy of the book.

We hope to get for the "Memorial" a picture of Mrs. Poe (Virginia) and one of Miss Royster (Mrs. Shelton).

I think the *Memorial* will be a very creditable thing, and will at all events, sell enough to cover all expenses, with which Miss Rice will be quite content. We shall use the Memoir from the International, the publisher agreeing for a *douceur* of $10.00 (this is *entre nous*), making the changes noted in your letter.[22]

And now I have a favor to ask of you. Will you ask, or empower, Messrs. Black of Edinburgh to let me have an electroplate from the wood-engraving of the cottage at Fordham (headpiece to your *Memoir*) to use in the *Memorial*? I shall write them today making the request, and saying that I have applied to you.

I enclose you (for your private eye only, and for your collection of Poeana) copy of a touching letter of Mrs. Clemm's, the original of which is in my hands. There never was greater devotion, nor greater fidelity than those of these two ladies (Mrs. Clemm and Virginia) to Poe, or than his to them.[23]

22. Ingram's article, "Edgar Allan Poe," had been printed in the *International Review*, II (March–April, 1875), 145–72.

23. Mrs. Clemm's letter, dated November 1, 1849, written from Lowell, Mass., where she was a guest in Annie Richmond's home, to Neilson Poe, in Baltimore, is printed as Letter 8 in this volume.

You have certainly achieved success with your defence of the poet. All over this country it is spoken of as "Ingram's Memoir," "the Ingram vindication," &c. I enclose a handbill from Widdleton (mark that, Master Brook!) in which he speaks not of "the Gill," but "the Ingram Memoir." Gill has been put where he belongs.

Very truly yours,
Wm. Hand Browne

Miss Sara Sigourney Rice, the Baltimore school teacher who had been the moving spirit behind the efforts to erect a suitable monument over Poe's remains, was at this time editing *Edgar Allan Poe: A Memorial Volume*, and apparently was fortunate enough to have Browne's assistance, even though his name does not appear as her coeditor. The pictures of Virginia Poe and Mrs. Shelton do not appear in the volume, but the wood engraving of the Fordham cottage does. For once, Ingram respected his correspondent's injunction that an item was for his private eye only, for he did not publish any portion of Letter 8 in this volume.

The memoir of Poe which prefaced Sara Rice's *Memorial Volume* was a condensation of Ingram's memoir which had prefaced his four-volume edition of Poe's works, published by A. & C. Black, Edinburg, 1874/75, and by W. J.Widdleton in New York, 1876. Ingram had made a few corrections and had added a few more facts to it before offering it to the *International Review*, where it appeared in abridged form in April, 1875.

William Fearing Gill had published an article called "Some New Facts About Edgar A. Poe," in *Laurel Leaves*, published by his father's firm in Boston, 1876. Subsequently, a violent quarrel erupted between him and Ingram over the duplicate use of materials they both had received from Mrs. Whitman.

Letter 28. **William Hand Browne, Baltimore, to John Ingram, London.** First printing. [Item 293]

June 6, 1876

My dear Ingram:—
Your letter of 25 May and the proofs arrived safely. Many thanks. I have written to the Librarian of Congress to know: 1., if we can copyright, and failing this: 2., if we can keep

others from copyrighting. It would be disagreeable to have the door slammed in our faces by burglarious intruders.

I dropped you a card to tell you that I had picked up a vol. for you containing *Burton's Gentms. Magazine*, Jany. to July 1840, with Poe's name as editor; and the last semester, without Poe's name, & with Graham as publisher. There are various reviews & other pieces by Poe in it. It is not in very good order, but may fill a hiatus in your library.

I have been shown today in the liby. of Maryland Histl. Socy. an 8 pp. pamphlet containing a satirical poem, called "The Musiad or Ninead." By Diabolus. Published by Me. Baltimore, 1830. It seems to be complete, and there are reference figures apparently referring to notes that are lost. I rather suspect it may be by Poe. There is a humorous prose preface, much in Poe's style; and Poe is mentioned by name in the poem as a young man of some merit, but at a disadvantage. The versification is extremely good, and a test word in it shows the writer to have been a scholar. Hast ever heard of it? The librarian is anxious to get a perfect copy.[24]

Thanks for promised attention to the electro. which I am desirous of getting hold of. "My" portrait of Poe—that is, Mr. Davidson's—I think you will admit when you see it, beats all the others[. . . .]

> Truly yours,
> Wm. Hand Browne

Letter 29. **William Hand Browne, Baltimore, to John Ingram, London.** First printing. [Item 360]

Oct. 16, 1880

My dear Ingram:—

I have been so busy, partly with the reopening of the Univy., and partly with things connected with the great

24. The late Thomas O. Mabbott thought it highly unlikely that Poe was the author of "The Musiad or Ninead." See T. O. Mabbott (ed.), *Collected Works of Edgar Allan Poe*, (Cambridge: Harvard University Press, 1969), I, 541.

holiday which Baltimore has been treating herself to all this week, that I could not write you: and even now I don't know when this letter will go off; but when it does go, it will carry the copies of Poe's letters. These I have made with the exactest care, scrupulously following even the punctuation. You will find them interesting. They were given to my friend, W. H. Carpenter, Ed. of Balto. "Sun," by the widow of Dr. Snodgrass. They have not been shown to anyone else; & indeed Mr. C. does not like to have them handled, as two are badly damaged by fire, & one by damp, and are really dropping to pieces. Mr. Carpenter first offered to lend them to me, thinking I might like to work them into a magazine paper. I declined to do this, but asked and obtained permission to take copies for you. Mr. Carpenter only stipulates that the copies should be shown to our common friend & his associate, E. Spencer, who may wish to refer to them in some article on Poe. He may, or may not, make some use of them: but in any case will not stale [*sic*] them to any great extent. Snodgrass's sketch of Poe in S[*aturday*] V[*isiter*] I will copy for you when I have time.[25]

   I will enclose also some reminiscences of P[oe] obtained from persons who knew him by my friend John B. Tabb of St. Charles Coll. Md.[. . . .]

Baltimore, 25 Oct., 1880

Since writing the other leaf, a new and very important Poe-annal has turned up among Dr. Snodgrass's papers. It is the letter from the *election-coop* asking Snodgrass to come to Poe's help—thus putting the "cooping" incident beyond a doubt. I have copied it from the original, & this is the text—

Baltimore City, Oct. 3d 1849

Dear Sir,—
   There is a gentleman, rather the worse for wear, at Ryan's 4th ward polls, who goes under the cognomen of Edgar A.

---

25. Dr. J. E. Snodgrass' biographical sketch of Poe occupied four columns in the Baltimore *Saturday Visiter* for July 29, 1843. [Item 494]

Poe, and who appears in great distress, & he says he is acquainted with you, and I assure you, he is in need of immediate assistance,

> Yours, in haste,
> Jos. W. Walker

To Dr. J. E. Snodgrass.

Spencer is hunting up all about Ryan's place, & will try to see if any of Poe's fellow-prisoners in that den can be now found. Walker was a printer, & is now dead. S[pencer] will then prepare a paper for one of the magazines, in which he will refer to these letters, as I wrote you before, & will doubtless make some extracts from them. I was wrong in saying that these letters were given to Mr. Carpenter: they were only lent to him by Mrs. Snodgrass with permission to make what use of them he chose; & has since returned them to her. Some of the old vindictiveness against Poe still crops up occasionally in the Northern papers—partly because they hate the South and everything Southern, and partly because some of the old "mutual-admiration" set still survive, and have never yet forgiven the man who told them the truth about themselves.

I have N. P. Willis' letter to Morris about Poe, cut from the *Home Journal* of Oct. 30, 1858. Have you it?[26]

> Truly yours,
> Wm. Hand Browne

Dr. Joseph Evans Snodgrass, a Baltimore physician and minor literary figure who edited with Nathan C. Brooks the *American Museum of Science* in 1839 and became the proprietor of the Baltimore *Saturday Visiter*, had probably known Poe since Poe's first real association with Baltimore, 1831-1835. Almost immediately after Dr. Snodgrass died in 1880, his widow released nine unpublished letters from Poe to her husband, plus the note Joseph W. Walker had written to Dr. Snodgrass after finding Poe in his sad condition at Ryan's Fourth Ward polls. W. H. Carpenter allowed Browne to make the copies for Ingram, plus a set of copies for himself, which he lent to Edward Spencer, his associate on the *Sun*.

26. A letter from N. P. Willis to George P. Morris, the coeditors of the New York *Mirror* when Poe joined their staff in late 1844, describes Poe's looks and manner at that time. [Item 526]

These letters are long and detailed accounts of Poe's plans and literary affairs, and there is in them more than a suggestion that Poe was playing the role of sycophant to Dr. Snodgrass. Ingram recognized the importance of these revealing letters, but they had arrived too late to be included in his 1880 *Life*, and for some unknown reason he did not follow his usual custom of rushing into print somewhere with new Poe material of this magnitude. He could have been too busy with other matters; he could have recognized that the letters, including Walker's note, put Poe in an unflattering light. Whatever the cause for his delay, he missed an important "first" publication about Poe, for to Ingram's surprise and anger, Edward Spencer published all of these letters in the New York *Herald* for March 27, 1881.[27] Ingram had felt that these letters were his alone, to publish when he pleased, and now that he had been anticipated in their publication, he reacted with his usual rage.

Browne had assured Ingram that he had made the copies "with exactest care," but a collation of the copies shows that he did make a number of errors, chiefly in punctuation. The press copies he made for Carpenter have disappeared, as have many of the originals; the copies Ingram received in 1880 and kept for inclusion in his last biography of Poe, finished in 1916, now serve as texts for the letters. For a detailed discussion of this Poe-Snodgrass correspondence, see John W. Ostrom's "A Poe Correspondence Re-edited," *Americana*, XXIV (July, 1940), 409–446.

Despite the trouble caused by Spencer's editing the Poe-Snodgrass correspondence, Browne's correspondence with Ingram continued for almost thirty more years. From time to time he sent Ingram important letters and items of interest in Poe affairs, among them a letter Poe had written to Messrs. J. H. Reinman & J. H. Walker accepting membership in the Philosophian Society of Wittenberg College, Springfield, Ohio. This letter was dated from New York, March 11, 1847. [Item 36] Ingram printed this letter first, in *Life*, II, 118, adding contemptuously that it was a "fair specimen of autograph hunters' success in 'drawing out' a distinguished contemporary." The original of this letter is apparently lost; Browne's copy and Ingram's printing of it remain the sources of its text. Ingram was able to achieve another first printing when Browne copied for him Mrs. Clemm's letter to Neilson Poe, November 1, 1849, reproduced in this volume as Letter 8, noted above.

27. [Item 802]

V

Marie Louise Shew Houghton Leads and Misleads Poe's Biographer

RUFUS GRISWOLD printed Poe's poem "To Mrs. M.L.S." under the title "To M.L.S." and placed it in the group of poems thought to have been written in Poe's youth. Inasmuch as Griswold knew who "M.L.S." was—and didn't like her—there was possibly some malice in his placing this poem with the sadly inferior early poems of Poe, who himself had said that "no poet wants to be remembered by his juvenile work." When Ingram began editing Poe's works in the early 1870s he had no idea to whom the poem had been written. He could get no help from any of his American correspondents, until he learned from a letter to him, dated November 24, 1874, from Mary Sargeant Gove Nichols, then living in London or nearby, that the poem had been written to Marie Louise Shew, and she gave Mrs. Shew's address to Ingram. [1]

Marie Louise Barney Shew was the daughter of a physician and was herself skilled in medicine and nursing. She had been married to Dr. Joel T. Shew, but had divorced him. In the winter of 1846, when Mrs. Nichols in New York had learned of the Poes' distressed condition in Fordham, she took Mrs. Shew along to see what help they might offer. They found Virginia dying in the Fordham cottage, and Mrs. Shew returned immediately to the City and started a collection of money, food, and clothing for the Poes. She returned with these and medicines and literally took charge of the distressed household, nursing Virginia until she died on January 30, 1847. Mrs. Shew then stayed to nurse Poe through a full month's sickness that followed Virginia's burial, returning to New York periodically to get supplies and to see about her own

1. [Item 183]

family. When Poe began to recover, he expressed his gratitude to Mrs. Shew in the lines "To Mrs. M.L.S." and in a poem beginning, "Not long ago the writer of these lines." Sometime later, he wrote still another poem to her which he called "The Beloved Physician," but which was never published, at least in its entirety.[2] Mrs. Shew was planning to marry the Reverend Roland S. Houghton, and it seems she was afraid the strong sentiments expressed in the poem would be recognized as directed to her; whatever her reason, she paid Poe $25 for the poem, which was subsequently lost and only the few lines she could remember of it were printed by Ingram many years later. Mrs. Shew did marry Houghton in 1850.

Ingram opened his correspondence with Mrs. Houghton early in 1875, and she responded quickly and generously, proving to be one of his most rewarding and the same time most confusing and difficult correspondents. At this time she was estranged from Houghton, had the care of a family, and was forced to make a living here and there as a practical nurse. She wrote to Ingram at odd moments as she watched over her patients, using whatever scraps of paper that were at hand; then for days afterwards she would add postscripts on pages of different sizes, and finally she would make a package of these undated, unnumbered pages and mail the package to Ingram.

Her accounts, memories, and reminiscences of Poe, Virginia, and Mrs. Clemm are at times so rambling, contradictory, and confused that the reader can only wish for revelation to make them completely intelligible. But her letters are always so warm and lively, intensely human in their emotions of love, dislike, asperity, and general sincerity, that the reader cannot but revel in them with joy and laughter.

It is impossible to assign limits and numbers to the letters Mrs. Houghton wrote to Ingram, for obviously some of her letters were removed from his files before they were shipped to the University of Virginia Library. All one can be sure of is that their correspondence began early in 1875 and ended sometime before her death on September 3, 1877.

Letter 30. E. Dora Houghton, Flushing, Long Island, to John Ingram, London. First printing. [Item 194]

2. [Item 977]

The Chestnuts
Jan. 9th, 1875

Mr. Ingram
Dear Sir

Your letter to my dear Mama was received this evening, it having been sent to Papa at Hartford, Conn. Mama desires me to say that she will do the best she can for you, and as soon as she can look over her papers will write to you herself. She has some of Mr. Poe's letters—and is familiar with the circumstances of the last years of his sad life. Mama also desires me to say that she will look over the Preface or biography written by Mr. Griswold and write you the points which are not only cruel and malicious but false. But as she has not seen any of the articles you mention, *it may have been done already* by some one more competent and with more leisure—of this you will please inform her—but be assured her heart is with you in this good work. To explain to you why Mama has not seen any of these articles I may add that at the breaking out of the war (twelve years ago) she retired to a remote country village taking with her her library of old books and baby Dora and for ten years seeing no new publications excepting an occasional newspaper. I may venture to enclose one of Mr. Poe's letters relating to his wife's last hours which I have in my possession and will keep a copy for you in case this letter should be lost in the mail.

Mrs. Clemm was very desolate after Mr. Poe's death and made her home with Mamma—*whenever she pleased*—until the publication of Mr. Poe's works by Mr. Griswold gave her a support. When the books were published her indignation and grief was heart-rending to witness, and after ineffectual efforts, to get justice—expressed herself as heartbroken and was said never to have smiled again. Mamma left New York about this time and lost sight or knowledge of her.

Will you be so kind as to forward the enclosed note to Mrs. Nichols whose address was mislaid in packing our books and papers.

Mamma is quite unnerved today by bad news from my brother which is my apology for being her amanuensis.

Yours very truly
E. Dora Houghton

Ingram had sent the first letter he addressed to Mrs. Houghton to James Wood Davidson in New York City, asking him to forward it if he could. Davidson apparently had located Dr. Roland S. Houghton* in Hartford, Connecticut, and he sent it to him to forward again to his former wife.

Nothing illustrates better Ingram's remarkable ability to touch the sympathies of Poe's friends and elicit from them their priceless keepsakes, by means of his forceful and impassioned letters, than this letter from E. Dora Houghton which included as a gift to Ingram from Mrs. Houghton the autograph letter Poe had addressed to Mrs. Shew on January 29, 1847, which began, "Kindest—Dearest Friend—My poor Virginia still lives." (See Ostrom, II, 340, for complete text.)

Dora Houghton's statement in this letter is the strongest evidence there is that Mrs. Clemm actually did receive considerable sums of money from the sales of Griswold's edition of Poe's works. But her statement that her mother left New York about the time the books came out in 1850 and lost sight of Mrs. Clemm thereafter is inaccurate; Mrs. Clemm certainly spent many months, on several occasions, as a guest in Mrs. Houghton's home during the 1850s.

Mary Gove Nichols and Mrs. Houghton had been personal friends and professional associates in New York City during the 1840s, and when Ingram gave Mrs. Houghton Mrs. Nichols' address in England, Mrs. Houghton promptly wrote to her, as she did to a number of the "Poe Circle," after getting their addresses from Ingram. (Notable among them was Sarah Helen Whitman.)

It is not known what the "bad news" was concerning Mrs. Houghton's only son, but during this period of her correspondence with Ingram Mrs. Houghton limped determinedly and vociferously from one crisis to another.

Letter 31. **Marie Louise Shew Houghton, Whitestone, Long Island, to John Ingram, London.** First printing. [Item 197]

Jan. 23, 1875

My dear Sir

My daughter Dora answered your letter enclosing one of Mr. Poe's notes to me at the time of his wifes [*sic*] death. I trust *the beautiful little gift to you* was not lost in the mail—I have not found many of Mr. Poe's letters but I enclose you one received by my uncle (who lived with me) about the time he wrote his "Eureka"—This was after he had risen from "Dispair's unhalowed bed" as he said in the verses addressed to me, who had been his nurse and Physician alternating my nights at his bedside with his "Muddie" as he called Mrs. Clemm. I am sorry I cannot serve you, as to *dates* but I never was a business person, and never had any discipline. I came up a country Doctor's only daughter, with a taste for painting and a heart for loving all the world—I saved Mr. Poe's life at this time, having been educated medicaly. I made my Diagnosis and went to the great Dr. Mott with it. I told him that *at best* when he was well Mr. Poe's pulse beat only ten regular beats after which it suspended or intermitted (as Doctors say). I decided that in his best health, he had leasion on one side of the brain, and as he could not bear stimulants or tonics, without producing insanity, I did not feel much hope, that he could be raised up from a brain fever, brought on by extreme suffering of mind and body, (actual want and hunger and cold, being borne by this heroic husband to supply food medicine and comforts to his dying wife) until exaustion and lifelessness was so near, and at every reaction of the fever—that sedatives even had to be administered with caution. I tell you all this to explain to you what followed— From the time his fever came on until I could reduce his pulse to 80 beats he talked to me *incessently* of the past, which was all new to me, and often he begged me to write for him his fancies for he said he had promised so many greedy pub-lishers his next efforts that they would not only say he did not keep his word but they would revenge themselves by writing "all sort of evil of him" if he should die—I have a great many pages of these penciled sayings *somewhere* part of them have been published I think one poem of touching pathos "the beloved Physician" he revised and prepared for publication, for I gave him the missing leaves, after he recovered. I asked him to wait a little, and gave him a check for his necessities as he said he had been offered twenty dollars for it. I gave him twenty five, & asked him to wait as every body would know, *who it was*, and it was so very personal and complimentary I dreaded the ordeal as I was about to be maried to a man, who had *old fashioned notions* of woman and her sphere—(a foolish idea of mine born of my great love, for this man—but which proved my great loss for I never *amounted* to anything —afterwards, having lost all my *individuality from that*

Jan. 23ʳ /75—

My dear Sir

      My daughter Doru answered your letter enclosing one of Mr. Poe's notes to me. at the time of his wifes death. I trust the beautiful little gift. to you. was not lost in the mail— I have not found many of Mr Poe's letters but I enclose you one received by my uncle (who lived with me) about the time he wrote his "Eureka"— this was after he had risen from "despair" unhalowed but "as he said on the verses addressed to me, who had been his nurse and Physician. alternating my nights at his bed side with his "Muddie" as he called Mrs Clemm I am sorry I cannot serve you, as to date but I never was a busines person. and never had any discipline I came up a country doctors only daughter. with a taste for painting, and a heart for loving all the world— I saved Mr Poe's life at this time. having been educated medically I made my diagnosis, and went to the

Marie Louise Shew Houghton to John Ingram, January 23, 1875
Letter 31

hour)—but this is diverging from my purpose which you will I trust forgive. If this poem, The beloved Physician could be found complete now, it would greatly delight you, and it would do me great good as I now support my two youngest children by practicing the healing art which in these days is so honourable and not at all novel, or new.

The poem was written in a singular strain, a verse discribing the Doctor, watching the pulse, etc. etc. and ending with a refrain of two lines—discribing the nurse—It was very curious as it was a picture of a highly wrought brain, in an over excited state. There was in every verse a line "The pulse beats ten and intermits" and in the refrain of the last verse (where he discribes me holding my watch and counting "so tired, so weary" and after I find that I have brought the pulse to the desired eighty beats—as low as I dared give sedatives) —I rested *and he did also* trying his best to sleep for my sake) in the refrain as I said before he adds, "The soft head bows, the sweet eyes close The large heart (a faithful heart) yields to sweet repose"   You can imagine it was a perfect thing as he revised it afterwards, discribing his visit to the great sergeon Dr. Mott (where I took him as soon as he was convelescent in a close[d] carriage to have the Doctor see my patient and *confirm, or not*, my Diagnosis as to *Mr. Poe's brain being diseased*! and also, to have him suggest such tonics as would not excite him to madness)—My impression is, that this poem of the beloved physician was given to Griswold, but as I went to see Griswold, and tried all my eloquence—and even offered to pay the expense of a change in the autobiography, which should be compiled by Mr. Willis* (or some one of three) Graham I think was one), and after promising me, and my leaving my watch and a diamond bracelet with him until something could be agreed upon, he went right on, and avoided writing me or seeing me, and afterwards I met him in Broadway one day in a crowd. I asked him what he was doing—that Mr. Willis would help us. He said very insultingly that the book *"would sell best as it was"*, and he had determined to let it be, and indeed it was all settled and I remember he said ["]Mr. Longfellow had given his approval and that Mrs. Clemm was reconsiled". *Which was not true* as you will see by some letters of Mrs. Clemm which I send you. Mr. Poe told me often that he had *never prospered by honest writing*. That when he wrote a really honest criticism of any author or work, he made himself enemies either from the publishers or the authors. He told me, that Mr. Longfellow would never forgive him for a truthful notice, he had once written of him, "that he would coldly stab his reputation when he was so far dead as not to rouse to defend himself" I remember what he said of Longfellow, from having made his acquaintance a few years before, and admiring the man and not being a judge of his poetry—or reader of it, I was interested—

Mr. Poe said "Longfellow was a *Plagiarist*, that he never wrote a poem without a model, that ideas and rhyme and rhythm were all borrowed that Americans were so superficial that they never recognized such stealing"—and he proved his words by taking down a book of old English Poets and illustrated his assertions &c. &c. I have always felt that Longfellow cruelly injured the dead Poe out of revenge, and that Griswold was a *misrable tool* to this end. Mr. Poe told me clearly that Griswold was his enemy that he (Poe) had offended him in his *weakest egotistic point*, that altho' he was obliged to treat him courteously from a promice given his Mother Mrs. C. (*who feared and asked favors of the man, in the same breath*) still he "always felt he was in the presence of a viper, who would sting him the first chance he got". It was the only point I remember his expressing anger towards this long suffering and loving Mother. But she would call on Griswold and receive favors of a pecuniary or literary nature from him—Mr. Poe wrote a criticism or lecture on Griswold's way of compiling and making books, for sale, which Griswold never forgot. He told me this himself—but I was so young and careless that I don't cannot recollect all the conversation.

I know nothing of Mrs. St. Leon Loud* altho' I might have done so if I had listened, for I heard a story or something was said of her to me both by Mr. Poe and Mrs. Clemm—but it is all a muddle now, perhaps I may recall it. There is an article in Harpers magazine September, 1872, *which is as near truth as I ever have seen published*, but I never in those days got a literary man to agree with me that Mr. Poe had brain disease, and that it was *physicaly impossible* for him to maintain an *equality* of action and feeling—and only the *Physicians* gave me credit for common sense in the matter. I have had a dear friend & companion, near me for years, with heart disease and at last the paroxyms of irregular action, were followed by temporary insanity, there being Leasion *of the brain, serious and fatal*. I often thought of Mr. Poe, when trying to soothe my sweet Lidie's fancies *and noticed* that no stimulant could be used without complete loss of reason—while she remained near me her attacks were controled, by sedatives *now* used, to control the action of the heart, but she lost her good sense, somewhat and did not realize that what served her truly and well under my personal supervision, would, or might, fail in the hands of a strange Doctor. This lovely young Lady was engaged to my eldest son, and I was as much in love with her *as he was*, she was such a true daughter to me in my exile of ten years, or more—I tried to save her to bless the world by her presence, but she gave up her engagement to Henry, for as her heart enlarged—*she knew that it must be so*, but she comforted herself that she would be a doctor. She went thru her three years reading with safety, but as I said before she left me, and came to N.Y. to graduate among strangers she died, before I could reach her, altho she said, "if she (Mrs. H.) had come, I could be saved" yet the northern roads were blocked with snow, and I was three hundred miles away! I loved her so dearly that my grief will never leave me, while I live, I mourn her daily as I do my own, my other daughter altho they both were angels here and are safe in Paradise, such fair and beautiful creatures so beautify this earth, they so relieve its cares and brighten its toils, their companionship is so sweet and cheering—that it is hard to part with them, even for the few years that remain before we go to our own rest; I mention my sweet friend and daughter Lidie Paulene to illustrate a medical fact however & to make my ideas understood as to Mr. Poe—even Mr. Hopkins, one of the most learned and noble ministers of the Church of England, will persist in saying Poe was intoxicated as you will see by my enclosed letter from him, which I asked as I know he will

serve me and mine to his utmost, and that he will not mention all this to any other person—His letter will enlighten
you, as to poor Edgars religion. When nearly gone with his
brain half gone (*a noble half* remaining). He Mr. Poe told me a
story of that matter *of theft*. I have it somewhere as he told it,
when in a calm and accountable mood. You must forgive my
scribling I write at intervals of waiting for a specific action of
remedies used among my sick, (or for the hour to come
round.)   and as I have very little leisure at home I must beg
you to excuse my want of continued ideas—I will answer
your questions as soon as I can.—I believe Mr. Griswolds
work a net of malicious misrepresentation and falsehoods
and I will carefully tell you where I know he is false. Mrs.
Clemm repeatedly calls him "a villian" in her letters to me,
some of which I send you, You ask of Mrs. Poe, I bought her
coffin, her grave clothes, and Edgars mourning, except the
little help Mary Star gave me She lies still in the vault at
Fordham I think. (I will go and see some day in March). Mrs.
Clemm died about two years ago, (I hear) and was buried
near her much loved "Eddie" in Baltimore. There is a monument in progress or finished, by a few American friends.
I will write and get the particulars (unless you have them)   I
learned from an old friend that Mrs. Clemm looked for me in
N.Y. to return me my watch which she wore after redeeming
it. The bracelet she sold for three hundred dollars, but used it
I presume, as it was intended to pay Griswold to keep his
infamous life or destroy it and make none but such as his Mr.
Poe's best friends approved. Not seeing Mrs. Clemm for many
years, I dont know of her circumstances but no doubt she had
a good income from those books for a while. I will look
Redfield up and others if they are alive, when I go to N.Y. I am
obliged to stay here until after April, as I said before. I have a
little volume of Poems entitled "The Raven and Other Poems
by Edgar A. Poe" & published in 1845 and dedicated to Miss
Elizabeth Barrett Barrett which I will send to you if you
desire it. I have also found a volume of Tales published at the
same time & by the same publishers (Wiley & Putnam)
Landor's Cottage is not in this collection. I know nothing of
his tales I never read them, and altho' I have read his poems,

they gave me (many of them) painful impressions—Their classical beauty and rhythm must delight scholars, I am under the impression Mr. Poe left West Point by resignation, and that if any action was taken by the Professors it was recorded, without being made public, indeed I know Mrs. Clemm said he resigned—Gen. Scott was very friendly to Mr. Poe, all his life, and it was thru his influence that Mr. Poe was admited to W. P. Gen. Scott was present once at the Union Club in N.Y. when a collection was taken up among the gentlemen, for his support & comfort after Mrs. Poe died and the old hero gave his share $5.00 and said, "Gentlemen I wish I could make it five hundred" and he was so ill I wrote to a gentleman, to mention the subject, and about one hundred dollars was collected, old debts were paid and necessaries provided with it. The Union Club in those days was only composed of college bred gentlemen. He [General Scott] also said "He believe Poe to be very much belied, that he had noble and generous traits which belonged to a gentleman of the old and better school, that true hearted Americans ought to take care of her poets as well as he[r] soldiers." Quite a speech for Gen. Scott. Mr. Chapin heard Gen. Scott, say it. Gen. Scott was a Mexican Hero about that time and rode thru New York sun burnt and bronzed, with war worn troops. If General Scott had got a bad impression from Poe's leaving West Point in disgrace, he would hardly have excused him so fully as to have spoken so often in his praise. It was his manner and bearing and grateful heart that Scott admired; and the pride and strength of intellect came in to make up the rest—combativeness is always a manly trait to a soldier of the stamp of Gen. Scott I know Mr. Poe could have won laurels as a soldier

Mr. Poe wrote the Bells at my house. He came in and said, "Marie Louise, I have to write a poem. I have no feeling, no sentiment, no inspiration—" I answered we will have supper and I will help you. So after tea had been served in a conservatory with the windows open, near a church—I playfully said, here is paper. A Bell (very jolly and sharp) rang at the corner of the street. He said I so dislike the noise of bells tonight. I cannot write. I have no subject. I am exhausted. So I took his pen and wrote "The Bells. By E. A. Poe, and I mimiced his style, and wrote the Bells, the little silver Bells &c. &c. he finishing each line

Then I said, The Heavy Iron Bells, "how solemn" and so on he helping me thru—Then he copied it, and he said he was satisfied. He called it my poem, because I said so much for him, "There floats from their throats," I feeling I could touch his ear, which was so peculiar—He afterwards added another verse, by my suggestion, after which he said, What a pity you had not been educated. You are a genius, You can wake the dead. My brother came in. I sent him to tell Mrs. C. "that her boy would stay in town and was well" and my brother took Mr. Poe to his own room and he slept twelve hours, and could hardly recall the evening's work. This showed his mind was injured nearly gone out, from want of food and disappointments (for he had not been drinking, and only a few hours from home—*evidently his vitality was low* and he was nearly insane while he slept we studied his pulse, which I so often had noticed. *The same symptoms* I called in old Dr. Francis who was one of our neighbors he said "he had heart disease and would die early in life according to the storms or sunshine of his environment", his own words. The old man was odd but very skillful, and a *noted* man   We did not wake him, until he slept it off, and after he had eaten his breakfast, I went down town with him, and drove him to Fordham in my coupa. He did not seem to realize that he had been ill—and wondered why "Madam Louise" had been so very good as to bring him home—His eyes were heavy, and his step unsteady, but he had not touched the cup

I could give many reminiscenses of Poe, from 47 to his death, but I am not certain as to dates & names. I prefer to find the notes I wrote for him—*if I can*—Some one relieved me of his portrait given me by his wife, but as I have no idea who took it   It being done during an abscence in the country I had to submit to its loss—I have a little jewel cace she (Mrs. Poe) gave me, which was Mr. Poe's mothers   He had a miniature of his mother, a (lovely intellectual face). I think it was saved at the Hospital where he died. I know his seal ring (which I had made for him) was restored to his family. Some Baltimore methodist preacher (a cousin of his) has it. I had it engraved with the motto of his family (Poes) upon it.

Poe's letter to Mrs. Houghton's uncle, Hiram Barney, was written probably in May, 1847; Barney was the senior member of the New York law firm Barney, Butler, and Parsons.

Poe's reference to rising from "Dispair's unhalowed bed" is in the eighth line of his poem "To Mrs. M.L.S."

Mrs. Houghton's remark in this letter about her coming up "with a taste for painting" is worth much consideration, for she almost certainly made the one water color painting of Virginia Poe that is in existence. Mrs. Houghton had been present at Virginia's death, after which she did the painting of Virginia propped up in the bed. The Baltimore Poes kept the painting from being reproduced as long as they could, for it takes only a glance for almost anyone to realize that the subject is indeed dead.

Dr. Valentine Mott was one of the leading members of the New York University School of Medicine.

Ingram wrote all there was to write about the lost poem, "The Beloved Physician," in a long article which he named "The Beautiful Physician" (apparently his post-Victorian notions of propriety led him to change the title), published nearly thirty-five years later in the Poe centenary number of the New York *Bookman*, January, 1909.

Mrs. Houghton's remarks in this letter about having attempted to pay Griswold to alter his biography of Poe and his reply that Mrs. Clemm was reconciled is all the evidence we have that both Mrs. Clemm and the then Mrs. Shew *anticipated* Griswold's slanders about Poe. This lead has never been followed, as far as I know; nothing has been done or written by any biographer about its possible truth. Griswold's "weakest egotistic point" could have been his method of compiling anthologies or it could have been his strong attraction to Mrs. Frances S. Osgood; Poe interfered in both. Mrs. Clemm's dealings with Griswold during Poe's lifetime were unwise enough; and after Poe's death they were disastrous to Poe's reputation.

Poe's unbalanced criticisms and judgments about Longfellow can be attributed, I think, to his knowing that he himself was writing some of the very best poetry being produced in America and was getting paid little or nothing for it, while Longfellow was successfully marketing much inferior verses.

Mrs. St. Leon Loud was a minor poetess of Philadelphia whose verse Poe had agreed to edit and was presumably on his way to do when he stopped over in Baltimore and died on October 7, 1849.

The Reverend J. H. Hopkins was a very close friend of Mrs. Houghton. In this letter to Ingram she enclosed the following letter from Hopkins to herself. This is a first complete printing of the letter:

> Plattsburg [N.Y.]
> Feb. 9: 1875

Dear Madam:

You ask for my recollections of a visit made by me to the late Edgar A. Poe, at his request in (I think) the year 1848. It was in regard to his brilliant lecture "Eureka," which I had heard on the occasion of its first delivery, and in which I was much interested, having made a report of it for one of the daily papers. He was thinking of printing it in book form. I did all I could to persuade him to omit the bold declaration of Pantheism at the close, which was not necessary to the completeness or beauty of the lecture. But I soon found that *that* was the dearest part of the whole to him; and we got into quite a discussion on the subject of Pantheism. For some time his tone and manner were very quiet, though slowly changing as we went on; until at last, a look of scornful pride worthy of Milton's Satan flashed over his pale, delicate face & broad brow, and a strange thrill nerved and dilated for an instant his slight figure, as he exclaimed, "My whole nature utterly *revolts* at the idea that there is any Being in the Universe superior to *myself*!" I knew then that there was no use in further argument. The subject was dropped, and there was nothing further in the interview that I can now recall. But that sentence, and the mode of its utterance, made an indelible impression.

I suppose that Mr. Ingram would not wish the details of the occasion when Dr. Houghton and I found him crazy-drunk in the hands of the police, and took him home to Fordham (eleven miles), where we found poor Mrs. Clemm waiting for him. He had been gone three days,—went to draw pay for an article, got into a spree, spent all, and we had to leave $5, with Mrs. Clemm for immediate necessities, as there was not a penny in the house. This, I think, was the same year with the above, only a little later in the season.

Yr. obt. servt.
J. H. Hopkins

P.S. There is one other incident that I recall concerning that visit to Mr. Poe. He was speaking of his near neighbors, the Jesuit Fathers at Fordham College, and praised them warmly, "They were highly cultivated gentlemen and scholars," he said, "smoked, drank, and played cards like gentlemen, and never said a word about religion."[3]

At this writing, Virginia Poe's body was still in the Valentine vault at Fordham; it was not until 1885 that her bones were brought to Baltimore and buried beside Edgar's.

"Mary Star" or "Starr" is still unidentified, though it is possible she was "Poe's Mary," as described in Augustus Van Cleef's article in *Harper's Magazine*, March, 1889.

Mrs. Clemm had been dead four years instead of two, when Mrs. Houghton wrote this letter. Mrs. Houghton's supposition that Mrs. Clemm had a "good

---

3. [Item 201]

income" or an income of any kind from the sale of Griswold's edition of Poe's works is unsupported except in Dora Houghton's letter to Ingram above.

"Redfield" was J. S. Redfield, the New York publisher who brought out Griswold's edition. Sometime in the 1860s he sold the copyright to W. J. Widdleton, who printed many more editions.

"Gen. Scott" was General Winfield Scott (1786–1866), who had something to do with Poe's appointment to West Point. Poe mentioned having seen him during his cadetship.

As proof of her story of the genesis of Poe's "The Bells," Mrs. Houghton later sent to Ingram the seventeen-line manuscript of the poem which Poe had indeed written in her home and had later given to her. Later she sent also her copies of Poe's *Tales* and *The Raven and Other Poems*, both published by Wiley and Putnam, New York, 1845. The letter from Mrs. Clemm enclosed in this package was written sometime in February, 1847, and is reproduced as Letter 1 in this volume. If Mrs. Houghton sent other letters or copies of letters to Ingram from Mrs. Clemm, he either destroyed them or returned them to her family who clamored for years to reclaim the "gifts" Mrs. Houghton had made to Ingram.

Letter 32.   **Marie Louise Shew Houghton, Whitestone, to John Ingram, London.** Mailed with another letter, dated January 23. First complete printings. [Item 197]

Feb. 16, 1875

Dear Mr. Ingram—

Your reply to our brief letter was very welcome and I will try and help in your noble work. I am sorry I was so heedless in noticing and remembering what I might have treasured up for you during the time I was so much with Edgar Poe. He talked over all the topics you mention, or nearly all of them, both when he was so ill and when he was so very certain of success, while writing his Eureka, and when he seemed calm and sane. But you will readily understand that I did not expect him to live long, and that I knew he was injured, that organic disease had been gaining upon his physical frame from the many trials and privations of his eventful life—I had told him in all candor that nothing would, or could, save him from a sudden death, but a prudent life, of calm with a woman fond enough—and strong enough to manage his work and its remunerations for his best good—I was often subjected to his irony, *for my lectures*—coming from a woman so little skilled in worldly troubles or cares as I was then for I was *not even intellectual*—He said I had never troubled myself to read his works or poems *which was true*, for my heart found so much sorrow to sympathize with in the griefs of those I came in contact with (a country girl coming to a city is too often startled out of all systematic reading, to minister to such sorrow as is *ever near* in cities), but I was a "rest for his spirit" for this very reason—He wrote a little poem about this which I hope I may find for you. My son has been robbed in the mines of Colorado. I trust however he left his trunks containing his papers with his friends in Denver. He has some of Mr. Poe's poems, two or three, written to me, which he particularly fancied   There is a lady living in N.Y. whose maiden name was Mary Star* or perhaps Helen, but I think it is Mary, her husband is a Merchant Tailor, (*just think of it*),   This Lady was the first love of Mr. Poe, and she belonged to a good Baltimore family, but for some reason unfortunate —She introduced herself to me at the time Mrs. Poe was dying and went with me to see them and kindly helped me to furnish clothes to Mr. Poe for suitable mourning. If I can only recall her husbands name, she had known Edgar at school, at home, & at different dates and times. She always looked up all his whereabouts, because she loved him in her bright youth. I know she spoke to me of his having so many enemies, and being so gentle and harmless in his disposition. I know she knows all about the scandles and wrongs you wish to clear up—You must ask Mrs. Nichols if she remembers the beautiful Mary Star. Her beauty was of the spanish sort, a gorgeous style; Her husband had a common name, so common, it might be Jones or Smith. I must look her up, for you, & to help brighten my careless memory. You must not think me stupid. I wept three years, of tears, *for a man*, and tried to forget *all I ever knew* but it was the proudest day of my life, when I presented myself before him, *emancipated*! and able to say, and do, all sorts of proper things *without a tear*—and now I have the courage of a Hero, *if my children are safe*—

Private, otherwise as you please   The only time I ever knew of his being intoxicated during the years I knew him, *was after dining with Mr. Griswold*, in an Eating house. whatever was given him, he became insane and unmanageble and he told the servant who tried to turn him out, (after the departure of this man, or fiend, Griswold) that his friends lived at 47 Bond St.—In this way I was notified, and sent Dr. Houghton & the Rev. Mr. Hopkins* to look for him, and they took him home—I afterwards learned the circumstances of his condition, during an illness which followed, and altho Mrs. Clemm knew it was true, she over looked this in Griswold, thinking it was unintentional, but I always believed (*and so said Mr. Poe*) that he would have been home with his hard earned money *but for Griswold*

In relating this circumstance you need not say who I sent to look for him, but that I sent a friend, or friends as Dr. Houghton is not as devoted a *cavalier* to me—as he *was then*, and would *think twice* before doing any service to any friend of mine now, because *they all think* he has failed in his duty to his family. The Rev. Dr. Hopkins, *knows he has*, for they were closely connected in the Church Journal for 17 years—Nothing has ever been made public *of all this*—in regard to my affairs and as *my family* is well known for high toned probity and loyalty to our own literary men, and as I belong to a family of gentlemen, representing the learned Professions, as my Father and all my Grandfathers, being noted Physicians, and my Uncles, Lawyers and divines—I have no need to look to the Houghtons for respectability or *reliability*—

My Uncle the Hon. Hiram Barney is my lawyer and defender—and N.Y. city has known this truly good and noble man for forty years, as he built up the firm of "Barney Butler & Parsons" by his forty years honest service to his laborious profession—His friends are among our greatest men, of every creed or party. Chief Justice Chace was his bosom friend. Governor Seymore another. indeed patriots and scholars of every stamp know him and love him—I do not wish to say that Dr. Houghton would wrong Mr. Poe. But I do not wish to mention him, *myself, nor have you*—unless from other sources. Mr. Hopkins was a great admirer of Mr. Poe, and often met him at my house, but when the question of pantheism came up, you see he thought him either insane or a hopeless infadel, and whenever I labored to prove my theory he would tell the story of that dreadful night when they took him home to Fordham, Mr. Poe reciting, "some unheard of jargon with glorious pathos—or deadly hate," as it suited the ideas at the time. *Of course I felt he was lost, either way*, and I could do nothing of any great service to him from my peculiar position after I married Dr. Houghton—I think Mrs. Clemm was left at Fordham when he went on his last journey and he was hastening home to bring her to his wedding. I never asked her questions about it, she was so full of grief and trials, but I do not believe Mr. Poe ever asked Griswold for money. I think *Mrs. Clemm did*. I never liked the heartless way she chose Griswold as Mr. Poe's biographer and I told her she was to blame I do not consider her intentionly so but she forgot the power could be used to injure her beloved son.

She had no haste. My house was open to her, and my domicil *wherever I was*, was hers but she saw her mistake too late—as you will perceive and probably know—You will see in the magazine (Harper) for September 1872[4]—that many things are uncertain, but I *think* he [Poe] told me his beautiful mother was born at sea, and I think he was born at Boston, indeed I will try to find his own account of it—(I have sent for my papers.) which are stored waiting the result of the chancery suit—I suppose I shall go to N.Y. in May to live in order to educate Dora with proper facilities for her great talents   She is a very marvelous musical genius but loves painting so much she neglects her music, indeed we are away from the world here, (being three women alone) just now. The ice is fearful in the Harbour now, and the ferries obstructed and in a dangerous condition—I trust I may help you in time however—Of course I will be very concise, when I get my papers together. Dora *gave you* the letter sent   She took a copy. Tell Mrs. Nichols I will answer [her] letter soon *please*   I have the origonal of the poem to M.L.S. and also the origonal of the valentine to Marie Louise   The poem to Mrs. M.L.S.

4. R. H. Stoddard had printed an article, "Edgar Allan Poe," in *Harper's New Monthly Magazine*, September, 1872.

was published in the Home Journal (Willis' and Morris's paper) *at the time it was written*. Mr. Willis was a friend of mine; but he is gone—too—

I enclose to you what was written first of the Bells, which he insisted was mine, because I mimiced his style to bring him into his subject—I will tell you soon about another subject, you enquire but now must say good night. Hoping I may not frighten you by my long and I fear useless letter I am yours sincerely

Marie L. Houghton

P.S. My dear Mr. Ingram

I trust you will not think me negligent, or, very-very— nearly wild! I am in an unusual state of work and trial—As to what I have told you of my visit to Griswold. I do not wish you to infer that he kept my valuables. I left them because he looked *so small and mean* (if I may be allowed the expression), and referred to the expense which had already been put in type—that carefully compiled string of testimony, to injure the dead!

I remember telling him, that he must be a lawyer— instead of a preacher, and many other childish ill natured things! but this was when I met him in the street after my first interview. I left Mrs. Clemm with him, and I suppose he gave her my valuables at what time he *did so*, I cannot remember, but I know she borrowed five hundred dollars on them, and offered it to Griswold to leave out any thing unkind or unpleasant or calculated to give any pain to her or any thing derogatory to his Mr. Poe's character as a gentleman. Mr. Griswold sneered at *my idea* of Brain disease, and I refered him to Dr. Mott*, who said there was a leasion of one side of the brain and a change going on slowly but surely, but this man Griswold had no heart or soul, and I was only a weak little woman, of no account, whatever; and everybody I met or spoke to about it, said I was *"unwise to meddle"* so I left it to Mrs. Clemm, to do as she saw fit—she left me and went to Mrs. Richmond at Lowel, as you see by her letter   I married Dr. Houghton, she returned and spent the winter with us, but before she left me she mentioned that "if she could get a proper Memoir published she would like to use the money she had raised on the diamonds, if needed" I answered yes—you can use it and *have it* for *this purpose—as no one will know of the obligation*,—I learned afterwards, as I have told you, that Mrs. Clemm looked for me before she died, to return me my watch, and that she mentioned having sold my bracelet for three hundred dollars!!! She said this to Miss MacQuaile (a former governess of ours) but I think Miss MacQuaile made a mistake, for the bracelet cost $500 and would bring its value, like gold—I speak of this not because I care, for the money, but to *prove to you*, that altho' Mr. Poe *was said* to have no friends and no one to love him, or his memory—*that I did what little* I could to spare him, that I nearly quarreled with Mrs. Clemm for giving her son's life into his Griswold's hands. That I offered to do even more, and only asked a month—to prepare, and even begged a statement of the whole expense and went home full of my intentions, but all the gentlemen of my household threw a wet blanket over it, and sent me to the country for a simpleton—This I think you can understand I knew Mr. Poe's *true nature*—was misunderstood. I grieved, *ever* for the great, for the bright—and brilliant intellect and glorious manhood so clouded and obscured at times—and *flashing out again*! and again! only to be *rudely quenched* and maligned, but I was not strong enough to do any thing really to help him. I had *no one* to stand with me. I was young with no self esteem—no firmness, no courage to battle for the right—(*as I have now*). I was not even fit for any great struggle, I had not been educated properly, my medical knowledge being the *only sensible* idea I had (which was really a fixed fact—not to be put down—or disputed)—I only wonder that Mrs. Clemm did not tell Mrs. Whitman, of some of these things, perhaps she did, and they did not think it of sufficient importance to mention to you I should think much more of Mrs. Clemm if she had returned me my watch (or Mr. Poe's ring) or *something* which would have showed she valued the generous love, that more than once made sacrifices for her children, or *sympathy strength*, and *personal service*—which money cannot repay—and only the memory, and gratitude of the recipient can in a *degree recompense*—That she wore the watch after redeeming it for many years I know, and it would have been a pleasure to me to have left it to the owner (as it was never appropriated to the purpose for which it was given) This, and *the fact that she* asked no service of me afterwards—goes to make an excuse for her long silence to me as my husband unkindly remarked, "She had got out of me all I could do for her,—and then it was a custom of poor human nature, to dislike those to whom they owe obligation", but this is not my nature, as Mrs. Nichols* will tell you, and I never could understand *it in others*. At first I did not intend to mention this to you, *this feeling of mine*, that Mrs. Clemm forgot her sworn, and oft repeated friendship to me—(it *is only a feeling I know nothing certain*) but I should never be able to get along with you, if I did not speak frankly, and I think my son, has Mrs. Clemm's letter written before her *gratitude had died out* which will make the matter perfectly clear to you, and beyond a doubt—you will see in Mr. Willis' Memoir (*or some one else's*) an allusion to this trait of worldly wisdom, and concealment —in Mrs. Clemm. I know the writer in Harper's Magazine Sep. /72 *mentions it*, and this article commands my respect for it (whoever he was) for he *well knew* in his heart that Mr. Poe *dispised him*—This same man was present at Mrs. Poe's funeral. I remember such a person who was very kind, and helped me to adjust the flowers and sprinkle the room with colonge, to brush Mr. Poe's old military cloak and cap which he would wear *after all my trouble to leave them out of sight*. The cloak had covered "Virginia's bed", *often* until I was sent—with a down comforter, from my own room, for her. (I think Mrs. Nichols told me of their destitution). I taught Mr. Poe to sit away from a heated *iron stove*, with a soap stone at his feet, and I taught him to eat fish and clams and oysters to supply brain power, by the phosphates lost in his much thinking, and I taught him to use wheat, prepared with all the phosphates saved, and Mrs. Clemm made bread of Hosfords yeast, which preserved supplied all the elements of nutriment necessary to brain work and supply and he recovered energy and strength to write after his sickness and if Mrs. Clemm had gone with him, in his last tour, he would have succeeded in some ways—with even her knowledge of his *necessities*—But from her ignorance of Physiology and want of faith in her young and womanly Doctor, (for such women never respect the intellect or judgement of their own sex) She trusted him alone, forgetting, that *where there is change of structure*, in *heart*, or *brain*, and *organic disease a fixed fact, recovery is only temporary*—and is dependent entirely upon a fixed routine of duties, *and habits, never* to be overlooked or infringed upon, at home, or abroad.

The medical profession know that a man who has a tendency to Peralysis may live years of usefulness, if he keeps up his usual care of himself, but if he *over works*, and is at the same time thoroughly chilled, congestion follows fatal in a few minutes as in the cace of our excellent Mayor of N.Y. last fall, who walked four miles facing a chilling wind, (*cars broke down* four miles from station) but if Mayor Havemeyer had been properly informed by his physician, he would have quietly remained in a shelter (however rude) untill a carriage could have been obtained.[5] It is all very well, to be *manly*, and *brave*, but when a human being has organic disease he is no longer, a perfect being, and he is a slave to his infirmity whatever it is—Those who suffer from irregular action of the heart cannot hurry, neither can they *hurry the circulation*, if *they do*, the blood cannot flow thru the obstructed vessels fast enough and the Brain (even a healthy brain) suffers congestion, or pressure, painful, and too often fatal to reason and responsibility—Such was the cace of Mr. Poe, I have never met the person who could say that Edgar Poe sought or even liked whiskey, or strong drink, or any one who ever saw him order or ask for it. Since his marriage he never was known to do it, until madness, or insanity had begun from other causes, or from some one else insinuating a glass of beer or wine had then begun the process—

He was not a sensualist in his mature manhood, but he was a wreck as to physical capacity with only half his brain in working order, and should have been watched and cared for

5. Mayor William Frederick Havemeyer died suddenly of apoplexy in his New York office on November 30, 1874.

accordingly, for common sense is the *first sense* lost, when disease attacks the brain,—and self esteem and self reliance run riot—to the exclusion of all prudence or caution. My husband often tells me I am a woman of strong mind, (because I have not lost my reason under the trial he has subjected me to, no doubt, this is the reason he comes to this conclusion) but happily *my brain is small*, and my heart large—and healthy, and when such a temperament as mine, suffers & tears, and a *conciousness of wishing no harm to others*, makes a quiet concience, and a sweet sleep which is natures sweet restorer. Mr. Poe never slept after taking stimulants, and days, and nights of ravings, was his doom! unless some redeeming influence or medicine, interupted the struggle and equilibrium was again established—It takes twice the nourishment to sustain a large brain, and I was happy in having a small one or I should have exaggerated all my woes, and lost my balance, as my sister in law did (who married Dr. Houghton's brother Fred,) and when troubles came from his family to poor Kate, she was paralized and sits now a hopeless cripple "in the shadow alone" can neither read—nor work, so much from having a large brain, for her troubles were not half as serious or agrevating as mine. Still she had not the equally balanced circulation of mind, and body that I had, and her large brain succumbed—You see I speak frankly to you life is too short for mysteries now—and I know you can get a *little sense* out of my overflow, with Mary's help   Mrs. Mary Gove Nichols, in London.

> Heaven bless you
> M. L. Houghton

I told you (in my first letter, enclosed) I met Mr. Griswold afterward, and he said Mrs. Clemm was reconsiled, &c. &c.

Mr. Ingram

This outside letter is a postscript to all I have written inside. I am sorry for you to have to wade thro' it all and I am deeply grieved and sorry that Mrs. Nichols has not her own eyes in their wonted power and beauty to help you, for she could read my mind without my speaking in old days.

M.L.H.

The children Dora and Mary send their kindest regards and best wishes to you.

M.L.H.

I will tell you, sometimes what he said of Rosalie   I have somewhere a letter, in which his sister is mentioned. I remember the sad regrets it contained well enough to describe it, but I prefer to find the letter—perhaps Henry has it. I know there is a reference to Byron, fancies and longings in it, also to an American poet, also, to Willis and his eldest child Imogen, the lovely womanly daughter of his (Willis') first wife, who was an English lady—The letter from Mr. Poe to his wife, *was not very nice to copy*, as it was written from his Mem. Book, but it was a good specimen of his notes to her as you will see by the copy—Perhaps the letter was not mailed I will look and enquire—I had a severe trial about the time I sent it—I may have mislaid it—if so it is in some of my boxes and will come to light again,   We all remember preparing the letter, and copying the two letters—
More when I have had a look at the post Office's register.

M.L.H.

The copies I enclose keep them, they are genuine and I hope the origonals will reach you, as I would like you fortified with Mrs. Clemm's to show to any Lewis woman that disputes the circumstances.

Even though Mrs. Houghton's seeming embarrassment over having sent such a mass of material for Ingram to "wade through" was probably matched by his frustration in trying to do so, he recognized and we now know she made important contributions to Poe biography in this particular package of pages, for the copy of Poe's letter to Virginia enclosed, dated June 12, 1846, is the only letter Poe wrote to his wife that has survived. (See Ostrom, II, 318, for complete text.) In addition, the letter Dora Houghton gave to Ingram, Poe's letter of January 29, 1847, addressed to Mrs. Shew, was so beautifully written that Ingram decided to reproduce the whole of it in facsimile in his *Life*, II, 107.

Mrs. Houghton later sent as gifts to Ingram the manuscripts of Poe's valentine to her and of the poem "To Mrs. M.L.S." The valentine, "To Marie Louise," had been printed in the *Columbian Magazine*, March, 1848; the poem, "To Mrs. M.L.S.," in N. P. Willis' *Home Journal*, March 13, 1847. Poe's first draft of "The Bells" was also an important and valuable gift to Ingram from Mrs. Houghton, for he used it again and again in his various publications about Poe.

Although Mrs. Houghton's account of her dealings with Rufus Griswold over the nature of his proposed biography of Poe and of her attempts to have his biography suppressed are disjointed and almost incoherent, they do have some ring of truth in them; and if they are true, even in part, Mrs. Clemm's roles in the affair are less than admirable. It certainly is true that her frequent and lengthy visits caused unhappiness and actual strife in the Houghton household. A number of other friends who sheltered Mrs. Clemm after Poe's death had causes to be unhappy with her, and several of them were vocal about what they saw as her duplicities, as has been seen in some of the letters above and will be seen again in the letters that follow.

In spite of Poe's ironical reactions to Mrs. Shew's advice that he seek a wife "fond enough and strong enough" to manage him and his affairs, very soon after Virginia's death he seems deliberately to have set about trying to remarry. When Poe left New York on his last journey to Richmond and Norfolk, Mrs. Clemm was scheduled to live with Mr. and Mrs. S. D. Lewis, but she rather quickly returned to the Fordham cottage. It has not been established that Poe was actually returning to Fordham to escort Mrs. Clemm to Richmond to be present at his wedding to Mrs. Shelton, when he died in Baltimore, but much evidence does indicate that such was very likely the case.

Mrs. Houghton's diagnoses and her explications of medical cases are interesting, to say the least, as are her simple and direct criticisms of Poe's fictions; and her firsthand accounts of Poe's physical symptoms of disease, his actions and reactions, are completely unique.

Mary Gove Nichols was afflicted with cataracts and was almost if not completely blind, at this writing.

Mrs. Houghton was always extremely anxious that nothing she said or wrote to Ingram be repeated in print that could possibly offend Dr. J. H. Hopkins, and nowhere is there any satisfactory reason given. She detested Stella Lewis when they both were intimately concerned with the distressed Poe household, and it appears that dislike had not faded; Mrs. Lewis returned Mrs. Houghton's dislike with interest.

Letter 33. **E. Dora Houghton, Flushing, to John Ingram, London.** First printing. [Item 209]

The Chestnuts
Good Friday, March 26, 1875

Dear Sir

Mamma received yours of the 11th and was glad you received safely such an incongruous mass of scribbling. We shall be delighted to have your photo & we shall be most happy to see you in person when you find the leisure to visit America.

Monday, March 29, 1875

Mamma desires me to say that although Mary Starr* was an early friend of Poe's & may be able (if alive) to give you new points about his early life & particularly about the hostility of his family. Mary Starr was an admirer of Mr. Poe for himself—his traits & personal character she defended & she is useful to you only in this respect just as Mamma would be if she had known him as long & like Mamma she never read Mr. Poe's Tales *appreciatively*, if at all. As Mamma knew her she was a lady-like, conventional, cold, & careful. Mamma admired her for her loyalty & fidelity to Mr. Poe & Mrs. Clemm. Mr. Poe spoke of her with just a little scorn as married to a merchant Tailor & evidently content with her lot. You must remember that Mamma has never seen any criticism of E.A.P. except those published in Mr. Griswold's books. (Mamma's books have not all arrived yet & she has not read Griswold's for many years) except the one you say is Stoddards (Mamma thinks Stoddard *was* at the funeral of Mrs. Poe "with green goggles over his eyes")   Will you please tell Mamma who gave you the account of Mrs. Poe's funeral. Mamma did not intend to complain of Mrs. Clemm's treatment of her, *you* are the first person to whom she has ever mentioned it; & did what she did willingly and with all her heart and never regretted it. Owing to an accident the books were not mailed until the 5th of March, & could hardly have reached you at the date of your last letter. Mamma is very glad if they will be of any service to you, & she has no doubt they will reach you safely; & is sorry she mislead you as to the date they were mailed. Mamma begs pardon for troubling you

with Mrs. Nichol's mail but she had an idea she was near
London or that you would see her soon   Mamma says you
have misunderstood her about some things but she will write
you herself about it. She is sorry she cannot be of more service
to you at present but we have to remain at home until after
April. I shall be overjoyed to receive the book on Flowers.[6]

> Yours sincerely,
> E. Dora Houghton

The books Mrs. Houghton had mailed to Ingram were original editions of Poe's
Tales and *The Raven and Other Poems*, both published by Wiley and Putnam,
New York, 1845.

The tone of R. H. Stoddard's* article, "Edgar Allan Poe," in *Harper's
Magazine* was distinctly hostile to Poe, and Ingram could not understand Mrs.
Houghton's approval of it.

Letter 34.   **Marie Louise Shew Houghton, Flushing, to John Ingram, London.** First printing. [Item 210]

> Easter Day
> March 28, 1875

Dear Mr. Ingram—

I think Dora has written you, but as she and her sister are
at church I cannot ask her and will say a few words to you. As
soon as I can leave home for any length of time, I will try to
find the lady who was **Mary Star**. I cannot recall her husband's name, but I will look in the directory for persons of his
business. The name is a common one, which is the difficulty. I
should have forgotten *hers*, if it had not been so odd. I believe
I told you that the lines "to Mrs. M.L.S." were written *to me*,
just after his sickness which I described to you. They were
published by Willis in the Home Journal, with the *Mrs.
attached* but I suppose Griswold or some other publisher has
dropped *the Mrs*. All the friends of Poe and most of the literary

---

6. The "book on flowers," Ingram's *Flora Symbolica: Or, the Language and Sentiment of Flowers*
1868).

persons in N.Y. knew *who* was so *extravagantly* praised—in those lines which was one reason I did not want the "Beloved Physician" printed. I hope I may find it for you. It is possible I have given it to Mr. Knowlton to copy for me. Poor Knowlton is dead! But his wife lives at "Sing-Sing." I will go and see her. I know Mr. Knowlton took some of my songs to copy, for Mr. Hopkins to set to music. I will look until I find it. I think Griswold wanted it at one time, but it is all a dream to me now—and I know Mr. Poe had a copy of it. If Griswold had it he suppressed [it], in enmity to me, but possibly he never saw it—I know I have the leaves from which Poe revised it, somewhere. We shall be happy to have your photograph and to see you, if you ever cross the Atlantic,—I am sorry for your sake my household goods and chattles are so scattered but I lost all interest in life for years, and tried to forget as much as possible the past   I have promised Dora the *Queens* book, in April Life of Prince Albert   I suppose it is expensive—This is her present desire, but I think it much cheaper here, than in England   Did you receve the books I sent you by mail? Congress has just passed a new law—doubling postage on books and heavy mail. It goes in our mail *now*, for one cent per ounce   When I spoke to you about Mr. Poe's poem doing me good, I ment *only*, as to my Diagnosis, of his disease, and skill in the same.

The Valentine enclosed was sent to me, a year after the Lines to M.L.S.   they were both Valentines but this last to Marie Louise was *so like a lover*, that it was never shown to but a few—I dont believe it was ever published, untill Griswold found it, among Mr. Poe's papers. These two Valentines please return to me, sometime, none of the others need be returned

Yours reced acknowledging package

> Yours sincerely
> M.L.H.

Yours of 16th just received

I shall expect my son in May   If he has any letters of any service to you I will get them   Most of Mr. Poe's notes to me are very like the one I sent you first, (or rather Dora sent it) The style and sentiments are the same. They show a gentle, grateful tender nature to those who are kind to him

The day before Mrs. Poe died I left to make some arrangements for her comfort. She called me to her bedside, took a picture of her husband from under her pillow kissed it and gave it to me. She opened her work box and gave me the little jewel cace I mentioned to you. She took from her portfolio a worn letter and showed it to her husband, he read it and weeping heavy tears gave it to me to read. It was a letter from *Mr. Allan's wife* after his death. It expressed a desire to see him, acknowledged that she alone had been the cause of his adopted Father's neglect, out of Jealousy that Mr. Poe really was a relative by blood to her husband. That if he would return to her at the end of her year of mourning, she would provide for him, &c. This letter he answered in scorn to her—and she replied "You was always a gentleman to me, *always*, until now—can you not forgive a fault so humbly acknowledged? This last was pinned to the first letter, & had been preserved by Mrs. Poe that the world might know her husband had treated this woman properly—She gave Mr. Poe the portfolio, and he put it in his desk,—She made him promise to preserve the letter and the few lines from another which she had saved from the flames, when received—

This is all that I know of the Allan matter, and as I remember it, it is not fit for publication. It is a delicate subject, as some of the Allan family still live. Possibly this horrid woman lives still in Richmond. Griswold must have got that letter, and could have used it—I suppose he was afraid of the Allans, as it was a cringing crawling confession of meanness, in the woman, but something might have been said in his defence, with this letter as proof—I cannot help you in time I fear. I cannot leave home until after the April term of court, as possession here is more than nine points of the law to me & mine. I am over worked and have a crushing load of care just now. You must expect little from a sad mother and struggling one

Yours ever truly
Marie L. Houghton

Mr. Poe told me a story of his experience once, which I'll try to remember & which founded the theft story!

Dearest John—

I enclose a letter which is from Mrs. Richmond of Lowel after my visit with her in N.Y. You see she speaks bitterly of Mrs. Clemm, who was like a cat, often, treacherous and cruel. She had a hard side to her nature like many Southern persons, who are, or have been brought up with slaves as servants and associates in childhood   Not that I wish to depreciate Southern Ladies for I have learned from *them* some of my greatest lessons of Humanity and Christian charity—but there are natures that grow hard from sorrow and cruelty creeps out and selfishness and in old age, a grasping sordid spirit which may the Lord preserve from me and mine—Yours

M.L.H.

Mrs. Clemm called me "Loui"—an abbreviation of Louise.

M.L.H.

I burned my Journal very injudiciously last summer. I had kept it hid for years thinking some child of mine would write my life, but I burned it nearly all

I found some leaves of it in a vase yesterday which described this letter of Mrs. Allan's—You make me curious to know, who you took to be M.L.S. I do not think it at all important to tell who Mr. Poe wrote his Poems for. He laughed over people's perplexities and amused Mrs. Osgood who said to me "(Mrs. S) Edgar will tell you anything you ask him. He says he could refuse you nothing. Do ask him questions" but I disliked people who asked questions   I am sorry now, but I had no curiosity which trait endeared me to many hearts

M.L.H.

The letter Mrs. Houghton enclosed to Ingram in this letter, from "Mrs. Richmond of Lowel," follows. First printing. [Item 79]

Lowell,
Feby 9 [18]53

My dear Loui,

So much has my time been occupied, since my return, in writing friends I neglected while in New York that I could not find an hour for you, although I have tried often so to do, and have twice commenced even writing to you.—

We arrived home in safety Sat. P.M. found all well, and glad to see us. The first thing I saw on entering the house was a letter from Mrs. Clemm in which she told me much concerning yourself and family—that you were soon to go to New York to reside. I immediately sat down and gave her a minute description of my delightful visit, expressing very freely my opinion of my acquaintances there, & particularly of her friend Dr. Houghton, but I did *not* tell her that I heard her name mentioned, during my sojourn among you—in her next I suppose she will enquire—Her letter was one of the most beautiful and affectionate I ever rec'd from her in my life. Oh, how hard it is to reconcile all we see & hear in this strange and selfish world of ours. Sometimes I fancy myself blessed with more kind and faithful friends than any earthly creature is deserving of—anon, I am striving in vain to find *one* I may venture to rely upon—such is life and such are some of the trials of my Everyday's Experience—Do you wonder I often doubt *everyone* & firmly resolve never again will I put it in the power of any human being to trifle with my heart's most sacred feelings. Not a secret (of my own) but I have confided in Mrs. Clemm—& what have I not suffered in consequence! God forgive her & enable me also to forgive the *cruel wrong* she has done the *dead* as well as the living—but I must drop this subject, lest my feelings get the better of my judgment, and I be left to say words of *bitterness* concerning one I have loved—Heaven only knows how devotedly—Caddie* sends much love & many thanks for the beautiful book from Marie—Please remember me very kindly to your husband & the children all—Have you seen Mr. [Wise ?] since I left & is his friend living yet? Do let me hear from you soon & believe me truly yours

Annie L. Richmond

Mrs. Louisa G. Allan was indeed still living in Richmond when Mrs. Houghton wrote this letter to Ingram. Ingram's attempts to communicate with her had failed utterly; his Richmond correspondents refused to try to deliver the letters Ingram addressed to her which he enclosed to them, on the grounds that she was adamant in her refusal to discuss anything concerning Edgar Poe. Mrs. Allan died on Sunday, April 24, 1881, in Richmond.

Mrs. Houghton is the sole authority for this story about Mrs. Allan's attempt to effect a reconcilation with Poe; but if there is any truth in Mrs. Houghton's account, it absolutely nullifies Griswold's statement in his *Memoir* that Poe had behaved badly if not indecently in the Allan household. Ingram published in his *Life* this whole story relayed by Mrs. Houghton, thereby adding to the speculation and confusion that has ever since surrounded Poe's relations with the second Mrs. Allan. It is probable that Mrs. Clemm destroyed these letters from Mrs. Allan, along with the "hundreds" she admittedly burned, after Poe's death.

Among the other confusions this letter from Mrs. Houghton caused in Poe biography are the accounts Mrs. Houghton sent Ingram from the "forty leaves" of the journal she had kept from the days and nights when Poe dictated to her concerning his supposed travels in France, his being wounded in a duel, his writing two poems and a novel while in France, and so on—none of which has ever been substantiated. Poe's love of hoaxing is probably as close to the truth of the matter as we shall ever come, just as his quixotic enjoyment in mystifying curious persons explains his attitude about naming the persons to whom he addressed his poems.

Mrs. Houghton was the only one of Ingram's correspondents who ever had the temerity to address him by his first name. Mrs. Whitman did on occasion banteringly call him "MacRaven," and "Don Felix"—because he once tartly informed her that "Ingram" meant "son of the Raven," and he had used the pseudonym "Don Felix de Salamanca" in signing articles he had written, in imitation of Poe, on the philosophy of handwriting—but Ingram was not amused. His personality did not encourage familiarity.

Virginia Poe's jewel case and the letters from Mrs. Allan, if they ever existed, are still unlocated.

Letter 35. **Marie Louise Shew Houghton, Flushing, to John Ingram, London,** including a letter from Poe to Mrs. Shew. First printing. [Item 213]

April 3 [1875]

Dear Mr. Ingram—

My books came yesterday and *yours also*. You may think it strange I could not get a copy of Poe's works here. Dora looked for it in the Public Library and several private ones, including the Rectory's at Flushing & Whitestone where my daughter is as much at home as any where, but your friend and my friend's Memoir was not there, in the full bookcases. I now have 2 copies of Griswold's edition (Mr. Chapin's* & mine). Shall I make a present of *one* of these to the Flushing Library? I could not tell which box the Poe's Memoir was packed in, but it came at last, *two copies*. I read your Memoir hurriedly last night while watching a sick neighbor. I recognized Mrs. Lewis whom you call an accomplished writer. Mr. Poe was indebted to her, that is, she paid Mrs. Clemm in advance, when they were needy, and poor Poe *had to notice* her writings, and praise them. He expressed to me the *great mortification it was to him*, and I child like I hated the fat gaudily dressed woman whom I often found sitting in Mrs. Clemm's little kitchen, waiting to see the man of genius, who had rushed out to escape her, to the fields and forest—or to the grounds of the Catholic school in the vicinity. I remember Mrs. C[lemm] sending me after him in great secrecy one day & I found him sitting on a favorite rock muttering his desire to die, and get rid of *Literary bores*. I tried to cheer him. He liked me for my ignorance and indifference, no doubt, to worldly honors, and lamented, in sincere sorrow when I grew like the rest of the world by my duties and position. I have two letters of his, "cowardly letters" he called them, as he said he saw me floating away from his sight, hence his bitterness to the student of divinity, whom he gave credit for instructing his friend in the duties of a mother, and as a child of the Church, in her example's avoiding "even the appearance of evil"! I never saw the reply to Mr. Hopkins article before (it must have been *him* as the *shirt collar described* him so accurately, but Mr. Poe wronged Mr. H.* I am sure, (*in his jealousy*) for Mr. Hopkins has an acute and fine perception of Mr. Poe's genius, and only attacked his so called Pantheism—as you know—He wrote a brilliant notice of Poe's lecture at the Society Library at *my house*, the same night. *This other article* I never heard of, before, evidently Mr. Poe *thought it was him, if it was not*.

The letters I mention are *Private*—extravagant in my praise and I did not send them. I will copy or get Dora to do any thing we find, but I am so nearly, *washed out*, *by sorrows* that the outlines are faint and unreliable, *as to dates and persons*—new things come to me daily, however. I hope you will forgive me if I say that your picture [of Poe, in Vol. I of Ingram's 1874/75 edition of Poe's works] is not as good as the one in Griswold's. I never saw this before that I remember. It may look as he did the last year (for he was very thin and worn when he went away) but Mr. Poe had *curling hair*, he wet it often to *straiten* it, and probably did so before this sitting (of your photo) but his hair *would curl as soon as dry*, around his ears. He had fine dark curling hair, blue eyes with dark lashes, or bluish grey—his mouth was small, *which was his only defect*, showing weakness. He was like his Mother, who wore her curls low on her forehead to conceal her broad intellectual forehead, or brain which was poor Edgars *inheritence*. He had a bundle of his Mothers letters, written in a round hand, very like Mr. Poe's, and two sketches of hers, one in pencil or indellible ink, the other in *water colors*, and represented Boston Harbour (I think from the Cambridge side) or view. On the back of this picture was a neatly written description, which ended in these words, which I copy from my journal. "For my little son Edgar, who should ever love Boston, the place of his birth, and where his mother found her *best*, and *most sympathetic* friends" Mrs. Clemm did not value "these antiquated specimens of art", as she called them in derision, and altho I had them neatly framed according to Virginias request of me, and hung in Mrs. Clemms room while at my house, after Edgars death, I think she must have given them away, I had her promice to give them to me, if they left the family. I cannot recall their fate, but only remember that she called them in jest "Loui Antiques" as I dont know where she died, I cannot say. they may have been given to the sister Rosalie. I wish I could find them. Mr. Hopkins said the water color sketch was lovely, Boston Harbour, morning, 1808. Mrs. Clemm was fond of new things, and *I of old*. She dressed very plainly herself, but if I was to take her out in my little coupa, she would give me a lecture on going out in white musline or on my childish simplicity, in not following fashions which neither suited my ideas or person, and I always had a lecture about it. This I mean when she was staying with me. The world was too much her Idol.

She covered over things which would have saved many sorrows, to have been known, for there were many noble souls in New York, among plain uneducated but wealthy people who would have willingly given of their wealth to have saved the immortal Poe—to finish his career in honor and comfort. I was too young then to know it, too *inexperienced and* undeveloped, but *now I know it well*—I have a picture which is very like the side view I copied of Mrs. Poe. Alma thinks it is one of Mr. Poe's mother, while ill in Richmond. I gave it to Alma, when she left home, with a book of autographs in which Mr. Poe wrote these lines "Like all true souls of noble birth" etc. I think the lines were sent me by Mrs. Nichols as a Valentine but they are carefully and beautifully copied, in Poe's handwriting in the book. I think he did it for a past time, and Mrs. Nichols is the author. It lies between them. I enclose them in the picture—which I think is very like the picture of Poe, in Griswold's edition, but not as intellectual as the side view I copied, and which I will send you when I find it. You can hardly imagine how broken my home is, with a few boxes here and a few there, but still we are a happy loving trio still—I think the registered post will be best for it and may not get it off, immediately so dont let me have you looking London over for it, please, as I found Mr. Poe's (or Griswold Memoir) & books in a box of my son Henry's. I may find a copy of the Beloved in his Boxes. Henry could repeat some verses of it, and called me "the Ancient Louisa" much to Lida's annoyance, the young lady who died, who also admired Mr. Poe's works, and the *beloved Physician in particular*. I have no letters here or papers of Poe, except the 2 letters of which I have or will send you copies. They are not useful to you except as explanatory. The following was his last, and was written in June 49 after my visit with Mr. Hopkins, the last time, Mr. H. went twice to see Poe. "The last time by appointment." "Can it be true Louise thay you have the *idea fixed* in your mind to desert your unhappy and unfortunate friend and patient. You did not say so, I know, but for months I have known you was deserting me, not willingly but none the less surely—my destiny—Disaster! following fast & following faster, & I have had premonitions of this for months   I expect, my good spirit, my loyal heart! Must this follow as a sequel to all the benefits and blessings you have so generously bestowed? Are you to vanish like all I love, or desire, from my darkened and 'lost soul'—I have read over your letter again, and again, and cannot make it possible with any degree of certainty, that you wrote it in your right mind *I know you did not without tears of anguish and regret*, is it possible your influence is lost to me? Such tender and true natures are ever loyal until death, but you are not dead, you are full of life and beauty! Louise you came in with the Parson, in your floating white robe "Good Morning Edgar" There was a touch of conventional coldness in your hurried manner and your attitude as you opened the kitchen door to find Muddie is *my last remembrance of you*. There was *love*, hope, and *sorrow* in your smile, instead of love, hope & *courage*, as ever before. Oh Louise how many sorrows are before you, Your ingenuous and sympathetic nature will be constantly wounded in contact with the hollow heartless world, and for me alas! unless some tender and pure womanly love saves me, I shall hardly last a year longer, alone! A few short months will tell, how far my strength, (physical, and moral), will carry me in Life here. How can I believe in Providence, when *you* look coldly upon me. Was it not you who renewed my hopes and faith in God? . . . & in humanity? Louise, I heard your voice as you passed out of my sight leaving me with the Parson, 'The man of God, The servant of the Most High!' He stood smiling and bowing at the madman Poe! *But that* I had invited him to my house, I would have rushed out into God's light and freedom! But I still listened to your voice! I heard you say with a sob, 'dear Muddie!' I heard you greet *my Caterina*, but it was only as a memory of—nothing escaped *my ear*. and I was convinced it was not your generous self that was repeating words so foreign to your nature, to your tender heart!—I heard you sob out your sense of duty to my mother, and I heard her reply— 'Yes, Loui,' 'Yes,' *it was the mother of* Alma, that child with the Madonna eyes! She is good and pure, and passably loving, but she is of her father type. She has not your nature. Why sacrifice your angelic perogative for a commonplace nature? Why turn your soul from its true work for the desolate, to the thankless and miserly world! Why I was not a priest, it is a mystery, for I feel I am now a prophet and I did then and *towered* in mind and body, over my invited guest in spite of the duties of hospitality and regard for your feelings, Louise, when he said grace and you said a low 'amen,' I felt my heart stop, and I was sure I was then to die before your eyes. Louise, it is well, it is fortunate you looked up, with a tear in your dear eyes, and raised the window and talked of the guava— you 'had brought for my sore throat'—Your instincts are better than a *strong man's reason* I trust they may be for yourself! Louise I feel I shall not prevail a shadow has already fallen upon your soul and is reflected in your eyes. It is *too late* you are floating away with the cruel tide. I am a coward to write this to you, but it is not a common trial, it is a fearful one to me. Such rare souls as yours, so beautify this earth! So relieve it of all that is repulsive and sordid, so brighten its toils and cares, it is hard to lose sight of them even for a short time, again I say I am a coward, to wound your loyal unselfish and womanly heart, but you must know and be *assured*, of my regret and my *sorrow* if aught I have ever written has hurt you! My *heart never wronged* you. I place you in *my esteem* in all *solemnity*, beside the friend of my boyhood, the mother of my school fellow, of whom I told you, and as I have repeated in the Poem the "Beloved Physician", as the truest, tenderest, of this worlds most womanly souls, and an angel to my for-lorn and darkened nature, I will not say 'Lost Soul' again, for your sake. I will try to over come my grief for the sake of your unselfish care of me in the past, and in life or death, I am ever yours gratefully & devotedly

June 1849 [1848]   Edgar A. Poe

Mr. Ingram

Mr. Poe always treated me with respect and I was to him a friend in need, and a friend indeed, but he was so excentric, and so unlike others, and I was also, that I had to define a position, I was bound to take, and it hurt his feelings, and after he was dead I deeply regreted my letter to him, as we all do, often to [*sic*] late.

Poor Edgar cannot but show how womanly and true I was

or was to him. Still I was only a "country maiden" and he could not reverence my intellect, poor fellow. He used to listen to my songs, written by myself and lament I had not learned greek and latin, still he would not change the songs, he said—

Mr. Ingram I believe I am the only correspondent of Mr. Poe to whom he called himself "cowardly" and a "Lost Soul" I never repeated this, or showed it to others, but generally burned such letters (as I was in duty bound). He did not believe that his soul was lost, it was only a sarcasm, he liked to repeat to express his sufferings, and dispair! I never saw a quotation from the Raven in any letter of his, but this. The whole stanza is written out after Disaster, following fast & following faster &c. (follow*ing* is used instead of followed)

I kept this letter and carried it in my memorandum book so long, (to grieve over) that it is nearly worn out. My son Henry is the only person I ever showed it to (except Dr. Houghton, at one time when I was looking for a letter for a date for him, after I was married to him, & he did not read it all. I read the passage about the valentine (for that is what Mr. Poe alluded to) in what he said as to what he *had written*, as it is the only thing he ever did or said that *could* be *construed* as wrong to me but I never thought it wrong. I think it a beautiful glorious valentine, and hope you will publish it, as I sent it, but it is best to take thought of its date as it is not dated, by him.   also I would not connect it in the Memoir as written to me. Let it stand as it is, to Marie Louise. How stupid of Griswold to leave out part of it. Do you not think so? I hope you will receive it safely. Dora did not register the letter as the postmaster could not be found to attend to it, in time for the mail. I only tell you my impression that it was written February 1848—and to save any possible accusation for or to his memory, in Mrs. Whitmans mind. I think the date better be omitted. We must be wise, we that love him, for his enemies are still alive. *Some friends of Griswolds* keeps these slanders circulating, so I am told—and now I hope you will not be startled. A man by the name of Jones, a bushy headed white livered creature had the *audacity* to stop at my gate or door yesterday, to enquire if I had any manuscript or poems of Poe that had not been published, "That an American publisher would like to know." I answered that I had yet to learn that any American publisher would do Mr. Poe the justice to *brand Griswold's edition* as an outrage, and a deliberate & *premeditated slander*, upon the dead poet, and as *this man* did not bring me any introduction I felt justified in shutting the door without giving him any reply, *but that I feared Griswold was not dead yet, as I had hoped he was, intellectually–morally–and physically.* I have never mentioned my correspondence with you to anyone, but your first letter, Mr. Davidson sent to Hartford and it went thro' Dr. Houghton's hands who knows I had some of Poe's poems years ago, he may have mentioned it to somebody, but I shall not give any information, and hope you will get your book out without meddlers or any other such specimens of greedy publishers, coming here to see me, for I am in no humour to meet with such creatures—now—I do not think Dr. Houghton, otherwise than friendly to Mr. Poe, but he is a friend of many publishers, and may have said something.

The *man who called*, remained in his carriage at the gate, and said he was lame, sent his driver to ask me to go out to him. I declined to go out to see a strange man, so he got out and hobbled to the door, & said hurriedly, "*My name is Jones madame*, and you are Mrs. Dr. Houghton." I said, yes. Then he repeated his business in the words I have written on the preceding page. Dora said that the man muttered "I thought so" as he got into his carriage, and she *scowled at* him, and told the man to "shut the gate, please."

M.L.H.

Note, When I spoke of the man Jones who called in the following sheet, I only intended to say that I hope no other book will get the credit, and profit you deserve

M.L.H.

Poe's mother's letters and the sketch and water color painting of Boston Harbor have not survived.

Mary Gove Nichols wrote the lines "Like all true souls of noble birth"; Poe simply copied them in Mrs. Shew's book of autographs. Several lines of Poe's valentine, "To Marie Louise," were omitted when it was first printed in the *Columbian Magazine*, and Griswold had followed that printing. Rufus Griswold had died on August 27, 1857.

When any one of Ingram's correspondents showed real signs of being a help to him, he flattered them by sending a set of his edition of Poe's works. The daguerreotype of Poe that Ingram had used as a frontispiece was actually an engraving made from a copy of a daguerreotype made in late 1848 in Providence, Rhode Island. Poe had given the original to Mrs. Whitman and she had furnished the copy to Ingram.

Apparently Poe was indeed jealous of the influence the divinity student J. H. Hopkins exerted over Mrs. Shew, feeling that Hopkins, seriously offended by Poe's pantheistic ideas, had warned Mrs. Shew that her association with Poe would endanger her both socially and spiritually. In many quarters, Poe's reputation was indeed not very good.

Mrs. Houghton's dislike for and jealousy of Stella Lewis are perfectly obvious, and they were shared by every other member of the "Poe Circle."

Of course, "Caterina" was the name of Poe's cat.

Letter 36. **Marie Louise Shew Houghton, Flushing, to John Ingram, London.** First complete printing. [Item 215]

April 9, 1875

Dear Mr. Ingram

I am sorry my letters are so long in getting off. I suppose when we miss a Saturday's mail the letters wait until the next Wednesday. I have made no enquiries as to the English mail and only judge from old times, when I had correspondence abroad, so you see how retisent I am, and how far behind the times. Mr. Hopkins has sent me the 40 pages. I received them last night. I see that Mr. Poe said in one conversation that he wrote a story that year which is a blank to you in his life, which was credited to Eugene Sue, and published afterwards as doubtful, still many believed it was Sue's. Mr. Poe said it was to much of the sensation character and he would not mix it up with his more studied writings. I don't give his own words *here* however in my Journal, only his ideas. This information was given in reply to my question why he didn't write stories like others, Bulwer, Dickens, and some others, as

I thought his tales so unsatisfactory and unpleasant. He said he was ill in a foreign port, once was insane, [illegible] in a fever, brought on from a sword wound, given him by an antagonist more skillful than himself, with whom he quarreled about a fair Lady—That he lay ill in a Lodging—that a noble Scotch woman of birth and culture, came to him, at the suggestion of a poor charwoman who had carried him food and heard his prayers and cries for water and ice that this Scotch Lady had followed her brother to this port, her brother having fallen into evil ways, gaming &c. That she cared for him, Mr. Poe, 13 weeks, providing him with everything he needed. (including a kind nurse) That she came daily with her brother to see him, and took the nurse's place while she slept. That he promised this angelic woman never to mention her name or service, except to those who had a right to know his whereabout. And then her name was not to be revealed, unless by her own request. He described her as a plain looking large featured maiden Lady, with no beauty but her eyes, which were heavenly blue with long dark lashes. That the [illegible] and intense trust & deep honest heart of sympathy, and trusting faith in God's ever present help, to those who believed in, and asked for mercy, was so expressed in this Lady['s] eyes, That he wrote a poem for her in parting called "Holy Eyes"—That he told her he intended to go home and follow or adopt journalism as a profession, And she said when he became great and noted, she would visit him in America, if she lived as long, and that she would have the poem published, after her affairs at home were settled. He also says he wrote a poem called Humanity which was sent to Paris and sold, and credited afterwards to "George Sands"— That his promise to this Scotch Florence Nightengale was the reason he never published these two poems, in America—The story he said was not to his taste and had too much of yellow covered novel style for him to be proud of, and besides "there were scenes and pictures, so personal, that it would have made him many enemies among his kindred who hated him for his vanity and pride already, and in some respects very justly, the fault of his early education." these were his own words.

M.L.H.

As near as I can make out Mr. Poe reffered to the time he left "West Point,"—The town was in France near the sea, and the Scotch Lady, and her brother, helped translate his novel, and sold it for him for *so many francs* equivalent to $100 dollars, which paid his passage home. The poem "Humanity" was not dedicated to George Sand but was *attributed to her pen* and was, (I think he said) published as hers in a collection—and the novel was attributed to *Sue*. He had the manuscript, but said he would destroy it. I begged him not to do so, but to rewrite it and make money as others did with everyday ordinary stories. He said he should detest himself as a yellow cover novelist—That the *truth* was more terrible than the fiction in it—&c. &c.

Note—

I fancy you will be able to make out now at *what time* the absence occured, when Mr. Poe was ill in a strange country, as very likely you can put your evidence together, as to his evident whereabouts from his relatives. They ought to know what became of his brother, whom Edgar said was a Secretary to some foreigner and afterwards "read law," as we say in America. He was a dashing gay cavalier, of tastes unsuited to the times he was bred in, or born to, and, with far more of the *Poe* nature than Edgar had—*coarser* rougher, and I fancy—very gay. Edgar mentioned him once to me the conversation I will recall and tell you, if I do not find the statement I wrote for him about it. What did Mrs. Clemm say about Mrs. Lewis. What does Mrs. L. do in London? Does she know you are writing me? I suppose I have done her injustice for it appears Mrs. Clemm *did* stay at her house before going to Baltimore. I have always *fully believed some one intercepted a letter* I wrote Mrs. Clemm to the care of her publishers, sometime /57 (in the summer of /57 I think) as it was taken from them by a lady with whom Mrs. C. was staying   I know so much, and it was just before she went to Baltimore.

M.L.H.

I see the story was written in the third person, and he called it "commonplace" and the name of it was at first called "Life of an Unfortunate Artist"—afterwards changed however, Life of an Artist at Home and Abroad and he supposed it would be compiled in Sue's works. He laughed at me for reading a book of George Sands. I think it was [illegible] and told me of his poem Humanity, as a nice little joke, because I did not admire *his style*. There is something else in this part of my Journal, *if you like the style* I will copy it but it is unsatisfactory, I not being a [practicle?] person, only wrote from memory what made my journal interesting, and I tell you *in confidence* that Mr. Hopkins one of the most learned men I ever knew, said it was a charming, womanly, record which he would never willingly see destroyed, but that it would take the place of, or was [equal?] in pathos, and power, to some correspondence, published by some German author of note. All of which is no matter now—I do not remember fully the title the story had at last, but it was similar to what I have written. I do not find any reference to the beloved Physician. Indeed these pages were written the winter after the sickness of Poe, Jan. Feb. and March, Apr. May & June of 1848. The Beloved Physician was written two months or more after Mrs. Poe's death, 1847. I will see what I can cull out for you in a few days. The reference to Bishop Hopkins family is not of a nature to send you and I shall return the Journal to Dr. Hopkins after I copy out for you what it reveals of Poe, and if you refer to what I say in the Journal you can say, This is from the Journal of his intimate friend, or Physician, and revealed during illness and gloom; and anything you please of Mrs. Houghtons Journal so you keep the "Parson" out

M.L.H.

[. . .]I heard your voice as you said Dear Muddie so tender and mournful, and then an allusion to greeting his cat, whom he calls *Caterina*. I copy this from a copy of the letter in my portfolio, for I sent my letters away to a safe, with some valuables belonging to the children yesterday,—you are right about the *was* and *were*! You must make what I write *good English* for I never was educated. I came up an only daughter, of a busy Doctor, who thought me too frail in health to *overtax* me with dicipline or learning and my old age is full of work and care   You have the *sense and meaning* and must supply the grammar

There is still a hiatus in our knowledge of Poe's whereabouts after he left West Point in February or March, 1831, but it is highly unlikely that this story of his being wounded in a duel in France has any basis in fact. Poe could have been delirious when he dictated these adventures to Mrs. Shew, or, more probably, he was simply enjoying spinning a romantic tale for her mystification. It is true that Poe's brother did go to sea, and it is possible that he reached Russia; but it is equally possible that Edgar assumed some of his brother's experiences as his own, just to amuse himself at Mrs. Shew's expense. Certainly no traces of any poems named "Holy Eyes" or "Humanity" have been found in the writings of George Sand, or anyone else for that matter; and no story resembling that told to Mrs. Shew has been located in the works of Eugene Sue.

After divorcing her husband, S. D. Lewis, in 1858, Stella Lewis moved to London. When Mrs. Houghton learned from Ingram that Mrs. Clemm had indeed been living with Mrs. Lewis in 1857, she surmised that Mrs. Lewis had intercepted her letter.

During the Civil War, Mrs. Houghton and her three children retired into the country, near the Canadian border, presumably without Dr. Houghton.

Mrs. Houghton's grammatical inaccuracies, as well as her ambiguities, her habits of leaving letters undated, pages unnumbered, and of adding endless postscripts that seem irrelevant are indeed frustrating at times—but John Ingram confessed himself charmed with her naïveté. He was himself not without grammatical sin.

Letter 37. Marie Louise Shew Houghton, Flushing, to John Ingram, London. First complete printing. [Item 218]

[*ca.* April 15, 1875]

Dear Mr. Ingram

I am sorry the books did not reach you in good condition. Books go by mail here to all parts of the United States safely. The Post Master advised me to send them in this way. They were carefully put up, and decently clean when they left us. You need not return them. The small one Mr. Poe gave me the first time I saw him and it was his last copy he said. If you ever come to see us, you can bring it [. . . .] I told you in my long letter that *Mr. Poe had* a miniature of his mother, and I was told by Mr. Chapin,* (who was an old resident of Baltimore) that Poe's satchel was given up by the Railroad Company, as he left it in the train, being entirely mad, that this portrait was in the bag and a slip of paper pasted upon the back, "My adored Mother! E. A. Poe, New York" with date of his departure from N.Y.

I copied it once on ivory myself, and some of my children have it, as I divided up many of my valuables but I did not mention this to you for fear I could not find it for you. You must have been mistaken or I may have forgotten. Dora says it may be in her boxes [. . . .] We will try to find something nice for you in the mean time. You must see we cannot serve you as well as we could wish, on account of our distracted surroundings at present. [The letter breaks off]

Dear Mr. Ingram
   [. . .] I must say in my own defense that I have slept only three nights out of six, for two months, having a sick neighbor with whom I have stayed on alternate nights, and *if I* write nonsense, or leave out half my words it is because I cannot see well, or as readily as I used to do, and also, I am weary and sleepy as most Doctors are [. . . .] While copying Mr. Poe's letter I was constantly interrupted and I did not read it over. Dora also copied one, which she hurried over, and she says it was all there, except the stars and punctuation, which she did not mind. What a pity! You probably can judge from these that his letters were of a confidential nature, and let it all go only, so you understand them—I see no more of the reminiscense of Poe in that 40 pages, except a reference to his coming to town to go to a midnight service with a Lady friend and myself. He went with us, followed the service like a "churchman", looking directly towards the chancel, and holding one side of my prayer book, sang the psalms with us, and to my astonishment struck up a tenor to our sopranos and, got along nicely during the first part of the sermon, which was on the subject of the sympathies of our Lord, to our wants. The passage being often repeated, "He was a man of sorrows and acquainted with grief." He begged me to stay quiet that he would wait for me outside, and he rushed out, *too excited to stay*. I knew he would not leave us to return home alone, (altho' my friend thought it doubtful), and so after the sermon as I began to feel anxious (as we were in a strange church) I looked back and saw his pale face, and as the congregation

rose to sing the Hymn, "Jesus Saviour of my soul," he appeared at my side, and sang the Hymn, without looking at the book, in a fine clear tenor. He looked inspired! And *no wonder. He imagined* he would have made a successful orator, and priest—I did not dare to ask him why he left, but he mentioned after we got home, that the subject *"was marvelously handled*, and ought to have melted many hard hearts" and ever after this he never passed Doctor Muhlenbergs 20th St. Free Church without going in, if the doors were open. He considered Dr. M. a wonderful man, "with a large heart for his kind, superlatively so!" as he proved to be, as we owe St. Luke's Hospital, to his influence and many other charities!!! —for fallen, as well as suffering humanity. Dora posted the letter containing the two original valentines, three weeks ago. It is time I heard of their safe arrival. I feel very sorry they were sent as they were beautiful specimens of art and poetry, and may be lost! The picture I sent, because I did not think it a good likeness, and too much like the portrait of Poe in Griswolds Memoir to *please you*, and besides a copy of a miniature [letter breaks off]

I copy or clip rather from a secular paper (The N.Y. Sun) the following notice or enclosed notice, of Dr. Muhlenberg*—

This Hymn was sung when my mother was dying, as it is in the prayer book, and I never could sing it from a nervous feeling of dread. He [Poe] said it was *originally* one of the most beautiful Hymns in the Language. That it had been simplified. That it was an Essay as well as a poem, and a thousand sermons could be written from it—for every thought contained numberless texts, to preach sermons from—*or for sermons*, and he repeated the *original* Hymn, which he learned when a little boy, from a newspaper copy and never forgot. I remember this as I thought seriously of asking a friend to introduce Mr. Poe to Dr. Muhlenberg, but was prevented at that time, and it never occurred. His wife told me that Edgar was not fond of forms of worship, but often went to hear Dr. M. from a sort of attraction "that he could not overcome and often remarked that he was a true and inspired teacher of the Gospel."

M.L.H.

Dear Mr. Ingram,

I have neglected to tell you that the Photograph or engraving in your Memoir improves as I have had it to look at, and I do not wish to discourage you as to its truthfulness.

What is Mrs. Whitman's address except Providence, R.I.? I will give her the jewel cace or something belonging to Mr. or Mrs. Poe, as she will value them. My life is almost over, and my children belong to another age. I enclose a slip from a Virginia Educational magazine about a monument to Edgar A. Poe.

Heaven bless you

M.L.H.

Don't speak of what I say about the jewel cace to Mrs. W. If you think it will please her I *know it will*. I will send it to her.

Yours very truly
M.L.H.

Ingram used the miniature of Poe's mother sent to him by Mrs. Houghton as a frontispiece for Volume II of his 1880 *Life of Poe*. He reproduced this account of Poe's going to church in an article called "Unpublished Correspondence of Edgar A. Poe," *Appleton's Journal*, May, 1878.

The two "original valentines" posted to Ingram by Dora Houghton were manuscripts of two poems Poe had written to her mother.

Ingram accepted as a gift the two volumes of Poe's tales and poems, on the basis of Mrs. Houghton's written "You need not return them." Later, her family resorted to every means known to them to get him to return these "gifts," but he resisted; and even after Ingram's death in 1916, they were trying to regain the items from the collection of Poe papers sold to the University of Virginia. Finally, Professor James Southall Wilson wrote the family a gentle and conciliatory letter explaining that almost all of the autograph letters and valuable items in the collection had been sold at various auctions by Ingram, after the persons who had given them to him had died. Ingram had insisted he had a right to sell the items, for he claimed he had devoted his life and fortune to redeeming Poe's name and he deserved the right to recoup what he could. At one sale, the British Museum bought several autograph Poe letters at a pound or two each; within a few years, autograph Poe letters were bringing as much as two hundred dollars each at auctions. Ingram was outraged, but helpless.

Mrs. Houghton did open a correspondence with Mrs. Whitman, but it is not known whether she sent to her the jewel case that had belonged to Poe's mother.

Letter 38.   Marie Louise Shew Houghton, Whitestone, to John Ingram, London. First printing. [Item 221]

May 2 [1875]

Dear Mr. Ingram,

   I suppose *you understand why* I have said *so much of Mr. Hopkins* to you. I did so because he was a frequent visitor at my house the year that Mrs. Poe died (and his father and brothers and sisters) and as you had only heard of my existence thro' Mrs. Nichols (who had not seen me for twelve years or more) I considered it best to mention some *reliable* person who had known me all this time also—I have said many things (in explanation) that it is not *usual to mention*, for instance about my journal. I do not think Mr. H. would like me to speak about his interest in it, for fear of misconception, but I have told you *why*—in all candor—and you must not mention or know anything thro' me, but my desire to do you some real service, and my memory will not give you proper dates unless I find the pencilled notes taken down from Mr. Poe's own lips, as dictation. You have not acknowledged the little note I sent you, given me by Mrs. Poe, in *his* picture or Deguerotype. It was not much but I sent it in March with a few lines telling you I had found it in my box of colors with a little bunch of flowers, very unexpectedly. It was a good specimen of his notes to his wife, as he always called her my dear Heart, &c. Dora kept a copy of it. I sent the original thinking you would like to have it as he wrote it, for your book—perhaps you think it too simple to notice—*if so*, I mistake your ideas and nature & I venture to mention it to you.

Marie L. Houghton

Monday [May] 3d [1875]

   Please send my letters hereafter until further notice to Box 72, Whitestone Queens Country, Long Island, as we give up the Flushing Box—after May 1st

   The note to Mrs. Poe was written on a leaf from his account book and sent by her mothers hand.

The original of the "little note" given to Mrs. Shew by Virginia Poe was Poe's note to Virginia dated June 12, 1846, telling her that he must stay in the city for the night. Ingram never received the original; only a copy made by Dora Houghton reached him. (See Ostrom, II, 318, for complete text.)

Reverend J. H. Hopkins (later Bishop Hopkins) was apparently very close indeed to Mrs. Houghton and her family. His interest in her journal was ostensibly appreciation for the charming wholesomeness of her personality therein expressed.

Letter 39.   Marie Louise Shew Houghton, Whitestone, to John Ingram, London. First complete printing. [Item 226]

May 16 [18]75

Dear Mr. Ingram—

Yours received *today*, ackowledging the little picture. You can keep the picture as long as you please. I told you that I did not feel satisfied about this picture. That I had a *side face* much more intellectual—*and this I should not have remembered* about but from my eldest daughter saying it was Mr. Poe's mother's picture, and she only valued it, from its resemblence to her great grandmother's portrait at her grandfather's house

Don't let the family (Poe family) know of your having this picture at present *and try to get the one* Edgar had with him when he died. You know portrait painters and miniature painters took great liberties (having no photographs in those days to help them in likenesses)   Find out first, if you can do better. I think you understood me as to Mrs. Allan. I know nothing only about those two letters mentioned and this I should have forgotten, if I had not mentioned it in my diary. Griswold must have returned those letters, or else Mrs. Clemm burned them. She burned a package of my letters to Mr. Poe *which he had preserved* carefully. She "burned them without opening them" she told me. This was very unwise for they would *now* be of use, in making dates out, and an angel might have seen them. They [illegible] from a true and loving friend and deserved a better fate. I wonder indeed! That what he cared for *so carefully* should have been *so carelessly distroyed*. I said to her "you might have returned them, and given me the privilege of disposing of what he chose to preserve" and as she said "tied up with white ribbon and a golden cord running through it"—The photograph is very good. It quite startled me, and at first I did not like it, but it is very like him indeed. I should like a large one if it would be as like, large enough to hang up in my "office", sometime. *You owe me nothing*, but patience and charity for my scriblings. Mr. Poe was the person who spent a year abroad and never betrayed his whereabouts to mortal. No one knew of the origin of the scar on his shoulder but Virginia, so Mrs. Clemm told me. She did not seem to know it then. I never talked with her about it, as she burned my letters so roughly and seemed to leave me out of all her plans except to make use of my loyalty and devotion, when she needed *personal protection* and *pecuniary* help. (This is between ourselves of course) Her letters are nearly all burned. Those I sent you *would have been* had they mentioned anything of obligations, as it was a sore subject with Dr. Houghton who did not like my help- ing Mrs. C. altho' nothing was ever said to me but in kindly warning of her ingratitude in those days, when I was his "Dearest Louise" his beloved wife his "Heart's Ever" his all". God help my elastic soul. It did not break or die, and I am thankful that I am emancipated from the love of this man, altho' he *is* the father of my children. His portrait hangs upon the wall before me beside mine of tender briliant beauty— His is cold and handsome. Nothing could induce the little girls to put a green sprig over it at Christmas. The only picture in the room without a touch of the time of rejoicing. Dora put up the motto "God with us" over the door near it, but it (the portrait) was passed by. I ventured to say "You have forgotten your father"—"*We remember him in our cold hands, our weary feet*, our daily *sufferings* and *deprivations*," Dora answered me thus, and I said no more—I am certain about the story of his illness abroad (Mr. Poe's) to change the subject and know that it is true, and it is probably the year he is said to have been in London which you refer to in your Memoir altho' I supposed it was after he left West Point, but as he published his poems and Hans Pfauall about that time in Baltimore. I am not certain *when* this occurred but know it is true. You speak of a writer who was intimate at Fordham page lxiv and lxv—*Who was this person*? I have told you the truth about the subscription and I think it was Mrs. Nichols that sent me to Mrs. Poe—who is this person "this writer" you speak of it as a man not a woman, and you certainly describe my work in part in this connection. I only wish to understand it, and do not wish notoriety. Still I think you see my meaning you ought to. Remember that you say in this Memoir that Mr. Poe's engagement to Mrs. Whitman *began* and *ended* in /48 and don't forget this again! And don't spoil the beautiful Valentine by dating it. I know Mrs. Clemm purposely kept me back to Mrs. Whitman for fear that Edgar's friendship (so foolishly fond) in always calling a married woman "Louise" as you know, and "Dear Louise" and some times "Dearest Louise" might *seem* to Mrs. Whitman to be a sort of ungovernable fickleness, unreliable and capable of being misunderstood,—my name being Shew, and myself being a childish undeveloped loving woman. No one that knew me well liked to call me Mrs. Shew. It seemed so inappropriate. And it was not noticed as it would be now. Still it was his way and everybody said what pretty letters he writes, and often ladies said "Is he not insane? Are you not afraid of him? I always answered he is as gentle as a child, and as tender as the most tender mother. I must have left out some of the words in the letter, Mr. Poe's cat always left her cushion to rub my hands and I had always to speak to the cat before it would retire to its place of rest again—He called her "Caterina". She seemed possessed and I was nervous and almost afraid of her, this wonderful cat. Mr. Poe would get up in the night to let her in, or out of the house or room, and the cat would not eat when he was away. The cat died while Mrs. Clemm was in an unsettled state, breaking up housekeeping. She found it dead when she returned for her last load of boxes. I was glad when I heard this cat was dead! As all she seemed to love was dead also. I did not copy the letters expecting you to use them. Dora thinks the *furniture letter* very patronizing and disagreeably so, *but I did not*, knowing the man who wrote it as I did. I think Graham's* letter in your Memoir so true and good and very much as I should write, if I was in his place. I am still in suspense about my affairs. You will not forget to acknowledge my letter, sent in March enclosing Mrs. Clemm's and Virginia's.

[. . .] I can not be certain as to dates, but after looking over the papers from my journal I see that he [Poe] returned to Richmond with two dollars in his portmanteau "a trunk of Books and manuscripts"—and "valise of clothes," having carried his mother's miniature thro' all in his "vest bosom"— I hardly think him mature enough at that time in 1827, to have done what he described to me so solemnly. I have seen the scar of the wound in the left shoulder, when helping Mrs. Clemm change his dress or clothes while ill. She said only Virginia knew about it. She did not. I asked him if he had been hurt—,in the region of the heart and he told me yes, and the rest as I wrote you. His head was also hurt but it is dark and I am asleep.

M.L.H.

I do not believe Mr. Poe's father deserted his wife, except for employment while she was ill, and that not for long.—Mr. Poe's (Edgar's) animosity towards some of his relatives was from their disrespect, (in one or two cases) of his mother, and her profession—Our next door neighbor, an old gentleman who lived 60 years in Washington, and is now 92 years of age, says that George Poe, Edgar's uncle, was very proud of his poet nephew, and often spoke of him, and his beauty & genius—

George Poe lived in Georgetown and had some lovely daughters. He does not remember any sons. Mr. Drake was Director in a Bank, with Mr. Poe, says he was a gentleman of wealth and culture, and a very good man, very much beloved by the old residents of Washington. Mr. Drake was a mechanic in his youth, but married a lovely southern lady, just after the *War of 1812* and built the new capitol or Presidents house, and from his great courage as a soldier, and goodness and skill in times of peace, took a high place as a citizen of Washington—

He lives now in retirement with his two maiden daughters, they having bought a place here during the Civil War, which disturbed many homes as you know at the South—Mr. Drake is too old to remember particulars, except something that happened long ago.—He says the Baltimore family seldom came to Washington, but he has seen Edgar's Father, and Aunt Maria and remembers their stately appearance at Church, with George, who was also tall and stately in personal appearance,—I think Edgar was very like his Mother *in his face*, and only had the tall stately statue of his father's people and he told me himself privately that he owed to his Mother "every good gift of his intellect, & his heart"—This alone ought to convince *you*, of the reason his kindred did not love him, another circumstance I remember, "that he burned the sweetest poem he ever wrote, *or conceived*" to please Mrs. Clemm and conciliate his *father's family*—That it was the regret of his life, that he had not vindicated his mother to the world, as pure, as angelic and altogether lovely, as any woman could be on earth." If you do not find *these Poes*, ready to give you better testimony than mine *that this is not so*, you must believe it as I say, for I promised his dying wife, I would listen to *his lamentation* patiently—and advise and sympathize with him to the best of my power—Mrs. Clemm reproved me for indulging *him in his fancies*, about his mother, and his *disappointments* and I had often to tell her of my promise to Virginia and my desire to do for him, while I could, an honest and true service—

So you have seen Mrs. Lewis—where is she living? Perhaps she thought me dead also! Alas! I was nearly swallowed up by the worlds falsehood—but God is good, and I live still

I have stated in this letter *somewhere* that I did not copy my last letters from Edgar expecting you to copy them, and was not as particular as I should have been, still you can use them as you see fit, they are *genuine*, only I may have left out some expression which was so very complimentary to myself I gave them as specimens, only for you to judge, of their availability to your purposes. Mrs. Nichols has written me twice since I asked you about her. She has had the operation for catract as I feared   What a pity she should not know enough to use vegetable alteratives as well as vegetable food!

> Your friend
> M.L.H.

I am glad Mr. Hopkins did not write the article on the Eureka but *I fear* Mr. Poe *thought* he did, as the description of "the turn down shirt collar" was so like the artistic habit of dress of Mr. Hopkins when he was a theological student. Dont—*I beg of you*, ever mention in print that I, or any one, attributed this to Dr. Hopkins for it would only injure Mr. Poe among literary men, and hurt Dr. Hopkins feelings. If Mr. Poe wrote this intending it as Dr. Hopkins, he did a spiteful unmanly act, and I grieve to see it in the Memoir for Mr. Hopkins when a student worked for Mr. Poe, and when he was ill and in trouble succored him—I hope Dr. H. will never read the article referred to—and I am sorry I mentioned it to you even.

P.S. I have copies of these letters, still I should prefer you to have had Mrs. Clemm's letter as it would so fix in your mind the situation, and so certainly silence any Lewis woman, who might annoy you, if any thing happened to me. Where is this Mrs. Lewis, whose name *was* Sarah Anna Lewis when I knew her, in the far away time? Poor creature so she is old and ugly, we all fade, but if the heart is true, and the *conscience clear* we need not become hideous. My children exult in my whitening hair, and I know I am but a wreck, but my *spirit* will not give up to be crushed! And my courage rises as my difficulties increase.

> Yours truly
> M. L. Houghton

By "the little picture" Mrs. Houghton almost certainly means the miniature of Poe's mother which she had sent to Ingram. Ingram had sent her, as a gift, a reproduction from one of the many daguerreotypes of Poe that he was accumulating. Mrs. Houghton's positive reply in this letter that he owed her no money for the many Poe letters, manuscripts, and the miniature that she had sent to him was to be of great help to Ingram after Mrs. Houghton died in 1877, and her family refused to believe that she had given such valuable Poe items to a "stranger in a foreign land."

Poe's third volume of poems was published in Baltimore in 1831, but his "Hans Pfaall" was not published until June, 1835, in the *Southern Literary Messenger*.

The writer who was "intimate" at Fordham, mentioned on pages 64–65 of Ingram's Memoir of Poe, was Mary Sargeant Gove Nichols. Mrs. Houghton's indignation was pronounced when Ingram credited other persons with the services she had herself rendered the Poes. At this point, Mrs. Houghton opened a correspondence with Sarah Helen Whitman in Providence, whom she never met, and protested to her. Mrs. Whitman was corresponding regularly with Ingram and she warned him of the danger of becoming entangled in a "coil" with the various ladies who had helped the Poes and who were now intensely jealous of their prerogatives.

The furniture letter was Poe's letter of May, 1847, to Mrs. Shew, complimenting her on the appearance and furnishings of her music room and library; in it he says he wonders how "a little country maiden like you had developed so classic a taste & atmosphere." (See Ostrom, II, 350–51, for complete text.) "Graham's letter" was the letter from George R. Graham to N. P. Willis, published in *Graham's Magazine*, March, 1850; it was a laudatory and understanding treatise on Poe's genius and personal character.

Two of the letters Mrs. Houghton received from J. H. Hopkins and forwarded to Ingram are reproduced in part below. They are Items 206 and 207 in the Ingram Poe Collection, and this is a first printing for both.

> Plattsburgh [N.Y.]
> March 10: 1875

My dear Mrs. Houghton,

    I remember that Dunn English was a scoundrel, but could not help you to answer any other of the points raised by Mr. Ingram. I have written to the Rev. Dr. Henry, one of the Editors of the New York Review & the sole survivor of them, to ask about Poe's connection therewith: which, I *suspect*, is groundless. I have not recd. his answer. I return Mr. Ingram's letter. . . .

> Yr. obdt. ser.
> J. H. Hopkins

> Stamford [Conn.]
> 13 Mar. 1875

Rev. & dear Sir:

    Edgar A. Poe was never "engaged as a writer on the New York Review."

    He contributed of his own accord *one* article. It was a review of

Stephen's Incidents of Travel in Egypt, Arabia Petrea & the Holy Land. It was published in the 2d. number of the *N.Y. Review* Oct. 1837.

Resptfly Yours,
C. S. Henry

The Rev. Dr. Hopkins

Mrs. Houghton's account is the only known record of Poe's having been injured "in the region of the heart" and having a scar on his left shoulder. It is indeed strange that Mrs. Clemm did not know how he came by the scar. George Poe, Jr., was a banker in Pittsburgh and Mobile; at one time he lent $100 to Edgar and Mrs. Clemm to start a boarding house in Richmond, but nothing came of their plan. Mrs. Lewis disliked her baptismal name of "Sarah Anna," so she dropped it in favor of "Estelle Anna" for a while, and abandoning that, settled finally on "Stella," which she used as a pen name and a given name and insisted that her friends do the same.

Mrs. Houghton's jealousy and distaste for Mrs. Lewis are amusing, at this distance. One can sense her satisfaction on learning from Ingram that Mrs. Lewis is now "old and ugly." Ingram disliked Mrs. Lewis too, but he saw to it that he stayed in her good graces, which was not an easy task.

Letter 40. **Marie Louise Shew Houghton, Whitestone, to John Ingram, London.** First printing. [Item 232]

Monday, June 7 [1875]

I wrote you a few days ago in which I mentioned Henry's admiration of Mr. Poe's poem "the Beloved" and copied his boyish verses, or one of them, *giving only one line of Poe's* "God shield the soul," or "God guide the soul" being in every verse of the *nine* Henry says is the number as cut down and prepared for publication, by Mr. Poe. Henry cannot write poetry, *never could* but Frank, my second son, is quite a rhymer. But Henry *appreciated poetry* far more and *Poets always*, and kept his old nurse Fanny busy, before he could read, clipping every verse he found and reading and saving it, for him. There is a closet in this house full of little rolls of poetry of "Master Henry clippings" which we light the fires with now. I have heard from my son. He will not come home yet. But has *given me an idea where to find the Poem!!!* among some boxes at Pierrepont Manor, (where Lida was buried and where little Mary was born) He says you shall have the Poem for your Memoir and a letter of Mr. Poes refering to it—which I had forgotten. He thinks it is safe in a desk Lida gave him—My three years of weeping and almost despair, after I went to live at the Manor, is all a dream to me and I have no recollection of his taking charge of some of my papers Sometime during the coming summer or *this* summer rather I will go to the Manor (where I have my china—some pictures—and furniture stored) and look up this paper for you. I am glad you like my son. The dear boy has had a sad experience. He longs to visit his old home here, he says, before it passes out of my hands—His old room (his sleeping room) upon the third story, had a raven nailed up over the door, which he put up, *fifteen years ago. No intruder* has ever offered to pull it down, as yet but it is a sad sight to me, now. It looks ominous of his fate. Misfortune and depressing care had ever followed my beautiful boy—and now he seems struggling in what he calls "hard luck" harder than ever it seems to me. He tries to cheer me "that it wont always be so," but I have a presentament that his fate will never change altho I dont tell him so—and I know he is more like me than any of the rest and *my faults* as well as other qualities he inherits "carries his heart upon his sleeve." &c. I have a great pity for him on this account   The *Manor* is three hundred miles away but it will be all in good time as you are *not* to publish it, except in the Memoir.

Given her usual inaccuracy as to dates, one can interpret Mrs. Houghton's "a few days ago" to mean her letter of May 16, in which she mentioned the poem, "The Beloved Physician" which Poe wrote for her and for which she paid him $25 for the manuscript. Unquestionably, many of the letters Mrs. Houghton wrote to Ingram have not survived. All of the letters herein reproduced can be dated accurately as having been written in 1875; Mrs. Houghton lived until September 3, 1877, and none of these letters reflects unhappiness or a "falling out" with Ingram, as was so often the case with his American correspondents. It is possible that her letters were removed from Ingram's files when he was defending his rights of ownership of the Poe items Mrs. Houghton had sent to him. The manuscript poem "The Beloved Physician" and Poe's letter referring to it have never been found. By "the Memoir"

Mrs. Houghton refers to Ingram's two-volume biography of Poe on which he was working in 1875 and which was brought out in 1880, by John Hogg, in London.

Here was a puzzle for Ingram. These letters from Mrs. Houghton were exciting, sincere, vivacious, and shot through with inaccuracies, myths, half-remembered facts mixed with hearsay and caution. What to do with them?

Ingram picked and chose throughout the lot, printing such incidents as made Poe appear fine and tender, and in so doing Ingram muddied the waters of Poe biography perhaps forever. There is just enough truth in some of these stories to make them acceptable, but not enough to allow proof to back them up.

The letters and editorial notes above show that Ingram was indebted to Mrs. Houghton for a number of Poe's autograph letters, letters from Mrs. Clemm, books written by Poe, the one remaining miniature of Poe's mother, and several manuscript copies of Poe's poems—as well as the only account that exists of Poe's lost poem, "The Beloved Physician."

Mrs. Houghton added a great deal that was true to Poe biography in her correspondence with Ingram, and, unfortunately, much that is imaginary or, at best, highly doubtful.

VI
Annie Richmond's Trust Is Betrayed

EDGAR POE went to Lowell, Massachusetts, in July, 1848, to deliver a public lecture on "The Poets and Poetry of America"; while there he met Mrs. Nancy Locke Heywood Richmond, with whom he was to fall in love, and to whom he addressed numerous letters and at least one great poem. He had been invited to lecture in Lowell through the kind office of Mrs. Frances Sargent Osgood, wife of the well-known portrait painter S. S. Osgood; his hostess in Lowell was to be Mrs. Osgood's cousin by marriage, Mrs. John G. Locke* (née Jane Ermina Starkweather). Poe had corresponded with Mrs. Locke, who was one of the more energetic female poets of the day and who was very proud to be entertaining the rather notorious Mr. Poe in her house, which she called "Wamesit Cottage." But when Poe's successful lecture was over, and he had been introduced to Mrs. Richmond, he went with the Richmonds to their Ames Street home and remained there for the rest of his visit in Lowell. This transfer of his person from the Lockes' home to the Richmonds' caused a rupture in the relations among all concerned.

Poe made at least three more visits to the Richmonds in Lowell and he celebrated Mrs. Richmond as "Annie" under a thin guise of fiction in his "Landor's Cottage," thereafter calling her by that name. Her husband, Charles B. Richmond, was a well-to-do paper manufacturer in Lowell and his tolerance of Poe's fervent addresses to his wife was threatened only by Mrs. Locke's machinations against Poe. On one occasion, Annie Richmond went to Fordham for the purpose of meeting Mrs. Clemm. After Poe's death, she cared for Mrs. Clemm in her Lowell home on numerous visits that lasted for months at the time.

Poe was thirty-nine years old when he met Annie, and she was twenty-eight. She was a handsome, pleasant, warm-hearted young matron enjoying social and economic distinction in Lowell, and busying herself with her family, numerous friends, activities in the Unitarian church, and local charities. She was not literary, as almost all the women around Poe aspired to be, and she brought to him a personality that he found refreshing and restful. His letters show that he quickly grew to love her, as a man loves the woman he wants to marry. As fascinated as she was by Poe's personality and genius, Mrs. Richmond had no intention of divorcing her husband and marrying Poe. That Poe knew this makes all the more pathetic his despairing wail to Mrs. Clemm in a letter written from Richmond shortly before he died, "Do not tell me anything about Annie—I cannot bear to hear it now—unless you can tell me that Mr. R. is dead." [1]

When Ingram opened his correspondence with Annie Richmond in 1876, he had long been in correspondence with several Americans who had known Poe intimately. Among these, perhaps the most helpful had been Sarah Helen Whitman and Marie Louise Shew Houghton. These ladies had given him names and addresses of other persons who had known Poe, and, as Ingram's correspondence multiplied, his pattern of behavior became set: when he had elicited all he thought the correspondent could or would give to him about Poe, or if the correspondent began to press or to bore him, he broke off the relationship.

Having learned from Mrs. Whitman that Annie Richmond was still alive, Ingram wrote his first letter to her in June, 1876. Mrs. Richmond was a fifty-six-year-old widow, her husband having died in the early 1870s, and she was living in Lowell with her only daughter, who was named Carrie. For twenty-seven years she had tearfully cherished Poe's memory and the letters he had written to her, remaining for the most part aloof from the controversies that had swirled around Poe's name, especially after his death. Her letter in reply to Ingram's first appeal is characteristic of her nature and disposition, mirroring as it does her warm-hearted, impulsive eagerness to help dispel the clouds over Poe's name. She deals in hyperbole always, it seems, but her erratic sentences, emotional language, and occasional misspellings do not obscure her genuine devotion to Poe's memory or her own fine character. Her confidences deserved better treatment, at the hands of a better man than was John Ingram.

---

1. August 28–29 (?). See John Ward Ostrom (ed.), *The Letters of Edgar Allan Poe* (2 vols.; Cambridge: Harvard University Press, 1948).

Letter 41. **Annie Richmond, Lowell, Massachusetts, to John Ingram, London.** First printing. [Item 297]

Aug. 15 [18]76

Dear Sir,

Ever since the receipt of your kind letter (late in June) I have been endeavoring to obtain possession of a manuscript sketch of Mr. Poe, which I loaned to a gentleman, who seemed anxious to do something toward redeeming his name from the odium Griswold had cast upon it—

It was returned to me yesterday, with a note saying it had not been used, but had been "copied for further reference." Under these circumstances, you would not I presume care for it—But there is one thing I *could* do for you, & were I to see you, I think I *would*—that is, to place my correspondence at your disposal—

I have said again & again, I could *never* do it, but for *his dear sake*, I *am* willing to make the sacrifice—I know that full justice *cannot* be done him by anyone, who has not seen the beauty & purity of his better nature, as revealed in these letters—

It may seem very strange to you, but I firmly believe they are without a parallel in the annals of love, & it seems like *sacrilege* to allow any human eye to look upon them, yet, for the sake of refuting the calumnies which have been heaped upon him through envy & jealousy, *I can bear it*—the letters themselves can bear the scrutiny of Heaven—! It is their *purity* that I shrink from revealing, to those who could not comprehend it. Is it not *possible* for me to see you? Are you not coming to our Centennial Exhibition? I could not let my treasures go out of my keeping for one moment, but if you will come where they are they shall be at your service. I have *not* seen your edition of Mr. Poe's works, but should be very glad to do so. I can never express the gratitude I feel, toward those who understand & appreciate him. Hoping to hear from you again, I am yours truly,

"Annie" L. Richmond

Lowell. Mass. Aug. 15th/79

Mr. J. H. Ingram,

Dear Sir,

Ever since the receipt of your kind letter (late in June) I have been endeavouring to obtain possession of a manuscript sketch of Mr Poe, which I loaned a gentleman, who seemed anxious to something toward redeeming his name from the odium Griswold had cast upon it—

It was returned to me yesterday, with a note saying, it had not been used, but had been "copied for future reference — under these circumstances, you would not I presume care for it — But there is one thing I could do for you, & were I to see you, I think I would — that is, to place my correspondence at your disposal — I have said again & again I could never do it, but for his dear sake, I am willing to make the sacrifice — I know that

Nancy Locke Heywood (Annie) Richmond to John Ingram
Letter 41

Mrs. Richmond's offer to let Ingram *see* her autograph letters from Poe was unprecedented; and it certainly attests to his ability to inspire great confidence and gain great favors through his impassioned letters. Mrs. Richmond did not indeed ever let her treasures out of her keeping, but she did make copies of them for Ingram, the only copies she ever made of her letters from Poe for anyone. The autograph letters themselves, for the greater part, have disappeared; almost certainly they were burned by Mrs. Richmond after Ingram printed a number of them. These copies then, that she so trustfully made for John Ingram, are the only sources we have for the texts of Poe's letters to her.

The "manuscript sketch of Mr. Poe" was written by Sarah H. Heywood, Annie Richmond's younger sister, and was called "Recollections of E. A. Poe." The gentleman to whom Mrs. Richmond had lent it was William F. Gill of Boston, and Gill printed it in his 1877 *Life of Poe*.

Letter 42.   **Annie Richmond, Lowell, to John Ingram, London.**
First printing. [Item 298]

Aug. 20th [18]/76

Mr. Ingram,
Dear Sir,

Since mailing my letter to you a few days since, I have re-read my sister's "recollections of Mr. Poe," & I cannot forbear sending them to you, for their uniqueness—Coming from a school girl then in her teens, I am sure they will *interest* you to say the least—In this connection I am tempted to copy for you also a note which she received from him, & which she cherishes among her most sacred treasures—It will give you some idea of the nature of my correspondence with him, which was never kept secret, from any member of my immediate family—

Yours very truly,
A. L. Richmond

Ingram printed Sarah Heywood's "Recollections of E. A. Poe" in his 1880 *Life*, referring to the article as "fresh and charming," although it had in fact been printed before in Gill's 1877 *Life of Poe*.[2]

2. William Fearing Gill, *Life of Edgar Allan Poe* (Boston: William F. Gill & Co., 1877), 209–213.

Mrs. Richmond did enclose a copy of Poe's letter of November 23, 1848, to Sarah Heywood; Ingram printed a portion of it in his article in *Appleton's Journal*, May, 1878, and in his *Life*, II, 195–96. (For complete text, see Ostrom, II, 405–406.)

At the end of her first letter to Ingram Annie Richmond had signed her name in quotes; in this letter, she uses her initials, "A.L." As a matter of fact, after her husband died in 1873, she had her name legally changed from "Nancy" to "Annie," because Poe had called her by that name and had so addressed her in his beautiful poem "To Annie."

Letter 43. **Annie Richmond, Lowell, to John Ingram, London.**
First printing. [Item 300]

Sept. 27th [18]76

Dear Mr. Ingram,

I herewith enclose a *small portion* of my long cherished & most precious treasures, trusting to your honor, that neither the *living* or the *dead* shall ever suffer in consequence, though I cannot help *feeling*, that it is a breach of trust for me to do it. But the deep gratitude I feel toward you for the noble work you have undertaken, (added to my own intense desire that it shall be *faithfully* done) has overcome my scruples, & I place these letters at your disposal, with unlimited confidence in your fidelity & discretion—I have some others that I *cannot* trust to cross the ocean, but I will send you copies of portions of them, when I hear that these have reached you in safety—I have a picture of Mr. Poe for which he sat when here, this is as good as could be taken in those days—I will have it copied at once & send it with Mrs. Clemm's—I do not know what became of the things she left, but she had in her possession letters, etc.—belonging to me, that I would be very glad to obtain were it possible to do so. I regret exceedingly that I could not have seen her during her last illness, but my husband was at that time an invalid, unable to go with me, & I did not like to leave him—Once since her death, I have passed through Baltimore, but was with a party & could not stop—If I knew it would be of any avail, I would go there, & try to get what information I could, but fear I should get very little satisfaction—Please accept my sincere thanks for your kind offer to send the Memoir & the picture—I am exceedingly desirous of seeing both & will write you as soon as they reach me. In one of the letters I enclose, Mr. Poe speaks of "The Bells" as coming out in a Review—but I think they were published in the "Flag of our Union"—I have the manuscript copy of that poem—the one "For Annie" & "A Dream within a dream", all of which he gave me, or sent me in his letters—

> Very truly yours,
> A. L. Richmond

Ingram reproduced in facsimile the manuscript of "A Dream Within a Dream," the last fifteen lines of Poe's poem "For Annie" in an article written especially for the Poe centenary number of the London *Bookman*, January, 1909, page 190. "For Annie" had appeared first in the *Flag of Our Union*, April 28, 1849, and Poe had sent the manuscript to Mrs. Richmond on March 23, 1849, saying the lines were "much the *best* I have ever written."

Poe's letter in which he spoke of "The Bells" coming out "in a Review" was written to Mrs. Richmond on February 8, 1849. (See Ostrom, II, 425, for complete text.) "The Bells" actually was first published in *Sartain's Union Magazine*, November, 1849, after Poe's death.

Beginning with this letter, Mrs. Richmond started enclosing copies of her letters from Poe and she continued until she had sent Ingram copies of them all. He betrayed her trust by printing them, although he did withhold her name and he made some elisions and modifications within the letters.

Ingram used the photograph of Mrs. Clemm that Mrs. Richmond sent to him, and it was immediately copied and recopied until it has become familiar to us all. Mrs. Clemm had lived with the Richmonds for many months at the time after Poe's death. While there she talked incessantly of Poe and Virginia, and enjoyed handling, reading, and crying over Poe's letters to Mrs. Richmond. On one occasion, when she left the Richmonds' home, some of Poe's letters were missing, but Mrs. Clemm insisted that she had returned them all to Annie. When Mrs. Clemm died in 1871 in the Episcopal Church Home in Baltimore, her few possessions went to her second cousin, Judge Neilson Poe* of Baltimore.

Letter 44.   Annie Richmond, Lowell, to John Ingram, London.
First printing. [Item 301]

Oct. 3d. [18]76

Dear Mr. Ingram,

I mailed you yesterday a valuable package (at least *I* considered it so) containing letters from Mrs. Clemm & from her gifted son, together with the photographs of them both —hers is very good, but Mr. Poe's does not do him justice— indeed, I have never seen a picture that did—his face was thin, & in the one I send, he looks very stout, & his features heavy, which makes it seem almost like a caricature —yet, he certainly sat for it, & the artist (if he deserves the title) is still living here, who had the privilege of taking it.

I shall feel not a little anxiety until I hear they are safe in your possession—the pictures you can keep as I have others— the letters of course you will not care for, after you have made extracts from them.

One question in your last letter I did not answer I think. Mr. Poe *did* tell me much of his early history at different times, but I can recall nothing that would have any particular interest, except to a personal friend—from his mother I learned much of the family, yet I could not be certain as to dates, names, etc—I have often regretted since, that I did not make notes of our conversations at the time—I was deeply interested in all that concerned him in any way, & she never cared to talk of anything else when she found an attentive listener.

The memoir of which you spoke, has not reached me as yet—I am looking for its arrival with pleasure saddened by the thought, that it comes *too late* for his dear "Muddie" to enjoy it with me—But I am very *very* thankful to know, that justice will be done his dear memory *at last*. When I hear that the letters have arrived, I will send more or copies at the least—

Very truly & gratefully
yours,
Annie L. Richmond

The photograph of Poe included in the package mailed on October 2 was taken from a daguerreotype that was later stolen from Mrs. Richmond's home.

Ingram used reproductions from these photographs in his 1880 *Life*. One can only speculate as to Ingram's reaction to Annie's inability to remember anything of Poe's early history, except that which would be of interest to a "personal friend."

Letter 45.   **Annie Richmond, Lowell, to John Ingram, London.**
First printing. [Item 304]

Nov. 21st 1876

My dear Mr. Ingram,
     Please accept my most sincere & grateful thanks for your kind letter of the 16th ult. together with a vol. of Mr. Poe's works containing your Memoir. They did not reach me until ten days ago, or I should have sooner acknowledged their arrival—There was some delay at the office, then my absence from home prevented my receiving them, as soon as I otherwise should—I am sorry to say I have not yet had time to read the Memoir *thoroughly*, I have been so occupied with an "orphan's Fair" for the past ten days—but I am satisfied that it contains a complete refutation of Griswold's vile calumnies which is a great relief to my mind—Nothing but my intense desire, to have full justice done to the memory of my dear friend, *could* have tempted me to put my correspondence with him into the hands of any human being—indeed, it seems even now almost a sacrilege, after keeping it inviolate all these long years to allow strange eyes to read it!—but I feel sure you are *his* friend at least, & for his dear sake, if for no other reason, you will never suffer it to be made public, or in any possible way used to his disadvantage. Since writing you last, I have been looking over my remaining letters intending to copy some of them for you, but they are so personal & contain so few allusions to matters that would interest you, that I hardly think it worth while to do it. If I ever have the opportunity of placing the originals in your hands, I will most certainly do so with pleasure, for I feel that you will understand & appreciate them. The Photo I sent you,

was copied from a daguerreotype Mr. Poe had taken the last time he visited me & the artist who took it is still living in this city. It is a poor picture, I know, but it was the best I could do at the time—the art was then in its infancy, & this man was the only one *here*, who took them so I had no other alternative. Mr. Poe promised to send me a better one, as soon as he arrived in New York—but it never came. I think the engraving in the Vol. you sent is perhaps quite as good as any that can be had, but it is not perfect. I am surprised to hear that my copy of "The Bells" is *not* the original, as he copied the entire poem while at my house, & I *supposed* left me the *first one*—however, it does not matter, the fact that it is in the author's handwriting is sufficient. I shall never cease to regret that I did not see Mrs. Clemm during her last illness, but it was almost an impossibility for me to go to Baltimore at that time—yet, if it were to do again, I should go, at the risk of my life. One very valuable letter was in her possession that belonged to me—she borrowed it, but for what purpose I never knew, nor do I know what became of it—many other things she promised me, which of course now I shall never get, but they would be invaluable. Please pardon this hastily written & unsatisfactory note—after I have read the Memoir I will write again. I am *very* weary with my last week's hard work.

Very truly yours,
Annie L. Richmond

Fortunately, Mrs. Richmond had had copies made of the daguerreotype taken of Poe on his last visit to Lowell, but she had cherished the original of it for many years and the theft of it from her home was greatly distressing.

It is easy to understand from her letters that Mrs. Richmond was indeed healthily active in civic, charitable, and church organizations in Lowell.

Her manuscript copy of "The Bells" was really the third draft of the poem. In the summer of 1848, Poe had written seventeen lines of the poem in Mrs. Shew's home, according to her story above, and with her help. He expanded this first version in his second draft, written about February 6, 1849; and he wrote the third and final draft at Mrs. Richmond's home in May, 1849. He even revised this last version, and the poem had 112 lines when it was published in *Sartain's Union Magazine*, in November, 1849.

Letter 46. **Sarah H. Heywood, Lowell, to John Ingram, London.** First printing. [Item 306]

Dec. 24, 1876

Mr. J. H. Ingram,

Dear Sir,

At the request of my sister, Mrs. Richmond, whose Christmas duties are numerous and imperative, I write the few words which will introduce to you Mr. Franklin Brown of London, a friend of the family, who leaves us today for his home.

He will hand you a package containing an early edition of Mr. Poe's works. It was found in the trunk which was forwarded to Mrs. Clemm from Baltimore, soon after his death.[3]

Mrs. Richmond will write very soon in reply to yours of the 5th inst. but she wishes me just to say that she will have the "Annie" Ms. photographed for you at an early day. She thinks you must have rec'd her somewhat tardy acknowledgement of the Memoir very soon after you wrote.

With great respect,
Yours very truly,
Sarah H. Heywood

Franklin E. Brown delivered by hand to Ingram in London the two-volume edition of Poe's *Tales of the Grotesque and Arabesque* (Philadelphia: Lea & Blanchard, 1840) that had been found in Poe's trunk when it reached Lowell, sent by Neilson Poe to Mrs. Clemm. Both Rosalie and Mrs. Clemm had engaged lawyers, free of charge, of course, to fight each other for Edgar's effects and estate; apparently Sylvanus D. Lewis* presented a stronger claim for Mrs. Clemm than John Reuben Thompson did for Rosalie.

---

3. This letter settles once and for all the long-standing and ridiculously bitter controversy of what finally became of Poe's trunk: Neilson Poe sent it to Mrs. Clemm in Lowell, Massachusetts. Since Mrs. Clemm detested Rosalie Poe so heartily and never saw her or corresponded with her after Edgar's death, it is most unlikely she would have allowed Rosalie to have the trunk or anything else that had belonged to her brother. The theory that Rosalie later owned the trunk and sold it or gave it to other persons is unfounded.

Letter 47. **Annie Richmond, Lowell, to John Ingram, London.**
Written on the back of a printed broadside, the prospectus for
Poe's "Stylus," dated New York City, April, 1848. First
printing. [Item 308]

Jan. 1, 1877

Before this reaches you, I hope you will have had a call
from Mr. Brown,* & have received the volumes I sent you by
him. He will tell you something of my cares just now—I have
three law-suits on hand, (which involves *time* & money more
or less,) besides, being connected with some charitable insti-
tutions here, that occupy & interest me more deeply than
ever, at the present time—I am *so thankful* for the bit of
Romance that found its way into the "web & woof" of my life
in the days of "auld lang syne," for it is so *intensely practical*
now-a-days, that I fear I should hardly be grateful for the
present, were it not for the sweet *sweet* memories that
brighten all the shadows, & make me feel that come what
may, I have had more than an average share of blessings, &
therewith *I will be content.* Pardon these scribblings & believe
me ever

Yours truly,
A.L.R.

Charles B. Richmond had been an energetic and successful businessman in
Lowell; after his death, Mrs. Richmond was frequently much distressed by
affairs involving lawsuits plus the financial complications arising from a severe
recession.

The "Romance" to which she refers was, of course, her meeting and
associating with Edgar Poe, his declared love for her, and the letters and poems
she had as proof.

Letter 48. **Annie Richmond, Lowell, to John Ingram, London.**
Notes appended to a copy of Poe's letter to Sarah Helen
Whitman, Providence, Rhode Island, dated January 21 (?) 25
(?), 1849. First printing. [Item 310]

Jany. 14th [18]77

My dear friend,

Yours of the 28th ult. together with the manuscript & Photo. reached me last evening.—I cannot reply to your letter in full for several days, but am anxious you should know it has arrived in safety—I enclose with this, a copy of another letter, to me, which I prepared to send you some time since, then decided *not* to do so. But your assurance that no harm shall come of it to *anyone*, re-assures me that I may trust you with *everything*!—The photograph copy of the Poem "For Annie" is perfect, *except* that where the original has turned *yellow* with age, the copy gives it *black*, making a *very* uninviting looking manuscript! I conclude however that you can remedy this—"Mr. Poe as a Cryptographer" was written by Rev. W. H. Cudworth* of East Boston who was then living in Lowell—I have written him for letters etc. but he has nothing left he says—I will write you at length in a few days—

Yours truly,
A.L.R.

I send you this copy of a letter written by Mr. Poe to Mrs. Whitman, my dear Mr. Ingram, in order to explain his letter to me, written about the same time, which would otherwise appear somewhat ambiguous, I fear—I also enclose a note from Charles Dicken's [*sic*] agent, (which accompanied a check for the amount named), which Mrs. Clemm received & acknowledged at the time.

[Mrs. Richmond copied here for Ingram her letter from Poe of January 21 (?), 1849, in which he had enclosed a letter addressed to Sarah Helen Whitman dated about the same time. She was instructed to read it, seal it with wax, and mail it from Boston. Poe's engagement to Mrs. Whitman had been broken in late December, 1848, and rumors were rife about his conduct in the matter. Quite disturbed about it all, Mrs. Richmond wrote to Poe, and he then quoted the following from her letter in his letter to Mrs. Whitman: "I will not repeat *all* her vile and slanderous words—you have doubtless heard them—but one thing she says that I cannot *deny* though I do not believe it—viz—that you had been *published to her once*, and that on the Sat. preceding the Sabbath on which you were to have been published for the *second time* she went herself to the Rev.

Mr. Crocker's and *after stating her reasons for so doing*, requested him to stop all further proceedings." By sending his letter through Annie, Poe hoped to preserve his good standing with her by showing her that he is asking Mrs. Whitman for a denial of the accusation that is referred to in this quoted passage. See Ostrom, II, 417–22, for as complete texts as exist of both these letters.]

> The quotation in this letter of course was written by me—not on my own account but to satisfy my friends—Mr. Richmond's family were at that time living in Providence & were continually sending him the gossip in circulation there, about this unhappy affair—In answer to their inquiries as to what "Mr. Poe said about it," I replied, that Mrs. W's statement was a false one, but nothing would do—they must have something more definite—of course I had no other alternative, but to tell him as briefly as I could, my reasons for troubling him, & ask some explanation—Mrs. W's reply exonerated him completely, yet I think they were inclined to discredit it & believe him still a very *unprincipled* man to say the least—A.L.R.

The "photograph copy" of the poem "For Annie" (the last 15 lines of "A Dream Within a Dream") had been made in Lowell for forwarding to Ingram.

The Rev. Warren H. Cudworth published his article, "Mr. Poe as a Cryptographer," in the Lowell *Journal*, April 19, 1850.

Occasionally Ingram sent proofs of his forthcoming articles on Poe to his correspondents and asked for their criticisms; this was merely an unsubtle way of flattering them, for he rarely paid any attention to their replies.

Letter 49. **Annie Richmond, Lowell, to John Ingram, London.**
First printing. [Item 312]

Jany. 31st [18]77

My dear kind friend,
    Your favor of the 13th Inst. together with the enclosure has just reached me, & I hasten to assure you of the safety of the manuscript, although not yet fully prepared to answer your last letters—For more than two weeks, I have been confined to the house with a severe cold or I should have

replied ere this to the questions in your letter of December 28th. I am quite certain that through a friend in Boston, I can obtain access to an old file of the "Flag of our Union", also may find the number of "Graham's" you desire—I will send you with this, *all* the letters I have from Mrs. Clemm, written previously to Mr. Poe's death—in one of them she speaks of Mr. Clark[e],* which is all I distinctly remember concerning him—of Mr. Graham * I know nothing—perhaps your friend Mr. Davidson* in N. York might be able to give some information on that point, as there must be those living there, who know of him—Mrs. Clemm mentions in one of her letters, sending "autographs" to Mr. Longfellow, which may or may not mean entire letters—two or three at least of *mine* are missing, & have been for many years—While Mrs. C. was with me she had access to all my letters, & was in the habit of looking them over (it was a privilege I could *not* deny her,) & after she went back to N. York, I missed some of them & asked her if they had not accidentally been carried away among her own—but she insisted upon it they had not been—& their disappearance has always been a mystery. She afterward *borrowed one*, which never came back, though she said she had mailed it to me—of Mr. Poe's early life, she used to talk, but I have no distinct remembrance of those conversations, except that I can readily substantiate what you have said. You have several times mentioned Mr. Gill*—I have seen him, but know very little of him except through the papers—I was introduced to him by a lady (well known among literary people here) who wished me to give him some facts about Mr. Poe, that he could incorporate into a lecture he was preparing, called "an evening with Poe & his critics"—of course I was interested to have some of the mistakes of the past corrected, & accordingly I gave him what information I thought necessary to make his lecture *correct* & attractive—the only *personal* matter he obtained was my sister's manuscript which he very soon returned—At the time he went to Baltimore to attend the Memorial services, he borrowed my manuscript of "The Bells," which he said he wished to have that he might read the poem with more effect! Since then I have heard (though not from him) that he was preparing a

Memoir that would come out this spring—he very likely has a photographic *copy* of my manuscript, taken while it was in his possession, but I certainly have the one *written by Mr. Poe*, which he gave me before it had appeared in print—Although I have so long & so ardently desired to see his name & honor vindicated, yet it was only by the urgent solicitations of the lady who introduced him to me, that I was induced to give aid to Mr. Gill, for I *wished* Mr. Poe's defense to come from his peers! How those who knew him *could* allow that *wicked* biography of Griswold's to go *unchallenged* has ever been & will ever be to me a profound & unfathomable mystery! I confess I was thankful to know there was *anybody* who could see his virtues & forget his faults—I think by this time *you* must understand something of what I have suffered, in all these long years, & can appreciate my gratitude, whenever I see written or hear uttered a single kindly word—I need hardly tell you, with what intense interest I look forward to your forthcoming Memoir, which I feel sure, will indeed be a "complete & thorough vindication," of that dear & tenderly cherished name, & I trust the confidence I have reposed in you gives assurance of my *sincerity* in making this statement —words can never express the gratitude I feel for what you have already done—I can hardly understand how anything *can* be more comprehensive or satisfactory—Many thanks for your kind offer to send me the remaining volumes—I shall be very glad to have the complete set of his works in this beautiful edition—As soon as I am able, shall go to Boston, & will do all in my power to procure for you the vol. dates, etc. of which you speak—the letters I enclose, you need not return—I regret now that I did not keep *all* her letters, for they would have been of use to you I am sure. In haste (for today's mail) & with grateful thanks,

> Yours very truly,
> A. L. Richmond

Ingram was suspicious of Mrs. Clemm's veracity, but he had to remember that she was after all the person who had been closest to Poe; he therefore generally quoted only portions of her letters directly or indirectly into whatever article of book about Poe he was working on when he received her letters or copies of them.

"Mr. Clark," mentioned by Mrs. Clemm, was Thomas Cottrell Clarke, owner and editor of the Philadelphia *Saturday Museum*, who had agreed in 1842 to furnish the money needed to start publishing Poe's long-dreamed-of magazine, *The Stylus*.

William Fearing Gill was certainly eager to redeem Poe's reputation from Griswold's slanders, but he was hampered by a diversity of interests and an impulsiveness that amounted to flightiness. He did, at his own request, recite some of Poe's poetry at the unveiling of the monument to Poe in Baltimore in November, 1875.

Letter 50. **Annie Richmond, Lowell, to John Ingram, London.**
First printing. [Item 314]

Feb. 5th, 1877

My dear Mr. Ingram,

A friend has just sent to me a bound vol. of "Graham" for /41 & 42, which has in it two chapters on "Autography", & an article on "secret writing" by Mr. Poe—would you like them? The Book belonged to a dear sister, & she does not like to part with it, but says I may cut out anything I wish & as neither of these articles are in his works, (or in the editions I have seen), I thought you might perhaps make some use of them—there is also, "A few words about Brainerd", that I do not remember having seen, besides a number of his stories, that *are* in his works—As yet, I have been unable to obtain the Nos. you mentioned, but think I shall find them in Boston. I take the liberty of sending this note to Mr. Brown,* as I have a letter ready to mail, thinking it may reach you in season for you to reply in your next—These chapters on "Autography" (having a fac-simile of each writer's hand who is mentioned) seem to me *very* interesting, & I am surprised that they have never been included, by any compiler of Mr. Poe's works—I wish it were possible for me to give you *all* the information you desire concerning him, but my memory of his conversations concerning his own history, is not sufficiently clear & comprehensive, to enable me to send you anything valuable—I often wish I had kept a diary, at that time, & had I realized *then* as I do *now* the *privileges* I enjoyed, I certainly should have done so—*wonder & admiration* so completely absorbed every other feeling, that I did not even comprehend the *rare* opportunity, with which I was blessed, or I should have better improved it—He seemed so *unlike* any other person, I had ever known, that I could not think of him in the same way—he was incomparable—not to be measured by any ordinary standard —& all the events of his life, which he narrated to me, had a flavor of *unreality* about them, just like his stories—who could repeat one of those! to do it *justice* I mean—but I did not intend writing you a letter—only to ask a question!—

Yours very truly,
A. L. Richmond

Mrs. Richmond's warmly reported impressions of Poe as a man are both sincerely human and unique.

Poe's "A Chapter on Autography" appeared in *Graham's* for November and December, 1841. "A Few Words on Secret Writing" appeared in the same magazine, in four installments: July, August, October, and December, 1841. "A Few Words About Brainerd" was in *Graham's* for January, 1842.

Letter 51. **Annie Richmond, Lowell, to John Ingram, London.**
First printing. [Item 318]

March 13, 1877

My dear Mr. Ingram,
    Your kind favor the the 24th ult. has just reached me—I am glad you do not stand upon ceremony, but write whenever you find it convenient & agreeable to do so. Your letters afford me much pleasure *always*, for there is no other person to whom I write, & rarely one to whom I speak, upon the theme which is the burden of our correspondence—they are therefore, the connecting link with the past—the *only one* which re-assures me that, "all we see or seem" *is not* "a dream within a dream." The *realities* of life are at present so

absorbing, so *very real*, that I sometimes wonder if I *have* ever known anything else, save what has come to me in dreams. I was sure the *romance* had all gone out of it, until a little sonnet came to me, as a New Year's greeting, which bore the sweet fragrance of "days that are no more." Then I felt *thankful* for the power we all possess to keep the *heart* perpetually & immortally young! But a truce to sentiment—*it is well for you*, my friend, (may I not call you so?) that I have so little leisure, or I should surely weary you by the frequency as well as the length of my epistles—Now I will try to answer a portion at least of your long neglected questions—I find that *all* the files of "The Flag of our Union," in which so many of Mr. Poe's articles were published, were destroyed in the late fire (/72 or 3 I forget which). Mr. Gleason, a former proprietor of the paper, told me he would willingly pay a fabulous sum to obtain even a portion of them—He spoke of Mr. Poe's contributions, & of having had some of his manuscript, which was also destroyed at the same time—It is barely possible, some person may have a copy on file, but scarcely probable—I have interested several friends in Boston, who will get them if they are to be found—As regard the Mag's I can only say now that I have heard where there is a collection of both the "Graham's" & "Gentleman's" & I am going down to look them over, some day this week—Should I find the Nos. you mention, will procure them & forward in the manner you suggest ("without the covers") unless it will answer your purpose to have merely Mr. Poe's articles detached & sent by themselves—I will wait until I hear from you again before sending any of them—I can as yet, get no trace of "Tamerlane etc."—"El Dorado" I am quite certain came out in "The Flag"—but the *date* I cannot tell, of *any of them*—"For Annie" even I am sorry to say—I sincerely regret that I did not keep the papers, as they came out—I had them all & might have done so—

I have often regretted also that I did not keep a *diary* at the time I knew Mr. Poe, & jot down conversations had with him on different subjects—it would be invaluable now—I remember well his speaking of his early life, but I can recall nothing distinctly, that differs materially from what has been published in the biographies—nor do I remember what he said concerning his school-days *particularly*, or of his foster parents, though he often mentioned being in England incidentally—I think he never mentioned the name of his *own* parents to me—Mr. Cudworth* had some conversation with him, about his visit to England I think, but seems not to have any distinct recollections, on the subject, more than myself— He has no letters written by Mr. Poe, & those of Mrs.Clemm I think contain nothing of value—I have made several efforts to find something of his, among the few autograph collectors that I know, but as yet have seen no one who has more than his simple signature—these were given by either Mrs. Clemm or myself—Of his life in Phila. I know nothing at all—indeed was not aware of his ever having passed any considerable portion of it in that city—did he meet "Almira Shelton" there? I never knew much about his acquaintance with her although I might have done so—but it did not interest me—I know Mrs. Clemm liked her very much & at one time was anxious Mr. Poe should marry her—Concerning the affair with Mrs. Whitman, there seems [sic] to be conflicting accounts —of course I had faith in *his* version of it, but it was the cause of more unhappiness to me than anything that ever occurred during the whole course of our acquaintance,—My husband was from Prov.[idence] & his father's family were living there at that time, & of course heard a great deal of the gossip connected with their names, & naturally enough sympathized with Mrs. Whitman—Their letters used to annoy Mr. Richmond exceedingly, for while he had the most implicit confidence in Mr. Poe, these constant allusions to his having acted dishonorably toward Mrs. W. had their effect, & really came very near putting an end to our correspondence—(I refer to the correspondence between Mr. Poe & myself) It caused him to write the only letter that really pained me & made me feel for the time, that our acquaintance *must* end—I think I will copy that letter for you, because it will show you how *honorably* he acted—indeed I do not think he was *capable* of a mean or dishonorable act toward any human being, & all imputations to the contrary, I firmly believe to be *cruel* & *unjust* in the extreme—he had the very personification of high-mindedness & true nobility as I understand those terms—The lines "For Annie" have never been out of my possession for a moment until I took them to the Photographers for you, & the plate is to be destroyed by my request—Mr. Gill,* (as I told you in a former letter) had "The Bells" for some time & I presume had a copy taken for himself.[4] I am quite certain he has no other & never has had *except* the one I lent him. I am sorry now, that he ever crossed my path—but my slight acquaintance with him was not of my own seeking, & I could not well have avoided doing as I did, under the circumstances. I hear his book is not coming out until autumn. I sincerely *wish* it may *never* come, but suppose I have no power to prevent it. Whether he has made use of the sketch loaned him by my sister, I cannot tell—she will write & request him *not* to publish it. On looking over your letter, I find several questions unanswered. I have heard Mr. Poe speak of Mrs. Stanard*—also of Mrs. Osgood* often, but do not imagine I could tell you anything about either of them that you do not know. Has "Mrs. Jane Ermina Locke" come under your notice? She was deeply in love with Mr. Poe, & went to Fordham to see him & afterward made arrangements for his lecture here. She it was who introduced him to me. I tell you this that you may understand his allusions to her, in the letter I am going to copy for you—he sent me a large package of her letters, but since her death I have destroyed them. I have just one memento of her, which I will enclose—please do not return it. Before closing this letter, I beg to thank you for all favors, & particularly for the promised set of your edition of Mr. Poe's works—hoping you will pardon my verbosity, I am dear sir,

> Yours very truly,
> A. L. Richmond

Have I ever told you that a manuscript copy of "A dream within a dream" is in the possession of a Mrs. Crane in East Boston? Mr. Poe sent it to me before it appeared in print, & many years ago, through the intercession of her pastor, the

---

4. Gill certainly did have a copy of "The Bells," and he reproduced it in his *The Life of Edgar Allan Poe* (New York: C. T. Dillingham; Boston: W. F. Gill Company, 1877), p. 207.

Rev. W. H. Cudworth (who is still in E.B.) I was induced to let her have it—I think you might by application to him, get a photograph of it, but I suppose it would be impossible to obtain the original although she promised if I outlived her, it should be returned to me—Autograph collectors have begged from me, everything I could detach from his letters, after the signatures were all gone.

The "one memento" of Mrs. Locke enclosed in this letter to Ingram was the manuscript of her poem, "Ermina's Gale," which is now in the Ingram Poe Collection, a four-page manuscript containing thirty-one four-line stanzas, with an appended note, presumably to Poe, asking that receipt of the manuscript be acknowledged.[5] If Mrs. Locke did go to Fordham to see Poe before inviting him to lecture in Lowell, he could not have been surprised to find her middle-aged and consumptive, the mother of four children and married to a man who was by no means wealthy—as Frederick W. Coburn* states in his article, "Poe As Seen By the Brother of Annie."

Frederick Gleason and Martin Murray Ballou established *The Flag of Our Union* as a weekly family paper in January, 1846, and it flourished until January, 1871, when it then merged with the *American Union*. All files of *The Flag* were thought to be lost, but Professor Killis Campbell discovered a complete set in the Library of Congress in 1909. "El Dorado" was published in *The Flag* on April 21, 1849; "For Annie" on April 28, 1849.

Stories of Poe's having behaved dishonorably in breaking his engagement to Mrs. Whitman were widely circulated, serving well many persons who enjoyed disparaging Poe.

A fire in the publishing house of which Gill's family were part owners delayed the publication of his *Life of Poe* until November, 1877.

The "little sonnet" that came to Mrs. Richmond as a New Year's greeting, returning romance to her life, was written by B. W. Ball of Boston. Sarah Heywood enclosed a copy of it, cut from an unidentified newspaper, in her letter of July 6, 1877, to John Ingram.

Mrs. Clemm, Mrs. Whitman, and Mrs. Richmond mutilated many of Poe's letters by cutting his signature from them, to please autograph hunters.

Letter 52.   **Annie Richmond, Lowell, to John Ingram, London.**
First printing. [Item 56]

5. [Item 44]

[*post* March 13, 1877]

Dear Mr. Ingram—

In justice to my dear husband, I feel in duty bound to tell you, that he *never* suspected Mr. Poe of anything dishonorable, though the Locke's [*sic*] did their best to poison him in every way, & make him believe their atrocious falsehoods— On receipt of this letter, he wrote them (the Lockes) denouncing them in the *strongest terms*, & the acquaintance ended then & there—He also requested me to *urge* Mrs. Clemm and Mr. Poe to come on, & said she was welcome to stay as long as she wished—If I ever see you I shall have many many things to tell you & to explain—

Yours always
A.L.R.

This short letter accompanied Mrs. Richmond's transcript of Poe's letter to herself, dated February 19, 1849, in which he offers to break their relationship and correspondence, since Mr. Richmond has either been influenced against him by the accusations of Mr. and Mrs. Locke or suspects Poe's motives in his addresses to his wife. In his letter Poe explains and refutes the charges and says he will not now plan to visit the Richmonds or board Mrs. Clemm with them while he is away on a business trip to Virginia. (See Ostrom, II, 429–32, for a complete text of the letter.)

Letter 53. **Annie Richmond, Lowell, to John Ingram, London.**
First printing. [Item 321]

May 27th [18]77

My dear friend

Ought I not to add neglected! I fear you must have felt so often, within the past two months, but I assure you it has not been wilfull neglect on my part—nor have I forgotten you, & the glorious work in which you are engaged, though my mind has been so distracted by cares & trials—sickness in my family, & business perplexities, of the most annoying kind, are what I have to offer in extenuation of my offence—Am I not forgiven? One *little* thing that has annoyed me I might as well mention here—It seems that Mr. Gill has in some (to me) mysterious way found out that I am in correspondence with you, & he has taken me to task for having furnished you aid in your Memoir of Mr. Poe, by sending you my sister's sketch of him! (I wonder if he thinks that is *all* I have sent you!) I suppose I am not doing quite right, as he particularly wished me to ask you *not* to use it (as he had already done so,) but without saying he had desired it! However I am under no obligation to obey his behest, & I shall therefore leave it with you to do as you see fit—he says if I have not seen it, "It is in print," & I shall see it very soon! I wrote him in reply, that until the *defenders* of the lamented poet outnumbered his *detractors*, I should feel at perfect liberty to aid anyone I chose, who would undertake to vindicate his name! Of course, it is not at all likely I shall ever be called upon, or if I am, that I shall be interested sufficiently to furnish any material—(indeed I have *nothing left*, that *could* be used now) but I was so determined to silence him once for all! How he could have got the information, seems the strangest thing, as no one knows *here* anything about my acquaintance with you, excepting my sister, & neither of us are acquainted with any of his friends. I will enclose you a P.S. from his last letter, in which he replied to my question of how he heard the fact he stated—I rather *doubt* his having heard it at all—am inclined to think he surmised it, & took that method of finding out if it were true. Enough of him. I enclose a copy of a letter I gave to a friend long ago, which I *know* is correct in every particular. I regret that the date is not given—the *year* I mean—perhaps you can find out, taken in connection with other letters in your possession. I *urged* him to send you the original, that you might copy it, but he did not like to trust it out of his sight. I am sure it is a *perfect copy*, for he is most reliable, & he assured me that every erasure & indeed *everything* was precisely like the original—he called to see Mr. Davidson * (at my request) to show him both the original & the copy, but did not find him. I have one letter more that I intend to copy for you very soon. It had allusions to Mrs. Locke,* which you will now understand, but until you knew something of her, I did not think it worth while to send it. I also enclose a poem, which *I* do not understand. Mrs. Clemm always said, that *Virginia* was the one for whom that poem was written, & it seemed to annoy her exceedingly, that *everyone* did not so understand it. I think myself, that it has very little significance, if it was intended for anyone else, but his bride. I have searched Boston in vain for the Mag. nos. you wish. I can find only a few—but a friend in New York is hoping to find more, which I will forward (if she is successful) with those I have. Many thanks for you kind offer of the remaining volumes of your edition of Poe, & I wish I knew some one who would take charge of them—but just now, I have no friends abroad, who are coming home, at least for some months. I hardly think we shall see Mr. Brown again, though he was very sure when he left us, that he should return in the spring! He may be able to assist you in forwarding a package to this country, as he is often sending to his uncle in Boston. But do not give yourself too much trouble—they will be very acceptable whenever you can conveniently get them to me. In the meantime, I am wondering how I can send you the magazines! They must be sent at different times—not all at once I suppose. I am not acquainted with anyone in Camden, but may find out what you wish through my friends in New York. I never heard either Mr. Poe or Mrs. Clemm speak of his having translated any tales from the French. I wish it were possible for you to see Mrs. Allan *—it seems to me *her* account would be of immense interest & value, if it could be obtained, for it would be in connection with a period in the poet's life that no one fully understands. His mother always spoke in the strongest terms of denunciation, of the treatment he received from that family—but I have felt that she either did not know, or would not reveal, the real truth about the matter. I cannot believe the Allans would have been guilty of the *injustice* she has charged them with—but nothing would satisfy me, except a statement from Mrs. Allan's own lips. I would see her if I could, *gladly*. Mrs. Whitman I have never cared to see, though I presume my prejudices are—many of them unfounded, but everything connected with *her*, has left a most painful impression upon me. Mrs. Shelton I would like so much to meet—also Mrs. Houghton—Mrs. Lewis is another person from whom I *shrink*, without being able to give any reason for it. I think we are often attracted & repelled *intuitively*, without having any reason for our likes or dislikes of people. Don't you think so? Hoping you will excuse this hurriedly written though *long* letter (for I never stop till I get to the end of my paper), I am, dear sir, your friend most truly, (though intuitively),

A.L.R.

The poem enclosed in this letter was probably "Annabel Lee," although why Mrs. Richmond could not understand it is not clear. Mrs. Clemm frequently insisted that Poe had written the poem only for his wife Virginia, but she also told Stella Lewis that Poe had really written it for her.

Mrs. Richmond's shrewd observations about Mrs. Clemm's denunciation of the Allan family show her acute perception of Mrs. Clemm's real nature.

This letter, perhaps more than any other, shows the warmth and charm of Annie Richmond's personality, as well as her strong desire to have Poe's name vindicated. Her distaste for Gill and her willingness to convey to Ingram Gill's attitudes and plans for writing on Poe are very similar to the attitudes quickly adopted by almost all of Ingram's American correspondents when they were approached by American writers who wanted to do the same job that Ingram was doing. Their almost fierce loyalty to Ingram is not easily explained.

Gill had learned of Mrs. Richmond's correspondence with Ingram almost certainly through Mrs. Whitman, for Ingram was writing and receiving letters from her with great regularity during this period, and he habitually gave her full accounts of his correspondents, his triumphs as well as his failures, in acquiring new materials about Poe.

Ingram had indeed tried to reach Mrs. Louisa G. Allan in Richmond, but without success. He had sent a letter to her through his loyal helper, E. V. Valentine of Richmond, but Valentine himself declined to offer it to her, even though he was on friendly visiting terms, since the subject of Edgar Poe was, as he bluntly wrote Ingram, "disagreeable to her." He did, however, give the letter to someone else to hand to her. She did not reply.

The friend to whom Mrs. Richmond had given the letter Poe wrote "long ago," to William E. Burton, June 1, 1840, and who made a "perfect copy" for Ingram, was William Rouse.*

Letter 54. **Sarah H. Heywood, Lowell, to John Ingram, London.** First printing. [Item 322]

July 6, 1877

Mr. Ingram,
Dear Sir,

Again Mrs. Richmond asks me to be her amanuensis, and acknowledge the receipt of yours dated 6/11 also of the 2nd vol. of Mr. Poe's Works. She will write you fully, as soon as this unusual business complication is adjusted. With her permission I add a few words respecting the "Sketch". You are certainly at liberty to use it in any way you like, and I heartily wish it had gone into no hands but yours. I understood that Mr. Gill was writing a *lecture*, & that he merely wished to read some little thing—anything that would help him form a mental picture—that he might write with more interest. I expected him to return the MS. As he did not do it, I sent for it. I have not sufficient confidence in Mr. Gill's scholarly ability or literary taste, to wish to aid him, even in a very small way, in a work of this kind.

I have often asked Annie to enclose to you a Sonnet "To A.L.R." written by B. W. Ball of Boston, several months ago. As I think she has not done so, I shall put it in with this.

I am, dear sir
Very truly yours—
Sarah H. Heywood

The sonnet enclosed in this letter, written by B. W. Ball of Boston as a New Year's present to Mrs. Richmond for 1877, when she was in her fifty-seventh year, is as follows:

To A.L.R.

A poet thee in other years did love,
Thy face was starlight to his fervid dreams;
And, of thy morning charms, still sunset gleams
Attest how potent was the spell they wove
Around thy glorious minstrel's lonely heart.
Thee in deathless verse did enshrine,
Thy name embalmed in many a burning line,
And of his wide renown gave thee a part.
Broken long since his heart and fitful lyre
By adverse fate; his threne long since was sung.
But more and more in every clime and tongue,

His fame is spread, which owns the poet's fire,
While still thou charm'st, e'en tho' no longer young,
As when thy minstrel's soul thou didst inspire.[6]

Letter 55.　**Annie Richmond, Lowell, to John Ingram, London.**
First printing. [Item 324]

Oct. 8th 1877

My dear friend Mr. Ingram—

I am not going to trouble you with a detailed account of *all* that has transpired to prevent my writing you for the past three months, though I am sure you would not wonder at my prolonged silence—suffice it to say your *last*, dated May 28th found me suffering from a severe attack of bronchitis, which still confines me to the house, though I am now able to leave my room—My business cares seemed almost insupportable, while in health, & as you will readily understand, are doubly wearing in a state of physical prostration—I am therefore, hardly in a condition to write an interesting letter, even upon the subject that is nearest & dearest to my heart—How I wish it were *possible*, for you to come here before your Memoir is published—I do so want to read & talk over Gill's book with you—It has provoked some adverse comments, yet on the whole, has been better received than it deserved to be—I know of *one* notice that was written for a consideration, & very likely others have been—there *is a way* of getting favorable notices, of the most unworthy book ever published, I find, & I think Mr. G. most *unscrupulous*. His audacity in using my sister's manuscript, after she had told him, she wished to prepare it for a Mag. article, shows him in his true light. I regret most sincerely that he ever crossed my path. I had hoarded my precious secret for *years*, & how it ever came to be revealed to *him*, passes my comprehension. Had I not been waiting *so long*, to hear that name vindicated, I should not have allowed him (Gill) even the few items of information he *did* extort, under pretense of preparing a lecture! But it

6. [Item 708]

was such a relief, to feel that one voice was to be raised in denunciation of Griswold & his wicked *Memoir*, that for a time I thought only how I might aid him, without betraying, what even then I felt was too sacred to be revealed, although *certain* that I held the key to many things that appeared inexplicable. I really wonder now sometimes, that he was not more successful—but I never liked the man—His *personality* was especially disagreeable—he repelled me constantly, & I felt, that even for the sake of having that dear name vindicated, I *could not* disclose my long treasured secret! How differently did I send forth the response to your first overture —it seemed to me, you *ought to know*—indeed that you *must* know, & that I must put those letters in your possession—for the first time, I fully realized the mistake I had made in allowing myself to yield, against my judgment, to the importunities of a —(shall I write it) mountebank! This must be "*subrosa*" for Mr. G. is a man who *might* make my acquaintance with Mr. Poe serve him with a weapon for *revenge*, if he were aware of my dislike—at all events, I would not trust him, & I therefore have just as little as possible to do with him in any way. I think it was a bitter disappointment to him, that I did not speak with enthusiasm of his Memoir. I could not say what I did *not* feel & I would not say, or thought it best not to say, what I *did* feel, consequently I merely thanked him for his attempts to vindicate the poet & said I hoped it would be well received. I had not read the book when I wrote this & told him so. Since reading it, I have neither seen him or written to him, & I hope & pray that our slight acquaintance may end here. Have you seen it—if not, I will send you a copy at once—by the way, I will go to Boston soon as I am able, & gather whatever numbers have been found, of the old Mags. you desired, & forward them to you by mail. I fear you will be disappointed for there are comparatively few of the dates I copied, that are to be found even in the oldest book-stores. I am told that very many such books & magazines were destroyed in the great fire, & I have no doubt it is true. "The Flag of our Union"* was entirely lost, & I have been unable to find a person who has a copy on file, though I have asked at least a dozen different people who were *supposed* to have them.

It was a miserable paper, & Mr. Poe used to say he was ashamed to write for it, but that they *paid well*. You speak of the "Burton letter," * & ask if there are any more. Mr. Rouse has nothing, except that letter, which I gave him many years ago, as a souvenir—could I have known you, previous to Mrs. Clemm's death, I could have done you a real service, for she would have given me all her letters & papers—indeed, she promised to leave them to me, & I have no doubt she *thought* arrangements had been made that would secure them to me—at the time of her death, my husband's health was much impaired & I could not leave home, even for a day, or I should have gone to Baltimore at once, & preferred my claims. I wrote to several persons, but got no satisfaction. Many thanks for the three Vols. (1–2 & 4) which have reached me safely, & in perfectly good condition. Is the Memoir to be connected with, or contained in the 3'd volume? I am more happy than you can understand, to feel that I have been able to aid you even a little, in your labors, & as I have said before, my only regret is that you could not have had *all*. But we all have to learn lessons from experience sometimes, very bitter those lessons prove. I sent a copy of "Eldorado," which I hope has reached you ere this—do not forget to tell me if you have Gill's book. I am very impatient to know how it impresses you. I mean the style—if it is not bungling & awkward, then I am no judge—my sister *Miss* Heywood sends kind regards. Excuse this stupid letter—I hope to feel better soon both in body & mind—there is a stray gleam of light to be seen in the business horizon I am told, & I think it may brighten for us all. I enclose the letter about "The Bells," which I think I mentioned to you.

Yours always very truly—
A.L.R.

Mrs. Richmond's enclosed "letter about 'The Bells'" was a copy of Poe's letter to her, February 8, 1849. (See Ostrom, II, 425–26, for complete text.)

Mrs. Richmond knew that Ingram was writing a new "memoir" of Poe, but she apparently did not understand that it was to be a full-scale biography, until the two volumes came out in 1880 and Ingram sent a set of them to her.

Ingram steadily regarded his work on Poe's true biography as a holy crusade in the cause of belated justice, and himself as the one person capable and equipped to storm and win that citadel; consequently, he took an extremely dim view of anyone else's efforts in that direction. He could be quite sharp with even his most active American helpers who had even a kind word to say about anyone's writing about Poe except his own. In this letter, Mrs. Richmond is obviously trying to ward off his displeasure over her having helped Gill. She, too, really believed that Ingram was the only person who could redeem Poe's besmirched personal reputation, as did Mrs. Whitman, Mrs. Houghton, and much later, Amelia Poe,* Neilson Poe's daughter.

Gill's *Life of Poe*, badly marred as it is with sentimentality and inept writing, has real historical importance, for he was close to the scenes of Poe's life and he met many persons who had known Poe and got from them a number of important Poe "firsts." He was extremely jealous and envious of Ingram's hold on some of Poe's friends and he resented Ingram's published statement that "no trustworthy biography of Poe has yet appeared in his own country," which he made in 1874. In his own preface, in 1877, Gill considered Ingram's snide remark refuted.

We know that Ingram had indeed seen a copy of Gill's recently published biography of Poe, for two days before Mrs. Richmond wrote this letter, Ingram's unsigned review of the book had been printed in the *Athenaeum*. In this slashing, contemptuous denunciation of Gill as a biographer and a person, wherein Ingram derisively attacked Gill's literary style and his ignorance of this subject, he even accused Gill of covert malignancy toward Poe, as well as stealing biographical materials from him, Ingram. Thus began the battle of Poe's biographers.

Letter 56. **Annie Richmond, Lowell, to John Ingram, London.**
First printing. [Item 325]

Nov. 25th 1877

My dear friend,

I am so *incensed* at the audacity (not to use a harsher expression) of Mr. Gill, that I can think of nothing else at present—In the first place, I never have heard of the Monthly you mention, & know not where to obtain a copy, but shall endeavor to get it, & see what it contains, then *ask* Mr. Gill where he found the extract! I have never seen him, except to pass him in the street, since that time he came to me some six or eight years ago, when he was preparing the lecture—I then read him some extracts from my letters, as I told you, but he never has seen them, *except in my hands*, for I never allowed him to take them, even in my presence! Of course, whatever he has, that he did *not* put in his memoir, must have been surreptitiously obtained, or he would have made use of it—How it is *possible* for him to have in his possession, *anything* from those letters, is something beyond my comprehension! They have never been loaned to any human being but yourself, & have never been read to anyone—I have occasionally in years past, read some few extracts to persons who admired Mr. Poe's genius, but deplored his weak & wicked nature, in order to prove to them the injustice that had been done him—At this moment I recall an instance, where I read some portions of them, to a would-be literary young lady, who expressed the most enthusiastic admiration of the *Poet*, but who firmly believed the *man* to have been unworthy the friendship of an honorable woman! Of course, I could not allow such accusations to pass without defending him—As this young lady has recently married a friend of Mr. Gill's, it is barely possible, he may have gathered this information from her, though it must be some eight or ten years since I have seen her, & the reading must have produced a strong impression upon her mind, if she can reproduce verbatim anything she heard so long ago—You remember perhaps, that I told you, several of my letters were missing—But I can hardly imagine they could have come into *his* hands! I cannot express to you how much this information *annoys* me. It makes me more unreconciled than ever, to the fact that the miserable man ever crossed my path! I am thankful that I *never* liked him, even tolerably well—I thought he might possibly, (if he were going into the lecture field) correct some of the cruel impressions made upon the public by Griswold, if he were able to say, he *knew* whereof he spoke. But we have to learn wisdom by bitter experience—(I ought to be wiser than Solomon!) Now I will *try* to answer some of your questions, though I am in a most *unenviable* frame of mind—I will write Mrs. Crane* for a photo of the poem, or a portion of it. I will also have "The Bells" photographed & forward them both to you, as soon as possible

—by the way, after all my searching, I have found only *three vols*. of the magazine, & lest these should not be among those you *particularly* care for, I will send you the dates, & leave it for you to decide—*Graham's Mag.* for 1843—1846, & 1848 —these are *entire*, from Jany. to Dec. *complete* (two vols. bound in one, making it all three volumes)—he, Mr. Burnham, antiquarian bookseller, has many others, but none of the dates you mention, & he *insists* that they cannot be found in Boston, for the reason that so many of the places where those things were preserved were destroyed by the great fire. I rather think he is correct, as I am told the same thing, wherever I go. He asks six dollars for the three volumes—is it too much for them? It seems to me so—though he says, he often has calls for these odd numbers.

To return again, *literally* to our *Mouton*! I have *not* seen the *Library Table's* comments on Mrs. Whitman's reply. I *did* see Gill's scandalous attack upon *you*, in the *Herald* last week (Boston Sunday *Herald*). I would not send it to you, because I considered it beneath your notice! "No respectable literary man" would condescend to write an article of *that* nature! Even for the *Herald*! (Oh dear, I loathe the very *name* of the miserable fellow).

Am sorry to hear of Mrs. Houghton's death just at this time, especially, as she could aid you in some respects, where *we* who are left cannot. I know very little concerning Mrs. Ellet,* except that Mr. Poe disliked her. I mean at the time I knew him—she was once his friend, but she exasperated him beyond forgiveness—*so he said*. In one of my missing letters, he had given me some details concerning her, & one or two other literary women, & I think *this* was the reason Mrs. Clemm wished to get possession of the letter—she borrowed it at one time & kept it a long while I remember, though I thought nothing of it, *then*. I have learned since to be—well —doubtful! I wish you *could* come to America before your book is published.

This is a most *unsatisfactory* letter—but I must send it.

Yours always, very truly,
A.L.R.

P.S. I have changed my P. Office Box, it is now No. 84. If you have not time to write a letter just send a postal telling me about the magazines please *at once*—

How Gill came by the extract he published from Poe's letter to Mrs. Richmond is not known, but it was from one of the letters "missing" from her collection of Poe's letters. Oddly enough, another of her letters from Poe made its way somehow to England, and was in Frederick Locker-Lampson's autograph collection by 1880, and Ingram was given permission by the owner to copy it on February 6. The letter really was but a brief note that Poe wrote from Fordham on October 8, 1848, introducing Mrs. Sarah Anna (Stella) Lewis to Mrs. Richmond.[7]

"Mrs. W's Reply" was a long letter by Sarah Helen Whitman to the New York *Tribune*, October 13, 1875,[8] in which she scathingly refuted Francis Gerry Fairfield's statement that Poe had been an epileptic, made in Fairfield's article, "A Madman of Letters," *Scribner's Magazine*, October, 1875.[9]

Gill's attack on Ingram, prompted by Ingram's brutal review of the Gill biography of Poe, was printed in the Boston *Sunday Herald*, November 18, 1877.

Mrs. Ellet remained one of Poe's bitterest and most relentless enemies until her death on June 3, 1877. Mrs. Houghton had died on September 3, 1877.

Letter 57. **Sarah H. Heywood, Lowell, to John Ingram, London.** First printing. [Item 326]

Dec. 24, 1877

Dear Sir,

The flow of Christmas-tide always finds me here in the capacity of "spare hand," and it is my habit—at this time—to do as I am bidden. Mrs. Richmond is busy at *"The Home"* today, and she asks me to say to you that she has received the third volume of the Memoir, also your letter of the 12th inst.

I think she is entirely willing to trust your judgment & taste in regard to the article of which you speak. But she will write you more particularly of that.

7. [Item 347]
8. [Item 619]
9. [Item 628]

The Photograph *I* sincerely hope you will be able to obtain. She has never sat for one, tho' we have often urged her doing so. Perhaps your request may prevail.

With cordial greeting from Mrs. Richmond, I am

> Very truly &c.
> S. H. Heywood

Ingram had asked Mrs. Richmond's opinion about some things in an article on Poe he was preparing for magazine publication, and it was the sweeping, overall permissions, such as this one in Sarah Heywood's letter, that helped him justify his printing almost verbatim the copies of Poe's letters that Mrs. Richmond had sent to him, "so that he would understand Poe better"—or at least Ingram used these statements as justification.

Someone must have persuaded Mrs. Richmond finally to sit for at least one photograph, for there is one of her reproduced in Mary E. Phillip's *Edgar Allan Poe: The Man*, II, 1294.

"The Home" was the Lowell orphanage.

Letter 58.   **Annie Richmond, Lowell, to John Ingram, London.**
First printing. [Item 327]

> Dec. 30th [18]77

My dear friend,

With many thanks, I return the papers you so kindly sent me—It is a mystery, I shall probably never fathom, how that extract came in Mr. G's* possession—I suspect he has nothing *more*, or he would have made use of it in his Memoir—No one can see my papers, except with my consent, as they are carefully locked up *always*—I feel that I am in your power, for you know *everything* connected with my acquaintance with Mr. Poe—but, as I have before told you, I also feel that I can trust you *implicitly*—not a human being, except my sister, knows what I have done, & no other person has ever had my unlimited confidence, beside yourself—In your biography of course I expect my name will appear, but if you write a sketch to be published *previously*, I would prefer *not* to be named, as it would undoubtedly be copied & have a wide circulation & it would be read by a different class of persons from those who would read the book. I hope you understand the feeling that prompts me to make this request. I would not restrict your use of the *material* in your possession but only ask, that my name be withheld. Believing that you have from the first comprehended the delicacy of my position & that you have understood my unwillingness to be brought before the public, *except* in vindication of a name *dearer to me than any other in the world*, & also, believe that you *will* be "careful," I leave myself in your hands, *confident* that I shall never have cause for regret—I met Mr. Gill at the "Old South Fair," & he would have been cordial, but I shrank from him as if he had been a reptile, & passed on, without giving him an opportunity to say anything, except, to express his "delight" at seeing me there! (Would that we had never met!) I enclose his scurrilous attack upon you, at your request, although I consider it beneath your notice—I am delighted at the prospect of seeing you, & *hope* the day is not far distant—next year—surely—If I can make up my mind to sit for a picture you shall have one—my sister forwarded my thanks for Vol. 3, I believe. I am writing hurriedly for I have a friend waiting, & I want to mail this tonight—Hoping the New Year will bring you blessings in abundance, & that we shall meet before its close, I am yours

> Always very truly
> Annie R.

Within a few months after this letter was written Mrs. Richmond learned how much she would indeed regret having sent Ingram copies of her letters from Poe and how little he understood or cared about the delicacy of her position; for he published a number of the copies of her letters almost verbatim in *Appleton's Journal*, along with other letters Poe had written during the same period. Mrs. Richmond was deeply hurt to see her letters in print; Mrs. Whitman had cherished for nearly thirty years the dream that she alone had been Poe's dearest love, but Ingram's publication of Poe's letters to Annie Richmond, with the dates that coincided with his letters to her, dispelled that dream.

Poe's letters to Mrs. Whitman are truly passionate literary love letters; his letters to Mrs. Richmond are passionate personal love letters. Ingram's publication served to break relations and correspondence with both ladies, but he already had in his possession all of the Poe materials anyone could hope to get from them.

Letter 59. **Annie Richmond, Lowell, to John Ingram, London.**
First printing. [Item 328]

Jany. 8th 1878

My dear friend,

I am sure you will sympathize with me most truly & deeply, when I tell you, that the enclosed is all that I have left, of my manuscript of "The Bells"! I took it to a Photographer, one of the oldest & most reliable in the city—he began the work, had got so far, was called away, forgot where he put it, & it has been stolen or lost! He has advertised it offering a large reward, but I doubt if it is ever found—he had with it, the "Dream within a dream" which was dedicated to me, & the only proof I have, or *had* that it was written for me! If he had only copied *that* before it was lost, I could have borne it better. But it has made me really ill—all my other trials, pecuniary embarrassments etc., seem trivial & of no account —time may bring all right, but this one—alas, there is no consolation for such grief, no compensation for such a loss! I cannot write at length today, I am too much depressed, to think of anything, but my great loss! The man feels so badly, that I cannot find it in my heart to say much to him—he says, he would give five hundred dollars in one moment, to put his eyes upon it once more, & restore it to me—I believe him—none of my family know it as yet, for I have not quite lost *all hope*, that the reward may bring it—excuse this hastily penned note & believe me

Yours ever
Annie L. R—

The lost manuscript of "The Bells" was Poe's third draft of the poem, written probably in late May of 1849, when he was visiting the Richmonds in Lowell. He had sent a manuscript of the last fifteen lines of "A Dream Within a

Dream," entitled "For Annie," to Mrs. Richmond earlier in 1849. The photographer, N. C. Sanborn, 50 Merrimack St., Lowell, advertised in the Lowell *Courier*, offering a liberal reward for the return of the lost poems, without saying what they were or to whom they belonged. The Detroit *Free Press* picked up the advertisement and jocularly advised the Lowell postmaster to prepare to wrestle with several tons of manuscript poetry, for every newspaper man in the United States would be glad to give freely from his treasured stock of manuscript poetry until Mr. Sanborn should cry "Hold! enough!"

Letter 60.   **Annie Richmond, Lowell, to John Ingram, London.**
First printing. [Item 330]

Feby. 5th [18]78

My dear friend,
The Gods be praised! My lost manuscripts have been recovered! They were found in the Post Office, among the "dead letters," but *how* they came there, is the great mystery! I have had the "Dream" copied, & will enclose it. "The Bells" are being done, & shall be forwarded at the earliest moment —so there is one bright spot upon my (at present) cloudy horizon—Your kind favor of the 7th ult. reached me on Saturday last (Feby. 2nd) & I should have replied *at once*, but thought the next steamer would bring me a reply to the letter which told you of my loss, as I mailed them so nearly together —but now that I have such good news, I will not delay a moment longer, hoping that the enclosure though late, will be in season for your sketch if you wish to use it. For a week past, I have been quite ill—under the care of a physician who wishes me *if possible* to keep quiet, & not *"worry"* about anything! I think the sight of my lost treasures, has done more for me than all his medicine, though it really overcame me, when they were put in my hand. It seemed almost incredible, that they would ever be found, & I felt as if I had received a message from the spirit world! Did I tell you about "The Dream"? It was sent me as you see it, in a sort of farewell

letter, (which is one of the missing ones, that I have mentioned to you) then afterward, the addition was made, & it was *published* in the "Flag of our Union"—As I have not the letter which accompanied it, I am unable to give you the precise date, but it was in connection with the Whitman affair, that the letter was written—I am rejoiced to know that there is a prospect of your coming here. I do *hope* nothing will occur, to prevent the carrying out of your plan for doing so. As regards what I said, about being in your power my dear friend, *understand me please*, I *am* in your power, but *willingly so*—all I ask is that you will use it just as *you* would wish *another* to use it, if it were your wife, or your sister, who occupied *my* position! Did I not feel *sure* that you thoroughly understand & comprehend the relation I sustained to Mr. Poe, I should be of all people most miserable, for I need not tell you, what *might* be made of that correspondence—indeed what nine out of ten persons, who should be given your opportunities, *would* make of it—I can hardly *realize* at times, that my inmost heart *has* been laid bare to a stranger! For a long time after I received your first letter, I delayed replying to it, trying to convince myself that it was *absurd* to say the least, to expect *anyone* would do us both justice, especially, one who was a stranger to us both! Do you not sometimes wonder, I *dared* so fully to trust you? But my impulse was too strong to be resisted, & I yielded for *his sake*, for, as I think I told you then, it seemed to me, his history could not be *justly* written, while the revelations contained in those letters, of his honor & purity, were unknown to his biographer—in haste for today's mail—

Very truly your friend
A.L.R.

The copy of "A Dream Within A Dream" enclosed in this letter was the last fifteen lines of that poem, here entitled "For Annie." Poe revised the poem still once more and published it as "A Dream Within A Dream" in *The Flag of Our Union*, March 31, 1849. Ingram reproduced this manuscript in the London *Bookman* for January, 1909. Ingram did not carry out his plan to visit Mrs. Richmond. She was shortly to regret, and bitterly, that she had laid bare her "inmost heart" to a stranger.

Letter 61.   Annie Richmond, Lowell, to John Ingram, London.
First printing. [Item 331]

Feby. 12th 1878

My dear friend—

I have a confession to make to you—I do not think I have *ever* fully appreciated your Memoir until now. Since I have been confined to the house, & obliged, to some extent, to give up my outside duties & cares, I have read more leisurely, & among other things, have re-read *very carefully*, your faithful & *just* tribute to my *precious* Eddie, for he was indeed *very* precious, & his affection for me, is the most precious *memory* my heart holds. It matters not to me, who were his friends— how many, or how dear they were, it is enough for me to feel *assured* that among those friends, *I had a place*—of course, the world would not, *could not*, understand our friendship, & I have always avoided speaking of him, *as a friend*, but only as an acquaintance, whom I met for the first time, when he came here to lecture. The loss of "The Bells" has given more publicity to our friendship, than anything previous, *even Mr. Gill's book*! When it was known, that the "missing manu-cript" was the *original* of that wonderful poem, there was great curiosity to know who *owned it*, & I told Mr. Sanborn I wished to have my name suppressed, but he could say, it belonged to a lady friend of the author. The Boston Sunday papers yesterday had the name, (however they found it out), which will I suspect, be a source of annoyance to Mr. Gill, as he wished it understood, that *he* was the fortunate possessor of it. But I have not told you, indeed, I fear I never *can* express all the exquisite joy & the boundless gratitude I felt, as I laid down your book, last night. I had only *one* regret—that I did not *know* what you were doing, *at the time*. However, it may be just as well now—by the way, there is a notice in the papers, that Mrs. John Weiss* has just published an account of the "last days of Edgar Poe"—whether in book form, or as a newspaper sketch, I do not yet know, but will try to get it for you, though I do not imagine it *can* contain anything really new. I am not surprised at *your* indignation at my loss. I could not feel as you did, because I knew Mr. Sanborn was, if possible, more grieved than ever I was—he was so overcome, that it seriously affected his health. He said if *money* could repair the loss, he would willingly give any amount he possessed—but his utter inability to make any reparation, was what made it so hard to bear. I really pitied him, & I told him I would rather be in my place than his—so I would—He took the roll every night, to a friend, just underneath his rooms, & had it locked in his fire proof safe—but the night he lost it, his friend had closed his store and gone, when he called, & he put it in his pocket to carry home—whether he himself put it into the P.O. Box with some other mail matter, or whether he dropped it *at* the office, & some one else picked it up, & put it in the Box, he does not know—he confesses, it was *terribly* careless—*unpardonably* so, & says it has learned him a lesson he shall *never* forget. But as it is *safe*, I have forgiven him, though it would have been very hard to do so, had it never been found. I am hoping yet to get the copy today—the weather has been so bad, he could not print it until yesterday. I suppose ere this reaches you, the "Dream" has been received. You will have the privilege of printing *one thing*, that has never appeared before—or rather, in the *original form*, which has never before been made public. I am so *very* thankful, Mr. Gill did not happen to get hold of it. Hoping to be able to send you the copy of "The Bells" by *tomorrow*, I am, dear sir, yours very truly,

Annie R.

Tuesday P.M.
[Feb. 12, 1878]
4 O'clock

The copy of "The Bells" has just been sent to me, & I mail it with this *today* in a *roll*. I did not like to fold it. Hope it will reach you safely, & prove satisfactory. I shall be anxious to hear from it—also, from the "Dream" mailed the 6th. I should write more, but am in haste to send this by the 5 o'clock N. York mail this P.M. Yours always,

A.L.R.

Gill had borrowed Mrs. Richmond's manuscript copy of "The Bells" so that he might read the poem with "better effect" at the dedication ceremonies for Poe's monument in Baltimore in November, 1875. He did have a facsimile of it made and reproduced it in his biography of Poe, facing page 206.

Mrs. Richmond is a day off when she says the Boston Sunday papers "yesterday" carried her name in connection with "The Bells" manuscript. February 12, 1878, the day she was writing to Ingram, fell on Tuesday. The Boston Sunday paper, probably the Boston *Sunday Herald*, would have been dated the tenth.

Mrs. John Weiss was Susan Archer Talley Weiss, who, as a girl, had met Poe in Richmond. Her long and valuable article, "The Last Days of Edgar A. Poe," was published in *Scribner's Monthly*, March, 1878, 707–716.

Letter 62.   Annie Richmond, Lowell, to John Ingram, London.
First printing. [Item 334]

March 17th 1878

My dear friend—

I beg pardon for having so long delayed replying to your kind favor of the 18th ult. It did not reach me, until three weeks after it was mailed, yet, it *should* have been answered at once, if only to thank you for the graceful & delicate manner in which you "ask" me a favor! Surely my friend, you will believe me, when I say, your proposition to associate my name, with the dearest one I have ever known, will be to me a most precious tribute, to the sweetest memory my heart holds. The manner in which it shall be done, I leave entirely to your own *taste*, with the same confidence that I have trusted everything pertaining to that acquaintance, to your *honor*—need I say more? Ere this you have doubtless received the copy of "The Bells," the "Radical Review," and the "Scribner," all of which I trust, will interest you. The notice I enclose from a religious (!) paper, seems to me the most *cruel* & *uncalled for*, of anything I have seen for years. How *can* a person *say* such things, even if they believe them to be true, especially of one who has *so few* left to defend him! I cannot understand it. I sincerely *hope* your paper *will* most effec-

tively "crush" these *"forgers, liars, and slanderers"*—God
forgive them, for "they know not what they do." I believe it
grieves me if possible, more than ever to read such things, for
it seems to me time to forget his failings, & remember only
his grand intellectual worth, if he had no virtues to be
remembered.

How soon will your article appear? What a pity "One who
knew him" is not here to receive his share of the castigation,
when it does come! Be sure & tell me how that notice of Gill's
book impresses you—I *think* you will enjoy it immensely—I
did!

The reminiscences of Mrs. Weiss are certainly very pleasant, & I feel grateful to her, for every kind word she has said. I
have thought of writing & telling her so, but have neglected it
so long now, that I may not at all.

You ask if I will part with my manuscripts. I certainly
have no intention of doing so, just at present—but I will
answer that question, more at length, when I see you—by the
way, have you a photograph of my friend Mr. Ingram, that
you could send me, so that I shall *know* him when he comes! I
should most certainly have complied with your request, if I
had ever sat for a picture. I have almost promised my family
that I will do so this spring—if I do, you shall be remembered.
My health is at present perfectly good—

Yours always—
Annie R.

Ingram's questions to Mrs. Richmond about parting with her manuscripts,
which would include her autograph letters from Poe, and her indication of her
willingness to talk about the subject when he came to America here take on
especial poignancy; for after Ingram printed Poe's letters to her in *Appleton's
Journal*, she destroyed almost all of her letters from Poe and other papers
relating to their relationship.

When Mrs. Richmond wrote this letter, she was fifty-eight years old, and
she had another twenty years to live. The one published photograph of her, in
Mary E. Phillips' *Edgar Allan Poe: The Man*, appears to have been made about
this age.

The *Radical Review*, printed in New Bedford, Massachusetts, probably
contained Gill's article on Poe in which he quoted an excerpt from one of
Poe's letters to Mrs. Richmond. The "religious paper" is unidentified, but the

clipping from it, enclosed in this letter, was a reprint of a portion of C. F. Briggs' posthumous article, "The Personality of Poe," and subtitled, "Poe as he was, by one who knew him," which had first appeared in *The Independent*, December, 13, 1877. Briggs had died on June 20,1877. In this article Briggs declared that Poe, when drunk, was a terror to his wife and mother-in-law.

Gill's *Life of Poe* had been reissued in January, 1878; the notice of it that Mrs. Richmond so markedly enjoyed must have been unfavorable.

Letter 63. Annie Richmond, Lowell, to John Ingram, London.
First printing. [Item 335]

April 1st 1878

Not yet heard from—
Roll of Manuscript—"The Bells"—
"Radical Review"—(New Bedford)
"Scribner's Monthly"—(article by Mrs. Weiss)
Letter dated March 17th with notice of "Poe as he was" by, "One who knew him"—Hope soon to hear, *all the above* are in your possession—

Yours truly—
Annie R.

The "roll of manuscript" had been mailed to Ingram from Lowell on February 12, 1878, and Mrs. Richmond's anxiety about it is understandable. But Ingram's correspondence was very heavy at this period, and he had to perform his daily duties in the English Civil Service, which made his replies sometimes tardier than his correspondents thought they should be.

Letter 64. Annie Richmond, Lowell, to John Ingram, London.
First printing. [Item 353]

May 19th 1880

My dear Sir—
Your postal has just reached me. I am glad to hear from you again, for I have been very anxious to know what you

would do about my letters. I *hope* they are not coming out in the new volume—yet, I suppose, I am "hoping against hope!" It will not surprise or shock me, as did their appearance in the magazine, but it will be a *life-long regret*! However, it is *too late* to discuss the matter now.

Mr. Davidson's address is the same as it used to be—Box 567, New York.

Thank you for the promise of the Memoir. I shall be anxious to see it—though I know it will bring a pang to my heart—

Yours truly—
A. L. Richmond

[on verso]

Mr. E. C. Stedman has a very fine sketch of Mr. Poe in *Scribner's Monthly*. Have you seen it? What he says of the poem "For Annie" pleased me.[10]

The formality of Mrs. Richmond's salutation to Ingram in this letter shows clearly that all cordiality on her part was over. She had been deeply wounded when her letters from Poe appeared in *Appleton's Journal* in 1878; and she knew that they would reappear in Ingram's biography of Poe.

There is a hiatus of more than two years between Letters 63 and 64; if she did write to Ingram between April 1, 1878, and May 19, 1880, her letters have not survived in Ingram's Poe collection. Ingram did try to reason with her through the mails, pointing out sentences and phrases in her letters that seemed to give him permission to do as he thought best with her letters. Apparently, she did not quarrel violently with him, but obviously all of her playfulness, her affectionate greetings and regard for him were things of the past when she wrote this letter.

By "promise of the Memoir," she certainly indicates that Ingram had just written to her, for his two-volume biography of Poe had just come from the press at this time.

Letter 65.   **Annie Richmond, Lowell, to John Ingram, London.**
First printing. [Item 357]

10. E. C. Stedman's article, "Edgar Allan Poe," appeared in *Scribner's Monthly*, May, 1880, pp. 107–124. [Item 769]

July 9th 1880

Dear Mr. Ingram—

Please accept my sincere & grateful thanks for your kind favors—the two beautiful volumes & your kind letter—all of which reached me in safety two weeks ago. I owe you an apology for this tardy acknowledgment of your kindness, but I was just starting for the seashore when I received them & had not time to write—or even to examine the Memoirs. I must confess, that the portion of my letter which you enclose—detached from its surrounding—seems to grant you a larger liberty, than I supposed could be obtained from anything which I had ever written to you—but even with this liberty, I think the injunction that you would give the public, what you would be willing they should know, if the letters had been addressed to your sister or your wife, *covered all the ground* with restrictions & confined it, to a very narrow limit. I supposed you would merely give the *ideas* of the writer, as you gathered them from reading the letters—but I did not dream of seeing them appear word for word as they were written! The shock was indeed a terrible one to me—it seemed *sacrilege* truly—I felt condemned, that I had allowed them to pass out of my hands. But it is useless to discuss the matter now. You evidently did not understand my feelings about them, or you would never have put them in print. I am very *very* thankful, that my name has been withheld—very few I think, even among my friends, will recognize them as addressed to me. Would you have published those addressed to Mrs. Whitman, had she been living? There are portions of her letters, as well as many things in mine, which can hardly be considered worthy of preserving for the author's sake, & which *might* be construed to his disadvantage. However, what is done is done cannot be undone—so here the matter must rest.

The vols. are very nicely gotten up & much of the material is exceedingly interesting. I hope you may come to America & that I shall see you, when we will talk this matter over, with more freedom than we can write.

Again thanking you for your kindness, I am, sir,

Yours very truly—
A. L. Richmond

After seeing her letters from Poe in print in Ingram's *Appleton's Journal* *
article, Mrs. Richmond was thereafter, for the next twenty years, inaccessible
to *anyone* seeking information about Poe.

Ingram had withheld her name in the *Appleton's Journal* article, but in the
"two beautiful volumes," which were of course his 1880 biography of Poe, he
had written a chapter which he entitled "Annie" (II, 187–221), in which he
reproduced all of Poe's letters to her, named the Richmond family in Lowell,
and had reprinted and assigned authorship of "Recollections of E. A. Poe," to
Mrs. Richmond's younger sister, Sarah Heywood. When Mrs. Richmond
thanks Ingram in this letter for withholding her name, it can only mean she
had not examined the books, much less read them closely.

Mrs. Whitman was living when Ingram's article was published and at first
she seemed to take the wound it gave her with equanimity, remarking that she
was already "ankle-deep in asphodels," and had not the time or energy left to
quarrel with John Ingram again. Later, it seems she changed her mind, for she
did publish her first attack on the article and Ingram in the Providence *Journal*
for May 4, 1878, fifty-four days before she died.

Mrs. Richmond's "the portion of my letter which you enclose" assuredly
refers to Ingram's having returned to her one of her frequently written effusive
permissions for him to use in any way he chose the Poe materials she was
sending to him so regularly. But her reservations had been strongly stated and
implied in many other letters.

Mrs. Richmond died in Lowell on February 9, 1898, after having mourned
for Poe for nearly half a century.

Annie Richmond's correspondence with John Ingram had begun on
August 15, 1876, and it lasted nearly two years. From the first letter,
her correspondence was marked by warmth, excitement, trust, and
gratitude, and with pleasure which deepened into strong partisanship
and even affection. But after twenty-two valuable letters to Ingram,
with three more that her sister wrote, the correspondence, on Mrs.
Richmond's side, stopped abruptly.

Why had John Ingram permitted this to happen? It is this writer's
opinion that there really was no lack of understanding on Ingram's part
about Mrs. Richmond's sending him copies of her letters from Poe or
how she really expected him to use them; nor do I think he failed to
understand clearly the personal awkwardness that would result for her
when it became public, as it certainly did, that Poe was addressing
passionate love letters to her when she was the wife of another man and
he was engaged to marry another woman. But Poe's letters to Mrs.
Richmond and her personal revelations about Poe and Mrs. Clemm

were simply too valuable to Poe biography for Ingram to keep them hidden, or even to use them in the manner she had made quite clear she expected.

By deliberately betraying Mrs. Richmond's trust, Ingram added very much indeed to our knowledge of Poe's personal life and feelings, and he certainly generated much interest in his biography of Poe. Foremost of the valuable outcomes of this correspondence were the many letters that Ingram was given access to. Through Mrs. Richmond's impulsive generosity he got copies of more unpublished Poe letters than any biographer of Poe had or ever has had: she sent him complete copies of the eight letters she had left from Poe (some were "missing" through Mrs. Clemm's handling of them). Of these, Ingram published portions of seven in his *Appleton's Journal* article in May, 1878; in his *Life* in 1880, he reproduced these again, with a few changes in the texts, and added an eighth, a short note in which Poe described to Annie the successful lecture he had delivered in Providence on "The Poetic Principle." In addition to these personal letters, he was able, through her copies, to publish for the first time Poe's letter to William E. Burton, June 1, 1840, which established Poe's authorship of "The Journal of Julius Rodman," one of Ingram's most important discoveries in Poe's canon of writings. He could print, too, for the first time, a letter Poe had written to Mrs. Jane Ermina Locke on March 10, 1847, replying to her letter of sympathy regarding his wife's death and in which she had taken occasion to enclose some of her verses asking for his critical opinions of them. Another unpublished letter Ingram was able to print was Poe's plea to Sarah Heywood, Annie's sister, dated November 23, 1848, in which he implores her to get Annie to write to him. And finally, Ingram was the first to print Poe's letter of January 25, 1849, to Mrs. Sarah Helen Whitman (See Ostrom, II, 420–22), since Poe had enclosed it to Annie for mailing to Mrs. Whitman and Annie had made a copy of it, which she sent to Ingram.

Other discoveries that Ingram came to through Annie Richmond were of major import:

Evidence that there was more than one manuscript version of "The Bells," which really was the third version. Ingram got a copy of this.

Copies of Poe's manuscripts of "A Dream Within a Dream," "For Annie," and "El Dorado."

A hitherto unknown daguerreotype of Poe.

Information about uncollected Poe articles on "Chapters on Autography" and "secret writing."

Evidence that should dispel forever the "mystery" of what actually became of the trunk Poe left in Balitmore in 1849.

Information about an interesting and fairly reliable article about Poe by Mrs. John (Susan Archer Talley) Weiss.

Tender, sincere, loving recollections of Poe's appearance, personality, manners, and behavior that could have come from no other source so concerned and so trustworthy.

With all of these letters and facts, intimate descriptions and recollections from Mrs. Richmond, Ingram was able to write a long and interesting chapter called "Annie" in his *Life*, which certainly added to the value of his biography. The fact that he betrayed her trust in him and took advantage of her warm, impulsive nature can be regretted, but it must be remembered that because he did so he was able to add a glorious chapter to Poe biography.

VII
George W. Eveleth Adds His "Mite"

EARLY IN 1874 Ingram learned from Sarah Helen Whitman that George W. Eveleth of Lewiston, Maine, had corresponded with Poe and after Poe's death had become something of his self-appointed champion. Ingram addressed to Eveleth on March 10 the earnest appeal for help that appears in the biographical sketch of Ingram in this volume. Eveleth did not reply directly, but he did send Ingram's letter with added remarks of his own to William Hand Browne, editor of the *Southern Magazine*, in Baltimore. Browne published Ingram's letter in the magazine for October, 1874 (XV, 428–30), and added his appeal to Ingram's and Eveleth's for all persons who could aid in the work of redeeming Poe's name to put themselves in communication with Ingram. Browne himself became one of Ingram's most valuable and enthusiastic correspondents.

Four years later, on October 1, 1878, Eveleth answered Ingram's letter by mailing to him a package containing forty-four pages of closely written copies of letters, a bundle of newsclippings, some of which had been sent to him by Poe, and a copy of Poe's addenda to *Eureka.* The letters were copies of those, or extracts from them, that had been sent to Eveleth in reply to his questions; from 1850 to 1875 he had corresponded with Mrs. Clemm, Mrs. Lewis, Mrs. Ellet,* Miss Anne E. Lynch,* Mrs. Shelton, Mrs. Whitman, John H. B. Latrobe, John P. Kennedy, and James Wood Davidson, in his efforts to collect material to refute Griswold's scandals about Poe's life. Also, there was a copy of a letter Eveleth had addressed on October 7, 1877, to the editor of *Scribner's Monthly,* protesting the validity of an article about Poe's drinking habits that had been published in that magazine. However good his intentions, Eveleth in fact never did present to the public an organized defense of Poe. Perhaps this is the reason he went to the great trouble of copying his materials and sending them to Ingram.

Eveleth was originally from Maryland, but he was a student in the Maine Medical School at Brunswick and his home was in Phillips, Maine, when he began writing to Edgar Poe in 1845. During the next four years he wrote at least thirteen letters to Poe; his last letter was returned to Mrs. Clemm after Poe's death. Poe replied to Eveleth at least seven times. Had not this unusual correspondence taken place, we would be without much valuable information about Poe; for Eveleth was intensely interested in Poe as a person as well as an artist, and his many questions were direct and extremely candid. Poe replied to them surprisingly enough in high spirits and with remarkable candor himself; it seemed he enjoyed Eveleth's brashness, a challenge from a highly intelligent young student.

Eveleth included in the package to Ingram copies of six of the seven letters he had received from Poe; at another time he sent a copy of the first letter he received, a short note in which Poe returned Eveleth's subscription money for the *Broadway Journal*.

The newsclippings enclosed in Eveleth's package to Ingram are in the Ingram Poe Collection. Copies of Maria Clemm's letters to Eveleth have been reproduced in this volume as Letters 9, 10, 11, and 12. The remaining nineteen letters and portions of letters are here printed as Eveleth copied them for Ingram, not as Ingram printed portions of them in his volumes on Poe.

Eveleth was strangely unwilling to appear before the public in his own name. When he forwarded Ingram's first appeal to him for help to the *Southern Magazine* in 1874, he signed his letter to the editor as "E. V. Theglew," which is, of course, an anagram of his real name. When he sent his materials to Ingram in 1878, he gave full permission for their use but forbade the use of his name in connection with them. Instead, he chose to use the initials "H.B.W." in his letters to Ingram and in signing many of his interpolated comments within the letters themselves. Eveleth's own explanation of why he chose these particular initials is given at the close of his letter to Ingram accompanying his package of Poe materials and is here printed as he wrote it.

Bracketed comments signed "H.B.W." are Eveleth's. Editorial comment is, in this one instance in this volume, enclosed in double brackets.

Letter 66. Stella Anna Lewis, Brooklyn, N.Y., to George W. Eveleth. Copied by Eveleth from the autograph letter. First complete printing. [Item 82]

Jan. 3, 1854

Your letter is before me. I am happy to say that Mrs. Clemm has been a member of my family for several months. She is in every way comfortable.

I knew much of Poe. As I knew him, I will speak of him. In my presence, he was always the refined gentleman—the scholar—the Poet. I place him among the greatest minds that this country has produced. Let me know precisely what you are going to write, and I will furnish you with any biographical items in my possession.

I know Griswold. I do not think he is in consumption. *Though he may be.*

Please tell me what condition Neal's work is in at present.

My prenomen is *not* Sarah Anna—though once or twice thus printed. *It was a mistake.* It is Stella Anna, or Estella Anna.

It is my intention to place the remains of Mr. Poe and his wife in Greenwood Cemetery [[Brooklyn]]. *This much done,* I think the literary friends would erect a monument over them. What do you think of this plan?

Will you be in Maine next summer? Tell Mr. Neal I should like to see him before he writes. I should like to see you before you publish anything about Poe. Who wrote that in *Graham*, for Feb? (P.S. The portrait *of Poe* in his works is the best).

[John Neal, of Portland, Maine. He proposed to make a critical survey of American Literature in general. Poe being one of his subjects. The design was not carried out—H.B.W.]

Sarah Anna Robinson Lewis was a minor poetess and the wife of a Brooklyn lawyer, Sylvanus D. Lewis. The Lewis family lived at 125 Dean Street at the time Poe was acquainted with them. Poe reviewed very favorably Mrs. Lewis' poems, apparently because she had already advanced payment to Mrs. Clemm, and he addressed to Mrs. Lewis a sonnet entitled "An Enigma," which embodied a "riddle" that could be solved by juxtaposing the first letter of the first line with the second letter of the second line, and so on until "Sarah Anna Lewis" was spelled out. It is a poor specimen of Poe's art. Poe apparently disliked Mrs. Lewis, and she felt his dislike; but his finances were in worse shape than usual at this time, and he grasped at straws. Mrs. Lewis pledged herself to take care of Mrs. Clemm while Poe was to be in Richmond in the summer of 1849, and Poe did leave her at the Lewis' home when he said his last goodbye, on June 29, but that arrangement did not work out; after perhaps a week, Mrs. Clemm betook herself home to the cottage at Fordham. She did, however, live in the Lewis household at various times during the 1850s, until she unfortunately took Mr. Lewis' side in a family argument that he lost, whereupon Mrs. Lewis ejected her permanently. Mr. and Mrs. Lewis were divorced in 1858. Mrs. Lewis traveled on the Continent for a while, finally settling in England where she lived until her death on November 24, 1880; her body was returned to America for burial.

Rufus Griswold died of a "throat infection" on August 27, 1857. Mrs. Lewis' name *was* Sarah Anna; after publishing her poems several times, she decided her name was unsuited to her personality and "fame." Mr. Lewis paid Rufus Griswold to change her name in the notice of her poetry scheduled to appear in Griswold's forthcoming *The Female Poets of America*; Mrs. Lewis wanted to be known as Estelle Anna, and the type had already been set. She later vacillated between Estelle Anna and Stella Anna, and finally settled on Stella. Her plan to move Poe's remains from Baltimore to Greenwood Cemetery in Brooklyn never succeeded, although at one time Neilson Poe, who had been in charge of burying Poe in Westminster churchyard, gave his consent, if Mrs. Clemm desired it.

Letter 67.   **Stella Anna Lewis, Brooklyn, to George W. Eveleth.**
Copied by Eveleth. First complete printing. [Item 83]

11 Feb., 1854

Your's of the 21st Jan. is before me. I have not time to write the Sketch of Poe now. I will prepare it the first leisure moment.

I do not believe that he was a drunkard. I do not believe that he could have been a very vulgar man under any circumstances. That Despair did sometimes lay her dark clutch on his heart and drag him to the very precipice of insanity, I have no doubt. That he shed bitter tears—that he heaped fiery curses on the heads of Wrong and Perfidy, at such hours, I have no doubt. But when I recall the depth of my agony, when wrong and misrepresentation have wound up my nerves to their highest tension, and remember that he was thus finely organised, I wonder that he was able to comport himself as well as he did. *May the God of Heaven be merciful to all liars!*

Edgar Poe dined with me at 3 o'clock, P.M., on the 29th of June, 1849, and left at 5, the same afternoon, for Richmond, Virginia. He never returned to New York again. He died on the 7th of the Oct. following, while on his way from Richmond to meet his mother at my house. She waited for him one *long* week; but alas! he never came.

Ingram used portions of these letters from Stella Lewis both in his *Life of Poe* (1880) and in a highly derisive article he wrote twenty-seven years later, "Edgar Allan Poe and 'Stella'," published in the *Albany Review*, July, 1907 (I, 4, pp. 417–23). He followed his usual method by breaking the letters up at will, failing to use quotation marks, and generally using the texts to make it quite clear to his readers that he distrusted if not despised Mrs. Lewis. He certainly made it clear that her word could not be trusted about Poe and his family, either when she knew them at Fordham or in her verbal and written communications about them when he met her in London.

Letter 68. **Stella Anna Lewis, Brooklyn, to George W. Eveleth.**
Copied by Eveleth. First complete printing. [Item 86]

6 Nov., 1854

Your favor of the 16th ult. is at hand. . . .

After looking over a bushel of letters, I found one from you dated Jan. 23 and one, Mar. 1st. I am almost certain that I replied to both.

To the letter of Mar. 1st, I reply thus: 1. I was in the habit of seeing Mr. Poe once or twice a month from Jan. 1847, to the 29th of June, 1849, on which day he dined with me, as I have previously informed you. I did see him in March, 1848. He did not leave for the South in Aug., but in June, /49. His last letter to you was three days prior to his departure. 2. I did tell Griswold that Mr. Poe expressed a desire that he should become his editor, in case of his death. *I did this in compliance* with Mr. Poe's own request. He had great confidence in Griswold's editorial ability; and as they had become friends prior to Poe's departure for the South, I do not wonder at the *appointment*. I do not comprehend Griswold, therefore could not tell you what kind of man he is.

["Sketch of Poe" never came—H.B.W.]

In this letter there is indeed an important and heretofore virtually unknown fact to add to Poe biography: Stella Lewis here admits freely that she, as well as Mrs. Clemm, told Griswold that Poe wanted him to edit his works, in the event of his death. Ingram had this copy of her letter, used portions of it in his *Life*, II, 219–20, but he did not bring out this fact. Mrs. Clemm has alone borne the blame for delivering such a message to Griswold and, it would seem, quickly and eagerly delivering to Griswold all of Poe's literary remains. She did these things, but it now is clear that she was encouraged, as was Griswold, by Stella Lewis.

Mrs. Lewis might not have "comprehended" Griswold, but she was on his side of things, even after his *Memoir* of Poe appeared. But Griswold died in 1857; the climate of opinion about Poe's deeds and misdeeds slowly began to change, largely due to Ingram's publications and the publications he evoked. By the late 1870s Poe was considered a celebrated American poet, even if not quite a socially acceptable one in his time. Mrs. Lewis had little trouble in switching sides smoothly, and addressing the following letter to Ingram. This is a first complete printing [Item 344]:

> 8 Bedford Place Russell Square
> 15 April, [18]79

Dear Ingram,

I read your Memoir of Edgar A. Poe in Black's Complete Edition of his works with profound pleasure. It is a noble vindication of the genius and character of the most cruelly slandered man since Lord Byron.

I have heard that you are now writing an exhaustive Life of the Author of *"The Raven"*, in which Poem his name will live as long as the language.

I saw much of Mr. Poe during the last year of his life. He was one of the most sensitive, gentle, and refined gentlemen I ever knew.

My *child-Poem*—"The Forsaken", made us acquainted.

He had seen it floating the round of the Press, and wrote to tell me how much he liked it—"*It is inexpressibly beautiful*," he said, and I should like to know the young author."

After the first call, he frequently dined with us, and passed the evening in playing whist or in reading to me his last poem.

The day before he left New York for Richmond, he came to dinner and stayed the night. He seemed very sad, and retired early. On leaving the next morning, he took my hand in his, and looking in my face said, with tears in his eyes, "Dear Stella—my best and most beloved friend on this earth, the only being that truly understands and appreciates me—I have a presentiment that I shall never see you again.

I leave for Richmond at 2 P.M. today. If I never return, write my life. You *only* can do me justice."

"I will!" I exclaimed. And we parted to meet no more in this life.

You, Dear Ingram, have done it far better than I could.

You have nobly vindicated his character, and placed him in his true light before the world.[[The letter breaks off, unsigned.]]

In Mrs. Lewis' letter of February 11, 1854, to George W. Eveleth, she says, "Edgar Poe dined with me at 3 o'clock P.M. on the 29th of June, 1849, and left at 5, the same afternoon, for Richmond, Virginia." When she wrote this to Eveleth, only four years had passed since the event; but when she wrote to Ingram thirty years had elapsed, and Poe's last visit to her had become an overnight one and he had left in the morning, saying he was leaving for Richmond at 2 P.M.

Poe's letter to Mrs. Lewis telling her how much he liked her child-poem is unlocated.

Mrs. Lewis died in London on November 24, 1880. Her obituary was printed in the *Athenaeum*, December 4, 1880. It is unsigned, but Ingram wrote it.

Letter 69. **Elizabeth Frieze Ellet, New York, to George W. Eveleth.** Copied by Eveleth. First printing. [Item 87]

April 5, 1856

. . .I always understood that Mr. E. A. Poe, though a man of genius, was intemperate, and subject to attacks of lunacy. He was frequently in the asylum. . . .[Take notice that every statement of the author's bad *habits* is simple *hearsay*— H.B.W.]

Mrs. Elizabeth Frieze Lummis Ellet was a sentimental minor poetess and translator who pursued Poe with her attentions until he scorned her. She then became his bitter, implacable enemy, persecuting him relentlessly, vocally and in print. After his death, and until her own in 1877, she never ceased her attacks.

That Poe was intemperate at times, and perhaps emotionally unstable at others, it is needless to deny. But he was never confined in any asylum.

Letter 70. **Miss Anne C. Lynch, New York, to George W. Eveleth.** Copied by Eveleth. First printing. [Item 84]

March 8, 1854

In reply to your letter of Feb. 27th, I would say that for the last two or three years of Mr. Poe's life, I saw very little of him—in consequence of a wide difference of opinion between us in reference to his treatment of another lady.[1] During the time that he habitually visited me, a period of two or three years, I saw him almost always on my reception evenings, when many other guests were present; and my relations with him were rather superficial than intimate.

In answer to your queries as to his private habits, I can only say that I never saw him under the influence of wine; and, with the exception of his course towards the lady alluded to, I knew nothing personally of him that was discreditable or unworthy of his remarkable genius. Mrs. Sarah H. Whitman, of Providence, to whom he was engaged after the death of his wife, would probably be the person to give you any information you might desire in respect to him.

Mrs. Anne Charlotte Lynch Botta (November 11, 1815–March 23, 1891) contributed undistinguished prose and verse to various magazines in America. Poe attended the soirées held at her home in 116 Waverly Place, near Washington Square, New York City, in 1846. After her marriage in 1855 to Professor Vincenzo Botta, she became the brilliant and popular hostess of what has been termed America's first literary salon. At one period in her life she had lived in Providence, Rhode Island, and had known Sarah Helen Whitman quite

---

1. This "treatment of another lady" refers to Miss Lynch's being one of a party of three who called at Poe's house in Fordham with the intention of securing the letters written to Poe by Mrs. Frances S. Osgood. Poe's angry reaction and subsequent regret for his remarks are told in the editorial commentary at the end of this letter.

well. Mrs. Whitman characterized her to Ingram, in a letter dated June 25, 1875, as "eminently practical, enterprising, prudent, circumspect and cautious." On March 10, 1874, Mrs. Whitman had written Ingram that Miss Lynch (Mrs. Botta) was "very much afraid of being compromised socially and likes to keep the peace with everybody." The "wide difference of opinion" between Poe and Miss Lynch was over Poe's angry reaction to Mrs. Ellet's interference with his correspondence with Mrs. Frances Sargent Osgood. On a visit to the Poe cottage at Fordham, Mrs. Ellet had seen a letter from Mrs. Osgood to Poe lying opened on the table. Mrs. Ellet returned to the city and persuaded Mrs. Osgood to send Anne Lynch and Margaret Fuller* to Fordham to reclaim her letters. Outraged, Poe retorted to them, "Mrs. Ellet had better come and look after her own letters." The affair caused quite a stir. Sarah Helen Whitman identified Miss Lynch as one of the two ladies who had called on Poe for the purpose of recovering Mrs. Osgood's letters, but Miss Lynch denied, in the 1870s, that she had ever heard of the episode. It is obvious in this letter, written in 1854, and in those that follow, that Miss Lynch is anxious to disassociate herself from Poe and to shunt Eveleth over to Mrs. Whitman. In spite of Poe's admitted genius, it was not quite respectable in some circles, for many years after his death, to have one's name associated with his. Miss Lynch belonged to one of those circles.

Letter 71. **Miss Anne C. Lynch, New York, N.Y., to George W. Eveleth.** Copied by Eveleth. First printing. [Item 85]

March 19th, [18]54

In reply to your last, I regret that I am unable to give you any further satisfaction, since I am obliged to confess that I never read the *Memoir* written by Griswold, therefore cannot judge of the spirit in which it was written. I know Mr. Griswold, personally, but have not spoken with him in reference to Poe for a long time. I did not see Poe at all, after he became acquainted with Mrs. Whitman; and it was not to me that he made the remark alluded to, though I did hear of his making it to another in reference to Mrs. Whitman.

In society, so far as my observation went, Poe had always the bearing and manners of a gentleman—interesting in conversation, but not monopolising; polite and engaging, and never, when I saw him, abstracted or dreamy. He was always elegant in his toilet, quiet and unaffected, unpretentious, in his manner; and he would not have attracted any particular attention from a stranger, except from his strikingly intellectual head and features, which bore the unmistakable character of genius. As I said before, I had no particular intimacy with him myself, but those who had, or many who had, were personally attached, and some *devoted*, to him. For myself, I was never under the influence of the fascination which he exercised over many; and, while I liked him and appreciated his genius, it was always with a certain degree of coldness, or at least, not enthusiasm. If he had any faults, I, for one, would let the grave cover them and let them be "interred with his bones", and the light of his genius alone "live after him".   I do not believe that the interests of truth require that the aberrations of genius should be held up to the gaze and criticism of those who can appreciate only the faults and errors of genius.

Mrs. Whitman I know personally. I know that she had, at one time, certainly, the highest admiration and regard for Poe; and I have no doubt that you would receive from her many interesting facts connected with him.

It is difficult to believe that curiosity did not impel Miss Lynch to read Griswold's biography of Poe. She knew both Griswold and Poe quite well, and she could be certain that her name would be mentioned in it. Poe became acquainted with Sarah Helen Whitman in 1848. The "remark alluded to" was a slighting reference Poe was supposed to have made regarding his intentions of marrying Mrs. Whitman. Miss Lynch's word picture of Poe is especially pleasant and engaging, coming as it does from one who knew him well and saw him quite often during the last years of his life. Her remark about Poe's "intellectual head and features, which bore the unmistakable character of genius" echoes the age's preoccupation with phrenology. Miss Lynch's anxious disavowal of any intimacy with Poe or fascination with him fits poorly with this portion of Mrs. Osgood's letter, printed in the correspondence of Rufus Griswold (Cambridge, 1898, pp. 256–57) and reproduced in Quinn, p. 499: "It is too cruel that I, the only one of those literary women who did not seek his acquaintance,—for Mrs. Ellet asked an introduction to him and followed him everywhere, Miss Lynch begged me to bring him there and called upon him at his lodgings; Mrs. Whitman besieged him with valentines and letters long before he took any notice of her; and all the others wrote poetry and letters to him,—it is too cruel that I should be singled out after his death as the only victim to suffer from the slanders of his mother."

Miss Lynch is using in this letter to Eveleth the weapons of hauteur and pretended ignorance, or, if one prefers bluntness, lying, to try to dissociate her name from Poe's. She might have succeeded, too, had not her letters been so carefully preserved, to be collated with other letters written by members of her circle. Ironically, too, it is Poe's fame that has given her almost all of the literary notice she now has.

Letter 72. Sarah Elmira Shelton, Richmond, Va., to George W. Eveleth. Copied by Eveleth. First printing. [Item 78]

Richmond, Virginia
December 22nd, 1852

Your's of the 10th, together with a short communication from Mr. Nelson Poe, not received until yesterday, owing to my absence from the city.

My acquaintance with the person in question commenced at a very early period in my life. I have always felt a deep interest in him, and still have the deepest respect for his memory. I have every reason to believe that he has been misrepresented, but would beg to be excused from communicating anything which might bring me before the public in any form whatever.

A few weeks since, I received a letter from Mrs. Clemm, similar to those sent to yourself; and I intend, as soon as an opportunity offers, to render her some assistance.

Sarah Elmira Royster possibly was Poe's boyhood sweetheart and it is possible they considered themselves engaged to be married when he left Richmond to enter the University of Virginia in February, 1826; however, when he returned to Richmond in December, he found her engaged to marry Mr. Shelton, whom she did marry when she was seventeen. Twenty-two years later Poe certainly asked her to marry him, for she was a widow with property and he was desperately following Mrs. Shew's advice to marry a woman strong enough and fond enough to take care of him and his affairs. After Poe's death, Mrs.

Shelton denied that she and Poe were planning to be married, but she certainly adopted a daughter-in-law-to-be attitude and tone in her letter to Mrs. Clemm on September 22, 1849 (see Quinn, 634–35). Her polite but definite refusal, in her letter to Eveleth, to allow her name to be used in connection with Poe's, or, for that matter, even to name Poe in her letter, may reflect, in part, the Virginia gentlewoman's traditional shrinking from public notice, but perhaps it indicates more strongly how aware she was of the unpleasant notoriety surrounding Poe's name in 1852. Twenty-eight years later Poe's literary fame was firmly established, and her attitude had changed markedly, when she wrote the following letter to Ingram: First printing. [Item 356]

> 414 North 10th Street
> Richmond, Virginia
> June 30th 1880

Mr. J. H. Ingram
Dear Sir:

    I take the earliest opportunity to acknowledge the receipt of your valuable, (and to me) very interesting book, on The Life, Letters, and Opinions of The Lamented Edgar A. Poe—I should have done so before this, but my health is extremely delicate, and I have been very sick recently—I assure you, that I am reading it, with deep interest, and find much in it, which revives many *sad* remembrances, as well as *very pleasant* ones, and am glad (after so many years) that one, has been found, to do him the justice, which he, (I believe) truly deserves—Please accept my warmest thanks, and believe me (Dear Sir)

> Yours Very truly
> Sarah E. Shelton

Mrs. Shelton died in Richmond in 1888, and was buried in Shockoe Hill Cemetery. The letter Mrs. Shelton mentions having received from Mrs. Clemm certainly contained a request for money, and since it was similar to those sent to Eveleth, the elisions he made in Mrs. Clemm's letters that he copied for Ingram must have been those requests.

    Mrs. Shelton did not respond as often or as generously as did Mrs. Whitman to Mrs. Clemm's pressuring letters, a fact that did not go unnoticed or uncommented upon by Mrs. Clemm.

Letter 73. **John H. B. Latrobe, Baltimore, to George W. Eveleth.** Copied by Eveleth. First complete printing. [Item 77]

Dec. 7th, 1852

I have your note of yesterday referring to Mr. Griswold's statement of the circumstances under which the late Edgar A. Poe received the prize offered by the *Baltimore Saturday Visiter*, at the hands of a committee, of which I was a member.

The point to which you call attention particularly, is the assertion that "it was unanimously decided that the prizes should be paid to the first of geniuses who had written legibly. Not another manuscript was unfolded." [[See Griswold's *Memoir*, xii]].

Certainly, the fact is not as is here asserted. I cannot be mistaken; for I was the reader on the occasion. The Mss., as received from the Editor, were laid in a pile upon the table. Each one was opened, as it came to hand. Sometimes, the first few sentences would condemn it as unworthy. Sometimes several pages were borne with. In some cases, the whole production was read. Two only of the prose pieces were laid aside for re-examination. I recollect them well. One was clever, but *watery*—evidently a woman's work. The other was terse—and the denouement terribly original. The poems were treated in the same way. But two of these were put by for review—one, "The Coliseum," by Poe; the other, to which the prize was awarded, by Mr. J. H. Hewitt,* though the authorship was not known till afterward. The loose Mss. having been gone through, I turned to the *Book*, which contained many tales, and *read it from beginning to end*. It was so far—so very far—superior to anything else before us, that we had no difficulty in awarding the first prize to the author. Our only difficulty was in selecting from the rich contents of the volume. We took the "MS. Found in a Bottle."

This was eighteen years ago, about. But the impression made on my mind by the wonderful power and originality of the writer is as vivid as an occurrence of yesterday. The calligraphy, to which Mr. Griswold refers, was certainly remarkable. It was not *writing*—it was *printing* with a pen. But it imparted no interest to the productions in the volume. It formed no part of the consideration on which the prize was bestowed—so far, at least, as I understood at the time, and now believe. The prize was recognized, and given, as the right of Genius. I have taxed my memory more than once, since Mr. Griswold's *Memoir* first appeared; but I can recall nothing that corresponds with his statement of the grounds on which Mr. Poe received the prize—not one thing.

The author of a new style, if it is a good one, or even, an exciting one, gives to us a new taste, which craves nourishment of the same sort—Originality creates its market, only to destroy it. The "MS. Found in a Bottle," "The Maelstrom", "The Murders of the Rue Morgue" are now every-day affairs [if the *letter* of the declaration carries the exact *spirit* intended, I enter a *dissent*—H.B.W.] To the Committee they were novelties, for which they were wholly unprepared. Hence, the admiration which, I well remember, the reading of them produced.

In this statement, I hardly think I can be mistaken, so far as the action of the Committee can be looked upon as a recognition of Mr. Poe's merits. Mr. Kennedy sent for him at once, and became his most valued friend. At my instance [*sic*], he called upon me sometimes, and entered at length into the discussion of subjects on which he proposed to employ his pen. When he warmed up, he was most eloquent. He spoke, at that time, with eager action; and, although, to judge from his outward mien, the world was then going hard with him, and his look was blasé, yet his appearance was forgotten, as he seemed to forget the world around him, as wild fancy, logical truth, mathematical analysis and wonderful combination of facts flowed, in strange commingling, from his lips, in words choice and appropriate, as though the result of the closest study. I remember being particularly struck with the power that he seemed to possess of identifying himself with whatever he was describing. He related to me all the facts of a voyage to the Moon, I think (which he proposed to put upon paper), with an accuracy of minute detail, and a truthfulness as regard philosophical phenomena, which impressed you with the idea that he had himself just returned from the journey, that existed only in his imagination.

I have been led into this detail, as a corroboration of my impression that Mr. Poe's merits as an author, on the occasion referred to were certainly not overlooked in the Committee's regard for his penmanship.

Here was victory indeed for John Ingram! He now had *written proof*, from an unimpeachable source, that Griswold *had lied* about Poe! And Ingram used this testimony for all it was worth, over and over again, in his future publications about Poe.

John Hazlehurst Boneval Latrobe was a lawyer, an inventor, and a distinguished public servant in Baltimore; he was joined on the committee to award the prizes offered by the Baltimore *Saturday Visiter*, by an equally distinguished lawyer, John Pendleton Kennedy, and J. H. Miller.

Poe always insisted that he did not win the prize offered for the best poem was simply that his tale had already been selected for the prize offered for prose, "A MS Found in a Bottle." When the winner of the prize for poetry, Henry Wilton, with a poem called "The Song of the Winds," was revealed to be John Hill Hewitt, an editor of the *Saturday Visiter* submitting an entry under a pseudonym, Poe was indignant.

The book containing "many tales" was Poe's unpublished "Tales of the Folio Club." Poe's handwriting has always excited much admiration; the beauty and symmetry of it certainly helps account for so many of his letters having been carefully preserved.

Letter 74. **John P. Kennedy, Baltimore, to George W. Eveleth.**
Copied by Eveleth. First complete printing. [Item 80]

Baltimore, Maryland
April 13, 1853

. . . .I had no time last winter, to write to you on the subject of your inquiries about Poe [He was, at the time, one of the President's Secretaries—Sec. of the Navy, I think—H.B.W.]. I coincided in the statement Latrobe sent me; and I suppose he so informed you.

As to the other questions respecting Poe, I can not say much. I lost sight of him after he broke off from Mr. White.* I have heard stories that he was dissipated and given to drink. White told me he could not be relied on for work; and Burton* has told me the same.

I did not see him when he was last in Baltimore, and know nothing of the facts to which you refer.

Excuse the brevity of this—I am too much of an invalid to write without pain.

Here, from a second eminent, highly respected man was corroborative evidence that Griswold had lied deliberately in his account of Poe's winning the 1833 *Saturday Visiter* prize for the best prose tale. Ingram was delighted. The rest of Kennedy's remarks about White's and Burton's testimony as to Poe's unreliability on the job, Ingram ignored.

John Pendleton Kennedy was a biographer, novelist, and an eminent lawyer. He had been of material help to Poe in Baltimore, after helping to award the prize to him, and had been instrumental in getting Poe his first job on a magazine, Thomas W. White's newly started *Southern Literary Messenger* in Richmond.

"Burton" was William E. Burton, owner and editor of *Burton's Gentleman's Magazine*.

Letter 75. **James Wood Davidson, New York, to George W. Eveleth.** Copied by Eveleth. First complete printing. [Item 101]

28th May 1866

I have just read the memoranda in *The Old Guard* for June [[1866]] under the title of "Poe and his Biographer, Griswold". I am grateful to you for putting in this form what I always felt to be true—that *so* much of Griswold's *Memoir* is utterly *untrue*. The fires of truth are gathering round, closer and closer, hemming in to consume him—this serpent-biographer —this Reverend Memoirist. I feel as if you had done *me* a personal favor; and you *have*, for somehow Poe-truth is personal to me.

Ingram could relish and respect this language! James Wood Davidson (1829–1905) was an author and journalist in Columbia, South Carolina , until his library was burned during Sherman's march to the sea. After the war, Davidson migrated to Washington, D.C. and then to New York City, where at one time he was a staff member of the New York *Evening Post.* He published *Living Writers of the South* in 1869. Much interested in Ingram's efforts to redeem

Poe's name, he became one of Ingram's most devoted helpers in the United States, and was himself active in print in Poe's defense: in November, 1857, he had published "Edgar Allan Poe," a thirteen-page unsigned article in *Russell's Magazine* (II, 2, pp. 161–73);[2] on September 27, 1860, he had published a broadside of thirty-four lines addressed "To Mrs. M.C."—The "More than Mother" of Edgar Poe;[3] and in 1871, *ca.* March 20, he published in the New York *Home Journal* a three-quarter column obituary of Maria Clemm, entitled "Poe's Guardian Angel."[4] Mrs. Clemm had died in Baltimore on February 16, 1871. Eveleth's series of letters to editors, paragraphs, and short articles in Poe's defense had begun even before Poe's death.

Letter 76. **James Wood Davidson, New York, to George W. Eveleth.** Copied by Eveleth. First complete printing. [Item 105]

8th Feb. 1869

. . . Mrs. Clemm told me, years ago, that E. A. Poe never was out of America, except while at Dr. B's school—that it was his *brother* who was the actor in the St. Petersburg affair—that he (E.A.) permitted the error to continue, from motives of delicacy, in that it was rather a *rum* affair—that St. P. bout. In connection with this view, do me the favor to remember (1) that such a course toward his brother was eminently in keeping with his mental bent; (2) that it is hard to fix upon a *convenient time* for this episode; (3) that he cared not a button for the Greeks, and still less, if possible, for liberty; (4) that he never *mentions* it; and (5) that St. Petersburg does not lie in the way of one going from *America* to *Greece*.

Griswold had written in his *Memoir* that Poe had been arrested for dissolute behavior in St. Petersburg, Russia, and had been rescued from the consequences by the American minister to St. Petersburg, Mr. Middleton of South Carolina. Ingram had had the files of the American consulate in St. Petersburg searched by staff members, but they had found no reference to Edgar or

2. [Item 525]
3. [Item 528]
4. [Item 555]

William Henry Leonard Poe. It is extremely doubtful that either was ever in Russia.

But for Ingram's purposes, this letter was a welcome addition to the bulk of evidence he was building against Griswold. It added strength from another source that Griswold's derogatory statements about Poe's personal behavior were all suspect. But Griswold had known what he was doing, for there was just enough truth in some of his statements about Poe to make it extremely difficult to clear Poe of *all* complicity in *all* of his charges. He had not, of course, counted on an English lad of eight years who would devote his life to proving him to be a liar and a forger.

"Dr. B." was Dr. Bransby, Headmaster of the Stoke Newington school which Poe attended while living in England with the Allan family.

Letter 77. James Wood Davidson, New York, to George W. Eveleth. Copied by Eveleth. First complete printing. [Item 114]

26th Nov., 1872

. . . concerning Poe's *Eureka*, I once felt that I knew what he means in it, but am not sufficiently familiar now to give you any clear reply to your criticism. It strikes me, however, I am free to confess, that the criticism is well put, and the point well taken. [The matter objected against is to be found in my friend's *Living Writers of the South*—page 464—in this passage:—"The author of *Eureka* held that the Creator of the Universe is '*one, individual, unconditional, irrelative and absolute Particle Proper*', which, by radiation, fills its sphere—the universe—with subdivisions of itself." My point was that *matter* and *mind*—the *particles created* and the the *Creator* of them—are kept entirely distinct all through the work quoted from—that Poe, himself, says, reverently, in substance:—"*Of the awful nature of the ether (the Soul) separating the distributed atoms, I venture not to speak*"—H.B.W.]

As to your own chirograph, you know that we—Mrs. Whitman and I—regarded it as almost identical with Poe's. That says a great deal. I think that your hand indicates less *ego-personality* than his; consequently you should bring in—lug in—personalities far less than he did. [Here, too, I have a *criticising* suggestion to throw in. The chirograph-reader has taken, unwittingly, of course, the very cue supplied to him by the Griswold *School of Memorialists*. He implies a charge that Poe was accustomed to *"lug in" himself* on on every possible occasion. Where, except in that School, does he get his support for the charge? *Not* in his own prior remark touching the same subject. On page 348 of *Living Writers* is this opinion:—"Captain McCabe's chirograph is one of the finest that I have seen. It indicates liberal and careful culture, an acutely sensitive aesthetical mind, and more originality than any other young writer in the South. In the quality of isolation of mind and in the faculty of *forgetting* personalities" (the italics are mine) "in literary estimates, and in literary work generally, I have not seen it surpassed since Edgar A. Poe." *There* we have the Chief of Egotists; *here*, the Standard of Impersonalities!—H.B.W.].

Stoddard's article in *Harper* is very readable. In a private letter since, he writes me:—"If I hadn't *seen* Poe personally, I don't know that I should believe in his existence." [This reference to that article, which I purpose to send to you, Mr. Ingram, gives excuse for another parenthesis. Stoddard employs the adjective "brutal", in commenting upon *The Literati of New York City*. I feel sure that the expression was not chosen in any, even remote, connection with a careful reading of the subject of the commentary, but was caught, as a kind of *parrott-echo* from the Griswold—*Chimney Sweepings* —H.B.W.].

Poe's *Eureka* had been published in the summer of 1848, probably in June. Eveleth was much interested in it, and in his letters to Poe he questioned sharply many of Poe's ideas expressed therein. In replies, Poe discussed his ideas and sent to Eveleth an addenda to *Eureka*. Eveleth was very proud of his handwriting resembling Poe's. Poe's series of personality sketches, *The Literati of New York City*, ran serially in *Godey's Lady's Book* from May through October, 1846.

Letter 78. **Sarah Helen Whitman, Providence, R.I., to George W. Eveleth.** Copied by Eveleth. First complete printing. [Item 96]

Dec. 15th, 1864

I left Providence for New York the day after I sent you the little volume—*Edgar Poe and his Critics*—and have been at home only a few days. I am glad to know that it interested you, as I learn by a letter from Phillips which I found on my return.

The quotation from Mr. Poe's writings which you have italicised, you will find in the *Tale of the Ragged Mountains*. I almost despaired of finding it, and had looked all through the *Marginalia* and the stories of *Ligeia, Morella, Eleanora* and *Berenice*, when I happened to remember some analogous speculations and experiences in the tale first named; and *there* I found the passage.

I cannot tell you, for I do not know, the time when the *marginal* note [numbered *sixteen* in Griswold's Collection—H.B.W.], to which you refer was first published.

You will have learned, from my little *offering*, how little reliance can be placed on Dr. Griswold's *Memoir*—I have abundant proof that Griswold *purposely falsified every anecdote and altered nearly every purported note or assumed Ms of his much maligned author*. The reason of his treachery is indicated in my work. I have been permitted to see a note which he wrote to a friend in New York, in the spring of 1850, in which he says:—"I am getting on rapidly with my *Life of Poe*, and *am trying hard to do him justice; for Fanny's* (Frances Sargent Osgood's) *spirit looks down on me while I write.*" The task was evidently too great for him. He could not forgive Poe the interest which he inspired in the person he [Griswold] most wished to please.

You will perhaps remember a paragraph in the *Memoir* in which it is said:—"He would have graduated with the highest honors, had not his gambling, intemperance and other vices induced his expulsion from the University". This passage, blindly accepted on the authority of Griswold, has passed through nearly all the European reviews, and has been again and again cited in proof of Poe's early and hopeless depravity. I have been favored with the perusal of letters from Dr. Maupin, Mr. Wertenbaker and other gentlemen of the Faculty of Charlottesville University, in which they affirm that he never at any time came under the censure of the University and that he did not *graduate* there, simply because the University, at that time, *conferred no degree*. I have also in my possession a letter from one of his class-mates (Mr. John Willis, of Orange County, Virginia), written on the 8th of April, 1861, confirmatory of their favorable statements.

In turning over the volume of "Tales" and "Poems", to find the passage quoted in your letter, I paused to read again a short sketch called "Landor's Cottage", with which some interesting memories are, in my mind, associated. In one of Mr. Poe's earlier letters to me, he spoke of the "Domain of Arnheim" as embodying some of his most interior and familiar tastes and aspirations. Two months afterward, while sitting with me in a room whose very simple and inexpensive arrangement and decoration seemed to charm his fancy, he expressed to me his intention of writing a "pendant" to the "Domain", in which the most charming effects should be attained by artistic combinations of familiar and unvalued materials. I remember that he noticed the delicate tints of the paper on the wall and spoke of the fine relief it gave to the pictures and to an antique oval mirror framed with ever-greens. When his collected stories were published, after his death, I saw, for the first time, "Landor's Cottage"—*A Pendant to the Domain of Arnheim*", and found that he had introduced into it the paper he had praised so much, with its "silver ground and faint-green cord running zig-zag through-out". I do not know whether the story (or sketch) had been previously published, but think *not*.

About my theory of the "correlation" and derivation of surnames (which furnished you with a theme for a humorous and ingenious article in one of the New York periodicals, some years ago), I might present a very plausible *show*, which might at least serve to amuse you. Assuming, for the present, a common derivation for the names *Poe* and *Poer*, which can be incontestibly established, I would remind you that Mark Anthony Lower, in his work on surnames, states that the name of *Power* [Mrs. Whitman's maiden name—H.B.W.], variously written as *Le Poer*, *Power*, *Poure*, and *Poore*, is of Norman origin. Gilbert de la *Poree* was the philosophical friend and colleague of Abelard. Again, the French Memoirs speak of

Gilbert *Poret*. Now, from *Poret* to P'ret the transition is easy—don't you see? [The name of my mother before her marriage was *Pratt*. I had traced this, and kindred words, to the Dutch *prat*, and so on, through various connections, to the Welsh *pert*, which, by transposition of the letters, becomes *pret*; and, upon the strength of the *literal* similarities, had claimed *blood*-relationship to her and Poe—H.B.W.].

Sarah Helen Power Whitman (1803–1878) was a highly intelligent poetess of Providence, Rhode Island. She was married in 1828 to a young lawyer who died in 1833. She was nearly forty-five when she met Poe and was seemingly content caring for her mother and mentally unbalanced sister, writing her verses, and sharing in the intellectual and literary life of her time. She was on friendly if not intimate terms with the more important literati of the day. After her brief engagement to Poe was dissolved in 1848, and his death in 1849, she became an ardent champion of Poe's reputation, working for many years with various would-be biographers, vainly hoping some one of them would one day be able to mitigate the slanders Griswold had so securely fastened to Poe's name. Her "little volume" forwarded to Eveleth was her book *Edgar Poe and his Critics*, dated 1860, but actually brought out late in 1859. Dr. Socrates Maupin, presiding officer of the University of Virginia faculty, directed William Wertenbaker, the university librarian (who had known Poe) on May 12, 1860, to draw up a statement about Poe's scholarship and behavior at the university in 1826. Included in this statement was the fact that Poe was entered on the university register as having been born on January 19, 1809. On May 22, 1860, Dr. Maupin appended a note attesting the validity of Wertenbaker's statements. Mrs. Whitman received these letters, or copies of them, from Sallie E. Robins, a young Ohio enthusiast who planned to write a complete vindication of Poe. "Landor's Cottage" had been published in *The Flag of Our Union* on June 9, 1849, before its inclusion in Griswold's edition.

Letter 79. **Sarah Helen Whitman, Providence, to George W. Eveleth.** Copied by Eveleth. First complete printing. [Item 98]

Jan. 15th, 1865

. . . It gratifies me that you liked my defense of "The Raven" [her appellation for the author of the poem thus entitled—H.B.W.], and that you read again the stories— *Ligeia*, *Eleonora*, etc.,—"with renewed interest", also that you found them enlightened by the "spiritual rays" thrown on them by my suggestions. It is strange that, in no notice of my book have I ever seen, an allusion, the most distant, to *this* part of the volume, which, to me, is the most significant and important feature in it [the feature associating Poe, somehow, with "spirit-manifestations"—H.B.W.]. Do you remember that I once wrote you a letter, in answer to some enquiries and suggestions of your's, in which I spoke of the strange spiritual energy or effluence which seemed to surround or ensphere "The Raven", and which acted on those who were *en-rapport* with him enhancing and intensifying the spiritual faculties of insight an impression, which suddenly flashed on me while in his presence, of the original identity of the names *Power* and *Poe*, an impression which I told you was afterward corroborated, if not authenticated? [The substance of her statement was that she was sitting with her eyes down-cast; that, upon the coming of the sudden thought, she looked up and met the fixed, intent gaze of Poe; and that, when she expressed to him her conviction of their kinship, he said:—"Helen, you startle me—therewith hangs a history!" Then he went into the *genealogy* already indicated—H.B.W.].

Mrs. Whitman was a firm believer in spirit manifestations and spiritualism in general, but she was careful not to associate herself with the then popular seances and mediums. Poe's humoring and playing up to her beliefs was, of course, part of his courtship.

Ingram had small patience with Mrs. Whitman's ideas about spiritualism; once when she told him that she had three initial letters that a spirit hand had written for her, he informed her bluntly that he wanted to hear no more of the matter.

Letter 80.   Sarah Helen Whitman, Providence, to George W. Eveleth. Copied by Eveleth. First complete printing. [Item 99]

Feb. 27th, 1865

You ask so many questions in your letter of the 19th, that I am at a loss where to begin with my answers. Perhaps it were best to take them in their order.—

Thirdly, "The Raven" *was* written before my acquaintance with its author. I think the line about the footfalls was altered by Mr. Poe himself, from the earlier version.

Fourthly: It is true, I believe, that Mr. Poe first saw me in 1845, when passing a night in Providence, on his way from Boston to New York. I think it was not after the delivery of his poem before the Boston Lyceum, but earlier in the season. Probably Dr. Griswold learned all that he knew of the matter from Mrs. Osgood, who was at the hotel in Providence, where Mr. Poe stopped on that "July midnight." Her account of the incident, given me in the autumn of 1848, agreed with what Mr. Poe had himself told me. Mrs. Osgood informed me that the night was exceedingly hot and sultry; that Mr. Poe told her, in the morning, he had passed the greater part of the night in rambling over the hills that command a fine view of the City from the east; that, at a late hour, he passed the house where I then lived, whose situation he had previously ascertained from her, and saw me walking up and down the lime-shaded side-walk in the neighborhood of my home. He told her that I wore a white dress, with a thin white shawl or scarf thrown over my head, and that he knew me through her description of me. The moon was at, or near, the full. I knew nothing of his having seen me at that time, till the summer of 1848, when he sent me, anonymously, the poem (in Ms) beginning:—"I saw thee once, once only—". About the same time (I think it was in June, 1848), he wrote a letter to my friend, Miss Anna Blackwell, then spending the summer in Providence, speaking of his interest in my writings, and saying that he had once seen me. In allusion to the "July Midnight", Mr. Poe afterward wrote:—"The poem which I sent you contains all the incidents of a dream which occurred to me soon after I first saw you".

Fifthly: Am I not "younger" than the "grim and ancient Raven"? If I am to believe the assertions of my "friends, lovers and countrymen", generally, I should answer "Yes." If I am to believe the written asservations of "The Raven", in particular, I should still answer, "Yes". But if I am to believe the figures, somewhat variously stated, of Dr. Griswold I should answer, "No." Or, if I am to believe "The Raven's" age to be correctly given by himself in the matriculation books of the University of Virginia, which made him four years older than (one of) the dates given by Dr. Griswold, I should still answer, "No". Or, more especially, If I am to believe the partially obscured date on the torn fly-leaf of an old family Bible, just come to light, I should say that I am, at least *ten years older*. The fly-leaf seems to indicate that I was born on the 19th of January 1803. The figure 3 is, to be sure, a little indefinite, and might be construed as an *8* or a *0* (an *eight* or a *naught*); but the three first figures *1 8 0*, are perfectly distinct, and would seem to show, *conclusively*, that I was born sometime within the present century. You will perceive, from what I have told you, that "The Raven" himself was of a very *"uncertain age"*, and seems at times to have affected the Mephistophelian longevity of Cagliostro, Cartaphilus, and other wandering Jew-ish *celebrities*.

Poe saw Mrs. Whitman for the first time in the summer of 1845, but he did not speak to her. He was in Providence, busily pursuing Mrs. Frances S. Osgood. He sent the manuscript of his second poem, later named "To Helen," to Mrs. Whitman early in June, 1848; his first meeting with her took place on September 21, 1848.

Poe's letter to Anna Blackwell, an English poetess he had met in New York City, was dated June 14, 1848; Miss Blackwell was spending the summer in Providence.

Poe's lecture before the Boston Lyceum was delivered on the evening of October 16, 1845.

On occasions, Poe gave 1809, 1811, and 1813 as the years of his birth. The matter was finally settled by Ingram in 1874, who, helped by documents sent to him by Mrs. Whitman, proved that Poe was actually born in 1809.

Mrs. Whitman's delightful persiflage notwithstanding, her date of birth was January 19, 1803, making her exactly six years older than Poe.

Letter 81. **Sarah Helen Whitman, Providence, to George W. Eveleth.** Copied by Eveleth. First complete printing. [Item 100]

Jan. 17, 1866

—I cannot, I think, stay long on this "bank and shoal of time." Before I go, I wish to put into your hand the accompanying statement about one of Griswold's myths. It is a statement which I have made, *in writing*, to but one person—and that one has met with a sad, strange fate; and the record is lost in oblivion. A rough sketch of it, made in 1860, follows. If you will, at some time when you are quite at leisure, copy it for me, and send me the copy, I shall be glad:—

To S.E.R.*—Dear Sir: It is not a little singular that, within a few days of your note, enclosed to me by Messrs. [[Rudd & Carleton]], of New York, I received a note from a gentleman of Philadelphia (who was to have been associated with Mr. Poe in the publication of *The Stylus*), announcing that he had prepared, and was intending soon to publish, a vindication of Edgar Poe. I do not think, from its scope and purpose, it will very soon make an appearance in print. He questioned me in regard to some of the charges brought against Mr. Poe by Dr. Griswold, and especially with respect to the story of *his riotous conduct at the house of a New England lady, rendering necessary a summoning of the police, etc., etc!!*

You will have seen that some of the critics of my little book have chosen to assume that, since I make no reference to this pleasant and piquant fiction, the story was undoubtedly a true one! If I had not wished my vindication of Edgar Poe to be entirely impersonal, in so far as regarded my own relations to him, I could most certainly have acquitted him of all the grosser charges brought against him in this most improbable narrative.

Mr. Poe came to Providence, on the occasion alluded to, by invitation of the Providence Lyceum, to deliver the second lecture of their course (Daniel Webster having delivered the first). Before leaving New York, Mr. Poe said to a lady of that city:—"I am going, this evening, to Providence". "To be married, I learn", rejoined the lady. "No—to deliver a lecture before the Providence Lyceum". On this slender foundation Dr. Griswold raised a fabric—a temple of fame—that has made me immortal—"You will go down to posterity", said a witty friend, "as the *brilliant New England lady who sent her Raven lover to prison on the evening of her bridal*".

Now for the *facts* of the case. In an interview with Mr. Poe, some three or four weeks previous to the giving of this lecture, he had vehemently urged me to an immediate marriage. As an additional reason for *delaying* a marriage which, under any circumstances, seemed to all my friends full of evil portents, I read to him some passages from a letter which I had recently received from one of his New York associates. He seemed deeply pained at the result of our interview, and left me abruptly, saying that, if we should meet again, it would be as strangers. He passed the evening in a bar-room of his hotel, and, after a night of delirious phrenzy, returned the next day to my mother's house in a state of great mental excitement and suffering, declaring that his welfare for time and eternity depended on me. A physician—Dr. A. H. Oakie—was sent for, by my mother, who, perceiving indications of brain-fever, advised his removal to the house of his friend W. J. Pabodie, of this city, where he was kindly cared for until his recovery. The incident naturally caused much talk and gossip, and was, I suppose, the basis of Dr. Griswold's distorted statement. "Only this, and nothing more."

It was soon after his return to New York, that he wrote me, in reference to these events, under date of Nov. 24, 1848, the words I have quoted on the 74th page of my book.

This further proof of Griswold's lying, *written out by the lady referred to* in Griswold's *Memoir* simply made Ingram's case against him the stronger.

Mrs. Whitman received a number of warning letters from various "friends" about the inadvisability of her marrying Poe. She was much influenced by her mother's strong opposition to the match also.

The statement in writing to "S.E.R." was to Sallie E. Robins. Her note to Mrs. Whitman was forwarded by Mrs. Whitman's New York publishers, Rudd & Carleton, as was John Ingram's first letter to that lady, in late 1873.

Thomas Cottrell Clarke was the "gentleman from Philadelphia" who was to have joined Poe in publishing the *Stylus* and who was gathering information also for a vindication of Poe's name; his plans did not materialize either.

William J. Pabodie was really a close friend and perhaps ardent admirer of Mrs. Whitman's. He was Poe's courteous host on his visits to Providence.

Mrs. Whitman eagerly looked forward to her death, or "de-materialization," as the spiritualists preferred to call it; but in spite of these anticipatory remarks, she still had twelve and a half years left to live. Death came for her on June 27, 1878.

Letter 82. **Sarah Helen Whitman, Providence, to George W. Eveleth.** Copied by Eveleth. First complete printing. [Item 103]

March 2nd, 1867

—You spoke of a paragraph in *The Round Table* in relation to "The Mystery of Marie Roget". By a strange coincidence, just after receiving your letter, I happened to see a number of that paper lying on the table of a friend. I borrowed it, and, on reverting to your letter, found that it was the one to which you referred me as containing your paragraph. It was the *only* copy of *The Round Table* that had ever chanced to fall my way!

Mr. Poe told me the fact there stated by you, and stated, moreover, that the name of the young "naval officer" was Spencer. I had entirely forgotten this, till your item brought it to my mind.

Poe had told Eveleth in his letter of January 4, 1848, that the "naval officer who committed the murder (rather, the accidental death arising from an attempt at abortion) *confessed* it. . . ."

Poe had evidently told Mrs. Whitman the same thing, and Eveleth's unlocated paragraph almost certainly was built around this fact concerning Poe's "The Mystery of Marie Rogêt."

Letter 83. **Sarah Helen Whitman, Providence, to George W. Eveleth.** Copied by Eveleth. First complete printing. [Item 173]

Sept. 30th, 1874

In your letter of Aug. 2nd, you asked whether I considered the picture of Poe, given with Stoddard's biographical sketch in *Harper's Magazine*, like him, as I knew him. It was taken from an engraving, which engraving was taken from a photograph which *does* resemble him, though never to me a satisfactory likeness; but in the woodcut in *Harper*, an impression from the steel engraving, all likeness is lost. Poe had two daguerreotypes taken in Providence, one of which will appear in Mr. Ingram's volume.[5] *He* thinks the engraving good. I hope it will prove so. This picture was once lithographed and enlarged by a Boston picture-dealer, I think, though the lithograph bears the name of a French artist. I have a copy of the enlarged lithograph, also a photograph of a *carte visite* size, which I had taken by a Providence photographer, last winter, from the large lithograph. But it gives no adequate idea of Poe's beautiful face and head. I will enclose you one—but, remember, it is *not good*. [I do, and shall, to the end of all the chapters, "remember" this, at any rate—that it is no true lens through which for *me* to peer into the wondrous, far-down depths of the mind-and-soul of him with whom I *thought* I was somewhat acquainted (from his writings, only—not personally), as "Edgar Allan Poe." If it is, really, a likeness of *any* Poe, I trust *not that one*—H.B.W.].

When Eveleth writes of the small photograph Mrs. Whitman sent to him being "a likeness of *any* Poe," he is toying with the fantastic idea that perhaps when Edgar posed for the picture, the likeness of his brother William Henry Leonard was actually recorded by the photographer! See Letter 84.

Letter 84. **Sarah Helen Whitman, Providence, to George W. Eveleth.** Copied by Eveleth. First complete printing. [Item 266]

Nov. 30th, 1875

I was very glad to receive your letter of the 19th inst. reminding me that I had not yet replied to your's of a year ago.

I think I can answer all your questions satisfactorily; and will do so *seriatim*.

In the first place, "Where did Mr. Stoddard and Mr. Ingram obtain the information that Poe's birth occurred in

5. This was used as a frontispiece to Volume I of Ingram's 1874 edition of Poe's works.

1809?" From the matriculation books of the University at Charlottesville. The only wonder is, that this source of information should have been so long overlooked by his biographers. *I* received the fact in 1860, from a correspondent in Ohio,[6] who sent me an autograph note from Dr. Stephen Maupin,[7] referring to and authenticating an account (accompanying the note) from Mr. Wertenbaker, Secretary of the Faculty of the University. . . .

Now, as to the discrepancy in dates respecting the year of the birth, I admit there is a difficulty. Mrs. Clemm wrote me that Poe never could retain dates in his memory, and always had to apply to *her*. There is no reason to doubt her *own* fallibility [It is this, or is it *in*—"fallibility" which is meant?—H.B.W.] on statistical matters. Poe had not seen Mrs. Clemm until after he left West Point, since his earliest years. She must (or *may*) have told him that he was two years younger than he imagined. And on her authority the dates given in Griswold's *American Poets* may have been founded. The subsequent story, in Griswold's "Memoir", *may* have been, probably *was*, a fabrication. I cannot think that Poe would consciously have misrepresented his age, when he knew that the Charlottesville record was open to all enquirers. What think you? [I am of opinion that, *if* he held out the idea that his birth took place at a time not the actual one, he did so "consciously"—deliberately—for a purpose—just as he was accustomed to bring up to sight the points in his *veritable* narratives—the "Narrative of Arthur Gordon Pym", for instance. Touching the *fact* of his birthday, I lean toward the belief—nay, am *convinced*—that its rightful place upon the record is that which was given in the first statement seen by me, before he, his friends and his enemies took into their individual and collective heads the freak of *leading the public imagination by the nose* (see number 27 of the *Marginalia*)—that is, the place between the names of Henry and Rosalie, Henry—1809; Edgar—1811; Rosalie—1813. I don't accept, at

---

6. This correspondent was Sallie E. Robins.

7. Mrs. Whitman gave Dr. Maupin's name incorrectly to Eveleth, and Ingram picked it up from this letter. His name was "Socrates," not "Stephen," and Ingram later had to make a correction in print.

all, the information of Mrs. Clemm (I mean, as this was applied by her), that one who dealt so carefully, so effectively, in details regarding other matters as Edgar A. always did deal, was at a loss when he came to guessing about his own age—H.B.W.].

As to the portrait in *Harper*, I *know* nothing. I supposed it to have been taken from the engraving prefixed to Redfield's illustrated octavo edition of Poe's poems, published in 1858. It does *not* resemble *either* of the Daguerreotypes taken in Providence. The one of those two which was taken expressly for *me*, was photographed (also in Providence) by Coleman and Remington sixteen months ago, and a copy of the photograph was sent to Mr. Ingram, and selected by him (from among a number of others) to illustrate his Memoir prefixed to Black's Edinburgh edition of Poe's complete works. It has been admirably engraved, and is thought, by those who remember Poe, to be more like him that any other of the portraits extant.

I fancy that Stoddard was right in saying that the daguerre, prefixed to his article, was taken in Richmond ten days before Poe's death. It resembles the portraits published in the Illustrated Papers, to accompany reports of the recent celebration at Baltimore [on occasion of the unveiling of Poe's monument], which portraits are claimed to have been taken from a daguerre in the possession of the original's Baltimore relatives "ten days before his death" [It seemed (*and seems*) to me that the portrait represented a much more youthful person than Poe was at the time indicated. Besides, the whole *out-look* of the countenance, general and particular, even including feature, as well as expression, struck me as being very different from what it ought to be, judging from other pictures which I had seen previously—for example, the picture in the first volume of Griswold's edition (which, as I infer, was taken when its subject was quite a young man) and that accompanying Lowell's biography, published in the number of *Graham's Magazine* for February, 1845. I confess that the last-named suits better my mental vision of him who etched so aptly the *Literati*; laid open *all the heart* of his matter, in his Criticisms generally; pulled out so skillfully the tangles in the *Murders of the Rue Morgue*; probed with so great effect the horrors of the *Man of Usher*; gave bodies so beautiful to the Souls of the *Northern Lights*, in Ulalume. Query—Whether it was not the image of the spirit of *Henry* Poe, which was caught upon that plate in Richmond, on Thursday, Sept. 27th, 1849—whether, indeed, it was not that same spirit, "materialized", that got into all the scrapes and cut all the curious capers put to the account of Edgar A.?—H.B.W.].

I agree with you in doubting Poe's *habitual* resort to intoxicating liquors. I think Mr. Ingram admits too much, and will see occasion to qualify his statement.

I find your question as to the disagreement in the item about *Ligeia* a very natural and pertinent one. Mr. Poe brought me, in the autumn of 1848, two bound volumes of *The Broadway Journal*. In these volumes were a few marginal notes penciled by him. Prefixed to the letter-press of the page on which was commenced the story of *Ligeia* were these lines, in pencil:—"The lines I sent you contained all the events of a dream which occurred to me soon after I knew you through Mrs. O's description. *Ligeia* was also suggested by a dream. Observe the eyes in both tale and poem"—that is to say, "*soon after I recognized you through Mrs. O's description.*"

I had been so importuned by friends and strangers for some single line (or even word) of Poe's writing, that, over-persuaded, I had often clipped to [*sic*] or three words from some fragment, to oblige the soliciter. In this instance, I had cut the passage:—"through Mrs. O's description" from the penciled lines on the upper margin of the page. In sending these volumes to Mr. Ingram, I pointed out the mutilated sentence, and gave him the concluding words. Probably, in his haste in preparing his notes for the press, he had mislaid my letter explaining the matter, and had published what he thought an interesting item without reflecting that, in their incomplete meaning, they contradicted the fact that the lines were written before our introduction by letter from Miss M. G. McIntosh. *I* noticed this apparent discrepancy, on reading Mr. Ingram's narrative, and long ago intended to point it out to him, but neglected to do so because the intention was frustrated by a press of other matters.

The registration entry for Poe at the University of Virginia was not in Poe's handwriting; it was probably written in by a proctor: "Edgar A. Poe," born "19 Jan. 1809."

Mrs. Clemm's positive statement that Edgar had to depend on her for accurate dates has caused much comment. She was herself notoriously inaccurate. But perhaps age and many troubled years were partially responsible. Poe was twenty-two when he left West Point and renewed his acquaintance with Mrs. Clemm.

Griswold's *The Poets and Poetry of America*, published in Philadelphia on April 18, 1842, contained three of Poe's poems and a brief, inaccurate sketch of Poe's life, which Griswold had paraphrased from notes given to him by Poe himself. At this time, Poe was better known in America as a critic and a tale writer than as a poet.

Eveleth's independence of thought notwithstanding, William H. L. Poe was born in 1807, Edgar in 1809, and Rosalie in 1810. Mrs. Poe had died on December 8, 1811.

The portrait of Poe used by Stoddard in his *Harper's* article had been reproduced from a daguerreotype of Poe made by Pratt in Richmond, sometime in September, 1849, perhaps three weeks before Poe's death. The portrait used by Griswold in his 1850 edition of Poe's works had been reproduced from the painting of Poe made by Samuel S. Osgood, husband of Frances S. Osgood, in New York about 1844; this painting is now owned by the New York Historical Society, and is supposed to represent Poe at thirty-five years of age. The reproduction used by Lowell in his biographical sketch of Poe in *Graham's Magazine*, February, 1845, was from a painting of Poe done by A. C. Smith. Many pictures of Poe, reproduced from daguerreotypes and paintings, were published in various magazines and newspapers reporting the ceremonies of Poe's monument unveiling in Baltimore in 1875.

The two bound volumes of *The Broadway Journal* given by Poe to Mrs. Whitman in 1848, were "lent" by her to Ingram in mid–1874, to be returned to her when she asked for them, which she said would probably not be before the "breaking of the seventh seal." Apparently Ingram thought this event remote enough to sell them to a London bookseller in the 1880s, after Mrs. Whitman's death. Frederick J. Halsey bought the volumes for $240 at a sale by Thomas J. McKee in 1909, in New York. They are now in the Huntington Library, San Marino, California.

Letter 85. **H.B.W.** [[George W. Eveleth]], **Nemonia** [[Maine?]], **United States, to the editor of** *Scribner's Monthly*. Copied by Eveleth from the autograph letter. First printing. [Item 323]

October 7th, 1877

Sir:

In your last (Oct.) number, you have a notice of Mr. Gill's *Life of Poe*, to the following passage from which I wish to call your attention:—"It is now well ascertained that Poe's intoxication was a thing caused by even the smallest quantity of wine, and took the form of terrible despondence or of strange and highly intellectual but deranged orations on abstruse subjects."

How has it been ascertained? From what source or sources, and through what channels, has the item of information come? Which are the witnesses to the "intoxication", and where—in whose keeping—are to be found the "deranged orations"?

As *I* have read the testimony—even that put in by Griswold himself, who is charged with having had a desire and a design to show the case of his subject in as bad a light (as black a shadow) as possible—no habitual use of intoxicating liquors is indicated—much less, *proved*. All the persons who are introduced upon the stand, whose names are vouchers for the truthfulness of their statements and for their ability to judge of the matter in hand—Willis, Graham, Mrs. Osgood, Mrs. Whitman—say, in substance, that during no one of their frequent interviews with their acquaintance did they discover a sign of the effects of *strong drink* in him, but that he was always the sober (in two senses, sober), rather sad, genial-hearted, intelligent (clear—not *wine*—or *brandy*—muddled—, headed) refined gentleman.

Those are only a few, from among the many, names which might have been (doubtless, now might be) cited. The evening *literary gatherings*, spoken of in Griswold's Memoir and in Mrs. Whitman's *Edgar Poe and his Critics* imply that a considerable number of the poet's associates are living, and could give evidence of his habits, particularly, evidence touching his *sensitiveness to wine*; for it is to be presumed that the spirit constituted a part of the furniture of the assemblies.

Then there are *The Literati of New York City*. In his "few words of personality" thus entitled (*Godey's Ladies Book* for 1846), Poe said that, with one or two exceptions, he was *personally* acquainted with those about whom he was gossiping. What answer to the question before the public have those deponents? Especially, what is their knowledge (or, lacking that, what their opinion) of this "smallest quantity of wine" affair? In *my* estimation, if it proves anything, it proves too much; for lo!—the man swallowed the first *drop*, which set him athirst—wild, craving, raving—for still other drops upon drops—and so on, hurrying, rushing, through his brief course. The natural inference is that his life would have been an almost unbroken series of confused, disconnected, unmeaning harangues from the way-side ditches.

But who, again, is the *revelator* of those harangues ("deranged orations")? Did the orator himself, or did any one for him, put the effusions in writing? If so, are they a portion, or all, of the contents of his printed volumes? If so, once more, then *I* join issue immediately, and declare that the *disorder* assumed—disorder, whether of thought or of expression—is nowhere throughout those contents manifest. Even where slackest rein is given to the imagination (say, in "The Black Cat"), there the regulator, analysis, keeps pace abreast, the two combining to throw a wonderful semblance of reality, yet a vivid strange coloring, about the narrative.

Professor Lowell says (*not* in the mangled mess which is offered under his name by Griswold, but in the original, genuine article, as it was printed in *Graham's Magazine* (No. for Feb., 1845) that Poe had two gifts which are rarely found united—those of analysis and imagination. *It was the former ingredient that made its possessor so good a critic. Nothing (save now and then a pet prejudice) could drive him off his scent–He watched, with an eye serene the very pulse of the machine; for such the thing under examination was to him, with wheels and cogs and piston-rods all working to a determinate end.*

That mental "eye serene" (always keen, as well as steady, *never* clouded by liquor-fumes) looks on me from out all its owner's productions which I have read. Mind, I am not to be understood as claiming that no *inaccuracies* ever occur in them. I do claim, however, that, when there are any, they are such as the productions of any well-balanced intellect will show. For instance, the errors (of calculation, simply) :·

Eureka are of the same nature as those which can be found in *Newton's Principea*. Indeed, the most notable of them grew out of the fact that too much reliance was place in the *unproved "principle* of Gravitation"—the later theorist took, for a part of his foundation, the reckoning of the earlier, without first having brought that analytic knife of his, ever sharp and sure, to bear upon it.

So I conclude with a reintimation of my unbelief in the story of *common drunkenness* and of the *crazing power of a drop of wine*.

[I will add here, and now (Oct. 1st, 1878), the opinion; formed long ago and still held by me, that Poe was willing— yes, that he coolly planned—to leave behind him the impression (for such as might be glad to receive it) of his having been almost anything or everything that was bad—a malign, unhealthful product of the soil of the evil latter times. I will state, farther, my strong persuasion, if not my full conviction, that those remarkable events (remarkable, from whatever point of view considered), which have been designated by many sincere people as messages from the "spirit world", had, somehow, their advent through the strange processes of his mental chemistry. My supposition is that the coming was foretokened in those "physical shadows of shadows" spoken of in the sixteenth number of the *Marginalia*. It was upon this supposition that I made inquiry (as indicated in one of the foregoing letters of Mrs. Whitman) about the time when the note first appeared in print. I have a half-recollection of seeing it in *Graham* in 1846 or '7. Perhaps some one can give the date; also can tell when, and upon the *margin* of what book, it was penned or penciled—?

H.B.W.]

Eveleth was much interested in Poe's *Eureka*, and he brings it into his writings about Poe wherever possible. We can be grateful to him for his pointed questions to Poe about it and his challenges, which led to Poe's writing out for Eveleth a long explanation and discussion of his theories contained therein. Poe's reply has been reprinted in ten closely reasoned pages as "Poe's Addenda to *Eureka*" in Harrison, XVI, 337 *seq*.

Poe writes about "shadows of shadows" in the fifth number of the

"Marginalia" in *Graham's*, March 1846.
"'Nemonia,' United States" is very likely an anagram for Maine.

Letter 86. **George W. Eveleth, Lewiston, Maine, to John Ingram, London.** First printing. [Item 340]

Oct. 1, 1878

John H. Ingram, Esqre,

There, my friend and partner in the Good Cause, you have my contribution toward the making-up of something like a true estimate of Poe. You will not complain of any lack in *quantity* of matter. Of *quality*, I will say nothing.

You say in your letter (which came duly) that Mrs. Whitman posted you pretty thoroughly about her relations with him. Nevertheless, I thought I would give you such of her letters in my possession, as have a bearing on the case—you *may* find an item or a hint which will be new.

I have written on both sides of the leaves, and with lines near together, in order that the bill for postage might be not very large, having taken for granted that you would re-copy for the press.

You perceive that I have taken the initials *H.B.W.*, instead of giving either my own initials or my full name. I ask you to *follow the same course*—that is, *not* to present me, in proper person, at all before the public. I have my reasons. It is fair that you should know whose initials I have appropriated— they are owned by a Mrs. Helen Bullock Webster. Mrs. Whitman once sent me a very interesting letter (to me interesting) which the lady had written her. I have a suspicion (it may be groundless) that Mrs. Webster is the author of *Prometheus in Atlantis*—Did you ever read it?

I did *not* see (in Aps. Journal) "Unknown Correspondence of Poe"—*How*, unknown?

I received your letter ('74); but was situated so (with no documents within reach) that I couldn't supply you with any information. Davidson* was so kind as to *lend* me your article in *Int'l Rev.* I am glad to put in *this* (my mite) without reference to *pay*; yet, if you can well afford, a trifle would be acceptable; for, as the Fates know, I am poor enough.

I mail, with this, a package of clippings—among them English *vs* Poe, and Poe in rejoinder.

Cordially—
G. W. Eveleth

The clippings, "English *vs.* Poe and Poe in Rejoinder," enclosed in this package to Ingram, had to do with accusations made by Thomas Dunn English* against Poe and Poe's reply to them; these clippings had appeared in the New York *Mirror*, June 23, 1846, and in the Philadelphia *Spirit of the Times*, July 10, 1846. Poe brought legal suit against the *Mirror*, and was awarded $225 damages.

Ingram replied quickly to Eveleth after receiving these forty-four closely written pages; for on October 30, 1878, Eveleth wrote him: "You 'presume' rightly that 'no one but 'Myself' possesses or may use—copies of 'those letters'—that is no one *may use*, unless with my permission *given hereafter*, which I have *now* no thought of giving. I have *not* 'parted with' the originals—prefer not to part with them just yet—think I shall send them to you by and by, if you intimate an acceptation of them. The matter of remuneration lies wholly with you—if none, no grumbling."

Ingram did not receive the autograph Poe letters. It is to be hoped, however, that he did send something more than "a trifle" to Eveleth for the work he had done for him, and for us.

Professor James Southall Wilson published Poe's letters to Eveleth from the copies Eveleth made for Ingram, and thus unavoidably reproduced errors in the letters made by Eveleth. John Ostrom first printed the letters correctly, from photostats of the originals which are now in the William H. Koester Collection, Baltimore, the Berg Collection in the New York Public Library, the Rosenbach Collection in Philadelphia, and the Morgan Library in New York City.

After his letter of October 30, 1878, written from Lewiston, Maine, to Ingram, Eveleth wrote at least six more letters to Ingram, dated between December 28, 1881 and April 24, 1889. All of these were written from Denver, Colorado, and all of them were consistently sharp, acrid comments on Ingram's writings about Poe. Then Eveleth was heard from no more.

Prometheus in Atlantis: a Prophecy of the Extinction of the Christian Civilization was published anonymously in New York City by G. W. Carleton in 1867.

The most important and valuable letters in this forty-four-page package received from Eveleth for Ingram's purpose of building Poe biography were, of course, the seven letters Eveleth copied for Ingram that he had received from Poe. Next in value, for Ingram's purposes, were the two flat denials by the judges of the contest for the prize story offered by the *Saturday Visiter* that the prize had been given to Poe in 1833 simply because his manuscript was the first legible one the judges picked up, as Griswold had stated as a fact in his *Memoir*. Equally as important, too, for controverting Griswold's statement that Poe's riotous conduct at the house of a New England lady had rendered necessary a summoning of the police, was Mrs. Whitman's denial of the statement and her account of what really had happened, in her letter to Sallie E. Robins, Letter 81 in this volume.

Portions of some of the other letters in this group served Ingram as he pleased to use them here and there in his *Life*, giving strength and depth wherever he felt his volumes needed them. The one letter from Mrs. Ellet, Letter 69, in which she accuses Poe of being frequently in the asylum for his attacks of lunacy, Ingram, of course, loftily ignored—but he filed it.

Ingram's handling of the seven letters Eveleth had received from Poe is nothing less than a study in confusion. Poe had answered Eveleth's brash, pointed questions generously; he wrote freely to the young man about his tales and poems, his criticisms, *The Conchologist's First Book, Eureka*, the libel suit he had initiated against Thomas Dunn English, his hopes and plans for his future, as well as his own personal affairs and his health. The peculiar intimacy with which Poe carried on his correspondence with his personally unknown admirer makes this segment of his personal letters striking and most unusual. Ingram was extraordinarily fortunate that Eveleth had made it possible for him to be the first to publish these letters.

Even though Ingram had complete copies of all seven of Poe's letters to Eveleth before him and was free to use them as he pleased, he by no means reprinted them in his 1880 *Life* as complete letters: he dismembered them into fourteen extracts which he quoted as having been written to "an unnamed correspondent," making it impossible to piece together the original letters in sequence; in some cases he left out places and dates, as well as phrases; in one instance, he even rearranged the paragraphs in one of Poe's letters. When Ingram's Poe papers reached the University of Virginia, this incredible mess was partially cleared up when Professor James Southall Wilson edited the seven letters Poe had written to Eveleth, exactly as Eveleth had copied them for Ingram. These letters were published in the University of Virginia

Alumni Bulletin, XVII, January, 1924, as "The Letters of Edgar A. Poe to George W. Eveleth"; later they were reprinted separately. [8]

In addition to these letters Eveleth copied serving Ingram's purpose of proving that Griswold had lied about Poe by providing three strong witnesses to that fact, they also serve to introduce the reader to Sarah Helen Whitman's charming, intelligent letter-writing style.

8. The late Professor T. O. Mabbott edited twelve of the thirteen letters Eveleth wrote to Poe and published them as "The Letters of George W. Eveleth to Edgar Allan Poe" in the *Bulletin of the New York Public Library*. This article, too, was separately reprinted.

VIII

John Henry Ingram Prepares to Write His Biography of Edgar Allan Poe

IN THE SHORT SPACE of one year John Ingram, working alone in London, had become a major figure in Poe scholarship. His memoir and his four-volume edition of Poe's works were before the public, and it mattered little whether the American critics and biographers were pleased or angry: they could not now ignore his work.

Ingram's first important magazine publication in 1875 was a twenty-seven page abridgment of his memoir published in the *International Review* and designed to reach readers in the United States, since copyright laws kept his edition of Poe's works from being published in this country until 1876. [1]

The first signal public recognition of Ingram's work on Poe came from the United States, and appropriately enough, from the University of Virginia, when in 1875 he was invited to attend a semi-centennial celebration of the university's founding. Enormously pleased by this accolade, Ingram saw to it that this honor was known to the English press, even though he had to answer with sincere regrets that his duties in England made it impossible for him to accept the university's invitation.

In a review of Henry Curwen's two volumes, *Sorrow and Song: Studies of Literary Struggle* (London: H. S. King & Co., 1875), Ingram devoted nearly half of the four columns allowed him to pointing out to the public and the author the errors made in Curwen's account of Edgar Poe, one of the six Grub Street authors Curwen had chosen as subjects. Ingram's tone in this review, printed in the *Academy* for March 13, 1875, [2] is that of a kind and patient mentor coaching a backward pupil,

---

1. W. J. Widdleton, a New York publisher, brought it out.
2. See the *Academy*, March 13, 1875, pp. 262–63.

but he used this review to place two new and startling facts about Poe affairs on the record. He wrote that Curwen had quoted excerpts from Poe's letter "which we do not hesitate to call forgeries." This was the first time Ingram had used the word "forgery," in connection with Griswold's manipulation of some of Poe's letters, and it caused enough excitement to start the investigation in America which, in the end, proved Ingram justified in using the term. And Ingram started still another controversy in this review which, though it still cannot be either proved or disproved, has certainly become part of Poe biography: using N. H. Morison's letter to himself, November 27, 1874,[3] he quoted Neilson Poe as saying that Edgar and Virginia were first married in Christ's Church, Baltimore, by the Reverend John Johns in 1834, but they did not live together for more than a year, Virginia continuing to reside with her mother until 1835, when Edgar and Virginia were again married in Richmond.

There was never anything very subtle about John Ingram, but this review showed that a change had taken place in his attitude. Gone, for the moment anyway, were his anger, his frequent use of epithets, his almost hysterical desire to convince his readers of Griswold's perfidy. In their place was an almost condescending manner bespeaking a new maturity and a sense of confidence.

By mid-summer of 1875 Ingram had sufficiently placated Stella Lewis for her to make him a present of Poe's manuscript of his unfinished drama, "Politian," of which only portions had been published, in the *Southern Literary Messenger* in December, 1835, and reprinted in *The Raven and Other Poems* in 1845. Using this newly acquired treasure, Ingram brought the year 1875 to a triumphant close by publishing the whole fragment, including at least four unpublished scenes, in the *London Magazine*. William Hand Browne gladly reprinted this article in the *Southern Magazine* in Baltimore for November, 1875. Ingram had achieved a real coup.

In his eagerness to put his memoir of Poe before the American public as quickly as possible, even before copyright laws permitted his full edition to be printed in the United States, Ingram had started a chain of events that was to culminate in an explosion of bitterness and hatred between and among English and American biographers of Poe, dividing them into hostile camps from which they issued accusations and counter-

3. [Item 184]

accusations of bad faith, double-dealing, and outright theft of each other's materials.

Immediately after Ingram's memoir was published in late 1874, Ingram suggested to a New York publisher, W. J. Widdleton, that he use it gratis, should he bring out another American edition of Poe's writings. When Widdleton announced in the spring of 1875 that he was issuing a memorial edition of Poe's poems, Ingram repeated his offer. Widdleton replied that he had been asked by William F. Gill not to use Ingram's memoir, as it covered materials taken from his own paper in a volume called *Lotus Leaves*.

The facts behind this request, which Ingram was unaware of at this time, were that before Mrs. Whitman had begun her correspondence with him in early 1874, she had lent to Gill some of her Poe materials, including excerpts from several of Poe's letters and a few newsclippings, for an article Gill had told her he was preparing for publication in *Lotus Leaves*. Having heard nothing from Gill for a very long time, Mrs. Whitman wrote to him and asked for the return of her materials. Gill did, in fact, return to her copies of some of them and he asked her not to help Ingram, for he thought the English writer would "take the wind out of his sails" in an article he wanted to publish in a companion volume to *Lotus Leaves*, to be called *Laurel Leaves*. Mrs. Whitman was by now of the opinion that Gill already "had too much wind in his sails for the amount of ballast on board," and she replied sharply, for her, that she would do as she saw fit with her materials about Poe.

The Widdleton memorial edition of *Poems and Essays* was out just after Christmas of 1875.[4] But at the close of of the prefatory note in the Introduction, an utterly false statement had been inserted:

> It should be stated that a considerable portion of Mr. Ingram's *Memoir* is gathered from material previously used by Mr. William F. Gill in his lecture, "The Romance of Edgar A. Poe," written in September, 1873, which formed the first complete vindication of Poe from the calumnies of Rufus W. Griswold. Mr. Gill has kindly permitted the use of the material derived from this source, in order that Mr. Ingram's *Memoir* might appear in its original form.

Ingram's composure and air of superiority vanished. Wild with rage, he composed and published in the *Athenaeum,* January 15, 1876, a long, bitter "Disclaimer," in which he castigated Gill as a person

---

4. Widdleton brought the book out but dated it 1876.

and a writer, called him a liar, and dared him to produce a shred of evidence to back up his claim to have "permitted the use of his materials in Mr. Ingram's *Memoir*"; and he saw to it that this "Disclaimer," bitter and ugly as it was, was widely circulated in American magazines and newspapers.

After a few short, angry exchanges in *Notes and Queries* with an unknown writer who signed himself "Uneda" and with J. Brander Matthews, both of whom had made erroneous and derogatory remarks about Poe's career in *Notes and Queries*, Ingram routed them from the field and turned his attention to his next new and important discovery in Poe affairs and the article that was to announce it to the world.

The existence of an 1827 volume of Poe's poems had long been debated among his biographers: Poe had said that in his 1829 and 1831 volumes he had included poems that were copied verbatim from the 1827 volume. Griswold at one time seemed to believe there had been such a volume, but later denied that it was so. R. H. Stoddard had openly written that it was "mendacious" of Poe to say that he had printed this early book of poems, when he had not.

John Ingram put an end to these discussions forever—and immeasurably increased his reputation as a Poe scholar and researcher—when he published in the *Belgravia Magazine* for June, 1876, an article called "The Suppressed Poetry of Poe," containing nearly the whole of Poe's 1827 volume of poems named *Tamerlane and Other Poems* (Boston: Calvin F. S. Thomas, Printer, 1827).

. This was indeed a bold stroke. The article added five new poems to the Poe canon, aroused considerable interest through reprints in England, France, and America, and allowed Ingram once more to belabor in print the dead Griswold and the living Stoddard for having doubted Poe's word.

Ingram had discovered this first copy of *Tamerlane* in the British Museum Library and had recognized it as Poe's 1827 volume, even though the front and the back covers had been torn off. This copy had been sent, probably in 1863, to the British Museum Library by an American bookseller, with many other pamphlets, and had been priced to the library at one shilling.

With this volume in hand, as well as the 1829 and 1831 volumes sent to him on loan by C. F. Harris, Mrs. Whitman's neighbor and a collector of early American poetry, and with the 1845 volume of Poe's *The Raven and Other Poems* still easily available in bookstalls, Ingram was able to prepare and publish very quickly—the month after his important article on Poe's suppressed poetry had appeared in the *Belgravia*—the first description and critical bibliography of all four of the volumes of poetry Poe had published in his lifetime.[5]

Meanwhile, with these triumphs on the record, Ingram felt that he could turn to his work on the great biography of Poe he had long planned; but, in America, another publishing venture was underway that was to tear him emotionally and put a strain on the relations between him and his gracious "Providence," Mrs. Whitman.

Eugene L. Didier of Baltimore, having calmly watched the wranglings among Gill, Stoddard, and Ingram, announced his intentions of presenting to the world an accurate memoir of Poe, not simply a denial of Griswold's, but one that should be the accepted "biography of 'The Raven.'" He, of course, applied to Mrs. Whitman for help. Remembering all too well the Ingram-Gill controversy, in which she had not been blameless, Mrs. Whitman very carefully asked Ingram's opinion in the matter. He replied diffidently enough, but seemed to encourage her participation, although he said he expected nothing important to come of the publication. Accordingly, Mrs. Whitman began a short note to Didier, which grew into a very long letter which Didier actually used as an introduction to his book and which Widdleton announced as the preface of the "Household Edition" of Poe's poems to be published in 1877.[6]

A few weeks later Ingram wrote Mrs. Whitman that he had lent her book to a "friend," who had reviewed it in London *Athenaeum* for February 10, 1877, and he suggested she read it in the Athenaeum Library in Providence; when she did not reply to his suggestion, he repeated it once more.

When Mrs. Whitman finally did look up a copy of that issue of the *Athenaeum* and read the long review, to her great surprise and unwilling belief she found it a brutally sarcastic attack on Didier, the book, and, remarkably enough, herself and her belief in spiritualism and prenatal influences! It was not signed, but she knew Ingram's writing and style too well not to be positive that he had written it, even though he continued to avow that he had "lent" her book to a friend who had

5. "The Bibliography of Edgar Poe," *Athenaeum*, July 29, 1876, pp. 145–46.
6. E. L. Didier, *The Life and Poems of Edgar Allan Poe* (New York: W. J. Widdleton, 1877).

actually written the review.[7] Mrs. Whitman had known for many years that Poe himself had employed this device and excuse to have a devastating review written of one of Griswold's anthologies, and had thereby incurred Griswold's undying enmity. Even if Ingram had indeed lent her copy of the book to a "friend," he had himself called her attention to the article *twice*. The time had come for a break with him, and she made it.

Within just a few months, still another American biography of Poe was to be published which would arouse even greater wrath in Ingram. William F. Gill's long-announced, many-times-delayed *The Life of Edgar Allan Poe* appeared in the summer of 1877, and in the Preface Gill suggested that his book "may also serve to answer the complaint of an English writer that no trustworthy biography of Poe has yet appeared in his own country."[8] Perhaps thinking this too gentle a reprimand, Gill wrote an estimate of Ingram's work in an appendix that could not but strike fire:

Mr. J. H. Ingram, of London, possessing both enterprise and determination, has written and published a memoir of Poe, which, considering the disadvantage of collecting literary material at the distance of three thousand miles from the poet's birthplace, is a creditable work, although, in some essential points, it is unreliable.[9]

---

7. This copy of Didier's book is now in the Rare Book Collection of the University of Virginia Library. Inscribed, "This copy given to me by Mrs. Whitman, JHI," it is copiously and angrily annotated by Ingram and contains as well some of Mrs. Whitman's penciled marginal notes. Someone, presumably Ingram, gleefully clipped from a newspaper and pasted the following six lines of doggerel at the end of the Preface:

> Dear D——, in your biography of Poe,
> The real cause for rue is,
> That what is true was published years ago,
> And what is new not true is;
> And the new poems that you tell about
> Upon the title-page, are all left out.
> Francis Gerry Fairfield

Ingram could not have afforded to return to Mrs. Whitman this copy of Didier's book which she had but lent to him; therefore, he told her that he had lent it to a "friend," who had used it to write the review. Saying that he could not get it back, he offered to buy her a new one in its place. Mrs. Whitman's sharp eyes were aging, but they would have detected Ingram's derisive marginal comments and notes. Internal evidence shows that the article as it appeared in the *Athenaeum* expresses Ingram's basic animosities; it is sprinkled with his favorite French phrases (one of the many writing habits Ingram tried to adopt in imitation of Poe's writing); and the whole thing, style and tone included, points to Ingram as the author of most of the sarcastic article, if indeed not the whole of it.

8. William F. Gill, *The Life of Edgar Allan Poe* (New York: C. T. Dillingham; Boston: W. F. Gill Company, 1877), 5.

9. *Ibid.*, 266.

If Gill really wanted to arouse Ingram, he succeeded admirably. The London *Athenaeum* for October 6, 1877, printed a long, blistering review of Gill's book, as did the Boston *Herald* on October 28, 1877 —the copy doubtlessly forwarded by Ingram, urging the reprint. Although the review is unsigned, it is beyond question that John Ingram wrote it, and he identifies himself as the same person who had written the scathing review of Didier's book. This, after having written to Mrs. Whitman, "I here declare that the words are not mine."

Even though active correspondence between Mrs. Whitman and Ingram had stopped, Ingram was to deliver a final, fell blow. He released it in *Appleton's Journal*, for May, 1878, in an article called "Unpublished Correspondence by Edgar A. Poe." Among the letters here first published were Poe's letters to Annie Richmond, in which he wrote slightingly of his engagement to Mrs. Whitman and announced his satisfaction at having at last been freed of his engagement to marry her. Ingram also printed here as authentic copies of Poe's letters to Mrs. Shew, copies which Mrs. Whitman had seen and had pronounced as doubtful, at best; and here Ingram had called Poe's relationship with Mrs. Shelton "as romantic as that ever penned by poet," and he styled that lady herself as "Poe's first and last love."

For thirty years Mrs. Whitman had cherished Poe's memory and had worked indefatigably with a number of persons to help clear Poe's name and to restore his good reputation. And she had believed for nearly thirty years that, after Virginia Poe's death, she was Edgar's only real love. Now Ingram had printed *dated* letters which told the world that Poe had been writing passionate personal love letters to another man's wife, while he had been writing, at the same time, passionate literary love letters to her.

Mrs. Whitman died in Providence on June 27, 1878, and Ingram, of course, wrote an appropriate obituary for her and published it in the *Athenaeum* for July 20, 1878.

During the distressing months that followed his final break with Mrs. Whitman, and before he published Poe's correspondence in *Appleton's Journal*, Ingram had made an extremely important discovery that was to add an important tale to the Poe canon. Mining the volumes of American magazines in the British Museum Library, he had found that the leading feature of the 1840 volume of *Burton's Gentleman's Magazine* was the beginning of a lengthy romance called "The Journal of Julius Rodman," with further installments there promised. This volume bore Burton's and Poe's names as joint editors, but the romance was not signed, nor had any of Poe's editors or biographers ever assigned it to Poe's pen. But Ingram knew that it was, for he had in his files a copy of a letter from Poe to Burton, dated June 1, 1840, which established the fact that Poe had written "Julius Rodman"; for Poe had written in that letter, "I can give you no definitive answer (respecting the continuation of Rodman's Journal) until I hear from you again."

Mrs. Richmond had sent Ingram this copy of Poe's letter to Burton by May 27, 1877. She almost certainly had received it from Mrs. Clemm, who had at one time promised to give to Mrs. Richmond all of her papers and letters. The original of Poe's letter to Burton has disappeared; this copy made upon Mrs. Richmond's request for Ingram by her friend William Rouse, to whom she had given it as a souvenir, is the sole authority for the text.

Ingram inexplicably chose to present his important discovery in a long, anonymous article, "'The Journal of Julius Rodman,' a Newly-Discovered Work by the Late Edgar A. Poe," printed in the London *Mirror of Literature* on November 3, 1877.[10] Of course, John Ingram was named in the article as the discoverer on this unknown work of Poe's, and no matter how loath American newspaper and Poe writers were to grant that the story was either a "romance," that it was "unknown," and that it was really nothing but a "fragment," this discovery by Ingram of the 25,000 word fragment, "The Journal of Julius Rodman," is regarded by one of the best of all Poe scholars, Professor Killis Campbell, as a major contribution to Poe scholarship.[11]

Poe's eye-catching, fun-inspired "Chapter on Autographs" had so fascinated Ingram when he discovered it while collecting materials for his 1874/75 edition of Poe's works, that now and then he prepared and published a similar series of sketches of the then reigning English and American literati, under the pseudonym of Don Felix de Salamanca.[12] The idea was still good and Ingram's articles excited enough interest and amusement for him to turn to producing a whole volume of them in late 1879, when his biography of Poe was apparently nearly ready for the press.

10. [Item 716] Four columns clipped from the *Mirror of Literature*.
11. Killis Campbell, *The Mind of Poe and Other Studies* (Cambridge: Harvard University Press, 1933), 189.
12. Ingram's use of a pseudonym is interesting here, but it is entirely in keeping with his efforts to do at one time or another everything that Poe had done. After he sent the first of these articles in proof to Mrs. Whitman for "approval," she playfully and affectionately addressed him as "Dear Don Felix" and attempted to analyze his own handwriting, but Ingram discouraged these things in her as tartly and abruptly as he did her beginning attempts to convert him to spiritualism.

The Philosophy of Handwriting, by Don Felix de Salamanca, was brought out by Chatto and Windus, London, October, 1879. It contained 135 facsimile autographs of persons of several nations who were distinguished in various professions. As a rule, the autographs were those of living persons, male and female, who were considered distinguished in their time, but Ingram did include a few of both sexes who had recently died.

Ingram's inclusion of autographs belonging to persons other than those of the literati is the only original feature of this volume, which was, of course, inspired by Poe and directly imitative of his style and manner. However, the differences between the two writers are clear: Ingram's imagination was earthbound by his ingrained habit and necessity of appealing to well-known authorities to justify what he says; hobbled by quotations, how could this book be expected to soar and glitter, as did Poe's? Ingram used satire and wit as a peasant uses his broadax; Poe had used them as a Cavalier used his rapier.

As the decade of the 1870s closed, Ingram could look back over it with real satisfaction over his important additions to the Poe canon and the position he had gained in Poe scholarship. When he had published the full account of and the unpublished scenes from "Politian," when he had discovered the first copy of *Tamerlane*, had written the first full bibliographical account of all four of Poe's volumes of poems, and when he had revealed the intimate letters Poe had written in the last years of his life, he had undeniably added more to the world's knowledge of Poe and his writings than had all of Poe's biographers combined, up to that time. Ingram's discoveries of such additional writings as "Julius Rodman," for instance, had appeared to some to be phenomenal luck, but actually he was able to accomplish so much because his researcher's keen instinct was wonderfully accompanied by unflagging zeal and ferocious energy. As both author and scholar, during this decade of the 1870s, Ingram could well be, and he was, proud of his accomplishments.

The six active, frantic years had taken a toll of him, however, and there were some painful and regrettable memories to plague him. He was certainly battle scarred by his quarrels with other Poe biographers, especially the American ones, and even though these public disputes had brought a certain prominence if not notoriety to him, their vehemence had cost him much in the time lost and the nervous strain he endured carrying them on. The snares and subterfuges he had encountered in his dealing with the ladies who had known Poe, and some who claimed they had, and on whom he was so completely dependent for source material, had kept him walking nervously, as on a knife edge, and had at times driven him quite close to that insanity which he daily feared. He could be ruthless with his correspondents when he had gotten from them all that he thought he could use in his work, but even he had not become so calloused or so completely obsessed with his work on Poe that he could see his long and intimate literary friendships with Mrs. Whitman and Mrs. Richmond come to their painful ends without feeling real compunction and regret.

In the six years between 1874 and 1880, Ingram had, in a real sense, presided over the dissolution of the "Poe Circle." He had met many of these friends and associates of Poe's personally or through correspondence, and he had established varying degrees of intimacy, sometimes bordering on proprietorship, over many of them just before they slipped away to their graves. By 1880, Mrs. Whitman, Mrs. Houghton, and "brave old" John Neal were gone; Stella Lewis was soon to follow; and Ingram was sorry they had not been able to stay to see his work on Poe finished. There was the other side, too, at these passings, at which the scholar-researcher part of his personality exulted openly: now that they were dead the whole stories of their associations of Poe could be told; he alone knew these stories, and he fully intended to tell them.

In the latter part of the decade, as Poe materials continued to pour into his hands daily, Ingram sorted, sifted, rejected, and accepted, with a canniness born of sometimes terrible and bitter experiences. At last, in the beginning of 1880, he turned over to the press manuscript and photographs enough to fill out a two-volume biography, *Edgar Allan Poe: His Life, Letters, and Opinions. With Portraits of Poe and His Mother*. The books were brought out by John Hogg, London, Paternoster Row, and they were off the press by mid-May, 1880.

Ingram was convinced that his volumes had the facts of Poe's life so buttressed with proofs, that they were so comprehensive and that they contained so much fresh materials on Poe that they would unquestionably provide the world with the long-needed authoritative account of the poet's life. He felt with equal sincerity that these two volumes would silence all of Poe's detractors, as well as his own, and would remove the necessity for anyone else ever to publish another biography of Poe.

Appendix
Names, topics, newsclippings, and letters frequently mentioned in the text

Allan, Louisa Gabriella Patterson (d. April 24, 1881): Second Mrs. John Allan; of Elizabeth, N.J. and Richmond; married John Allan on October 5, 1830; adamantly refused to talk about Edgar Poe.

Botta, Mrs. Anne Charlotte Lynch (1815–1891): Member of the New York literati, at Waverly Place; Poe knew her as Miss Anne Lynch; she married Professor Vincenzo Botta in 1855; tried very hard, after Poe's death, to disassociate her name from Poe's; generally conceded to be the hostess of the first American salon.

Briggs, Charles Frederick (1804–1877): Journalist, author, novelist; founded *Broadway Journal*, with which Poe was briefly associated as editor; friend of Lowell's, enemy of Poe's.

Brooks, Nathan Covington: Editor, with Dr. J. E. Snodgrass, of the *American Museum of Science, Literature, and the Arts*, in Baltimore, to which Poe contributed from its beginning in September, 1838, through its concluding issue in June, 1839.

Brown, Franklin E.: Of London, England; friend of the Richmonds in Lowell; on returning home from a visit with relatives in the United States carried by hand Mrs. Richmond's gift to Ingram, the two-volume edition of Poe's *Tales of the Grotesque and Arabesque*, found in Poe's trunk when it was forwarded after Poe's death from Baltimore, by Neilson Poe, to Mrs. Clemm in Lowell.

Browne, William Hand (1828–1912): of Baltimore; author, editor, educator; founded and edited the *Southern Review*, the *New Eclectic Magazine* (later called the *Southern Magazine*); ardent defender of Poe; faithful friend and correspondent of Ingram's for nearly thirty-five years.

"Burton Letter": Poe's letter of June 1, 1840, to William E. Burton; Mrs. Richmond gave the letter to her friend William Rouse as a souvenir of Poe;

Rouse copied it for Ingram in May, 1877; by means of this letter Ingram was able to prove that Poe wrote "The Journal of Julius Rodman," and add that 25,000-word fragment to the Poe canon.

Burton, William Evans (1804–1860): Author, actor; appeared on stage in Philadelphia, 1834–1838; published *Burton's Gentleman's Magazine* in Philadelphia, 1837–1840, with Poe as editor, part of the time; managed theaters in Philadelphia, Baltimore, and Washington, D.C., 1841–1848.

Caddie (also called "Caddy," "Carrie," and "Abby"): daughter and only child of Charles B. and Annie Richmond.

Childs, George William (1829–1894): Publisher, author, philanthropist; sent check for fifty dollars to Rosalie Poe, which she received a few minutes before she died; underwrote expense of Poe's monument in Westminster Churchyard, Baltimore.

Clarke, Thomas Cottrell (d. 1874): Owner and editor of the Philadelphia *Saturday Museum*; at one time agreed to furnish necessary money to start Poe's long-dreamed-of magazine, the *Stylus*; later withdrew his backing; after Poe's death Clarke collected materials for many years with the idea of writing a biography refuting Griswold's; nothing came of his efforts.

Clemm, Maria Poe (also called "Muddy" and "Muddie") 1790–1871: Poe's aunt (sister to Poe's father, David) and mother-in-law.

Coburn, Frederick W.: Author of article, "Poe as Seen by the Brother of 'Annie.'" in *New England Quarterly*, XVI (September, 1943), 468–76.

Crane, Mrs.: A friend of Annie Richmond's to whom she gave as a souvenir of Poe the manuscript of "A Dream Within a Dream."

Cudworth, the Reverend Warren H.: Of East Boston; friend and former pastor of Annie Richmond; published an article, "Mr. Poe as a Cryptographer," in the Lowell *Journal*, April 19, 1850.

Davidson, James Wood (1829–1905): Of South Carolina and New York City; editor and author; wrote a defense of Poe's character, printed in *Russell's Magazine*, November, 1857; author of *Living Writers of the South*, 1869; eager, helpful correspondent of Ingram's for many years.

Didier, Eugene Lemoine (1838–1913): Of Baltimore; gave up commercial life to become an author; published *Life and Poems of E. A. Poe* in 1877; *The Poe Cult*, 1909; accused Ingram of stealing Poe items from the Houghton family.

Ellet, Mrs. Elizabeth Frieze Lummis (1818–1877): Of Columbia, S.C., and New York City; translator, sentimental poetess, member of the New York literati; at one time an ardent admirer of Poe's, but after he discouraged her she became his bitter, relentless enemy.

English, Thomas Dunn (1819–1902): Physician, lawyer, author; Poe called him "Thomas Dunn Brown," and "an ass"; the quarrel that resulted ended in court. Poe sued the *Mirror*, in which English's reply had been printed, along with his dare to Poe to sue; as a result Poe was awarded $225 damages for English's libels.

Eveleth, George W.: Of Lewiston, Maine; corresponded with Poe as a young medical student; Poe replied to his letters at least seven times; they never met; sent Ingram forty-four closely copied pages of correspondence he had amassed over the years to help Poe's defense; has been called "the first Poe specialist."

Flag of Our Union: A weekly family newspaper established in 1846 by Frederick Gleason and Martin Murray Ballou; by 1850 its circulation was 100,000; in 1871 it was merged with the *American Union*; a fire destroyed all files of *The Flag*, it was thought, in 1872 or 1873; however, in 1909 Professor Killis Campbell discovered a complete set for 1849 in the Library of Congress.

Fuller, Sarah Margaret (1810–1850): Journalist, social reformer, intellectual, editor of the *Dial* with Emerson and George Ripley; main interest lay in potentialities of women in modern society.

Gill's "Reply": Answer to Ingram's "Disclaimer," in *The Athenaeum*, January 15, 1876; appeared in the *American Bookseller*, February (?), 1876, and in Boston Sunday *Herald*, November 18, 1877; Ingram's "Rejoinder" was printed in the *Bookseller, ca*. April, 1876.

Gill, William Fearing (1844–1917): Son of publishing family Shepard & Gill, Boston; impulsive admirer of Poe's works; became bitter antagonist of Ingram's; published in 1877 a badly written but important early biography of Poe; rescued the Poe cottage at Fordham from threatened destruction in 1889, and the Poe Park resulted; founded the Poe Society in 1903; coined the phrase, "the Sixth Sense" in the New York *Graphic* in 1880.

Godey, Louis Antoine (1804–1878): Publisher, with Charles Alexander, of *Godey's Ladies Book*, Philadelphia, 1830; Poe contributed articles of literary criticism and his "Literati."

Graham, George Rex (1813–1894): Of Philadelphia; owner of *Graham's Magazine*, of which Poe was editor; longtime friend and defender of Poe; published in his own magazine, March, 1850, a long letter to N. P. Willis which is one of the strongest defenses ever written against Griswold's slanders.

Griswold, Rufus Wilmot (1815–1857): Editor, critic, author; licensed to preach by the Baptist Church in 1837, but never held a regular pastorate; assistant editor of *Graham's* 1842–1843, succeeding Poe; wrote obituary of Poe signed "Ludwig," in the New York *Daily Tribune*, October 9, 1849; named Poe's literary executor by Mrs. Clemm and Stella Lewis; edited first edition of Poe's works in 1850–1856.

Hewitt, John Hill (1801–1890): Of Baltimore; journalist, poet, editor; won poetry competition, under assumed name, over Poe in *Saturday Visiter*, 1833.

Hewitt, Mary Elizabeth Moore: Poetess, member of the New York literati; Poe reviewed her verses favorably; she told the story of Poe's saying his marriage to Mrs. Whitman would never take place; married first to James L. Hewitt, brother of John Hill Hewitt, later to a Mr. Stebbins.

Heywood, Sarah H.: Annie Richmond's younger sister who lived in nearby Westford, Mass., but spent much time in the Richmonds' Lowell home; later married Charles P. Trumbull.

Hopkins, John H. (1820–1891): Of New York; a divinity student when he met Poe through Marie Louise Shew; detested Poe's pantheistic ideas, as expressed in *Eureka*; was afraid Poe's ideas would be morally and socially dangerous for Mrs. Houghton; became a bishop.

Houghton, Dora: Daughter of Marie Louise Shew Houghton who assisted her mother with the correspondence to Ingram.

Houghton, Mrs. Marie Louise Shew (d. September 3, 1877): Of New York City; daughter and granddaughter of well-known physicians; married Dr. Joel Shew; was divorced from him when Mary Gove Nichols introduced her into the Poe household during Virginia's last sickness in 1847; Poe wrote several poems to her; proved to be a valuable if somewhat confusing correspondent of Ingram's; sent him many Poe items of inestimable value.

Houghton, the Reverend Roland Stebbins (d. March 23, 1876): Married Marie Louise Shew in 1850; they were estranged when she corresponded with Ingram in 1875, but some communication existed between them.

Kennedy, John Pendleton (1795–1870): Of Baltimore; biographer, novelist, eminent lawyer, Secretary of Navy in President Fillmore's cabinet; helped Poe materially.

Latrobe, John Hazelhurst Boneval (1803–1891): Lawyer, inventor; one of the three judges of the *Saturday Visiter* contest for prose and poetry in which Poe won the prize for prose in 1833.

Lewis, Mrs. Sarah Anna Blanche Robinson (1824–1880): Also known as "Estelle Anna," "Stella Anna," and "Stella"; a minor literary figure; wife, until they were divorced in 1858, of Sylvanus D. Lewis, a Brooklyn lawyer; furnished both money and hospitality to Mrs. Clemm and Poe after 1847, principally for Poe's favorable reviews of her pedestrian verses. Ingram met her after she moved to London and succeeded in obtaining from her by gift and legacy very important items to add to Poe biography.

Lewis, Sylvanus D.: Of Brooklyn; husband of "Stella"; lawyer who helped Mrs. Clemm fight Rosalie Poe's claim for Poe's estate; succeeded in getting Neilson Poe to ship Poe's trunk from Baltimore to Mrs. Clemm in Lowell.

Locke, Mrs. Jane Ermina Starkweather (d. *ca.* 1859): A minor poetess of Lowell, Mass., in whose home Poe was a guest until his lecture, where he met and promptly moved into the house of Mr. and Mrs. Charles B. Richmond; probably Poe's bitterest, most relentless enemy thereafter; cousin by marriage of Mrs. Frances S. Osgood.

Loud, Margaret St. Leon: Minor poetess of Philadelphia whose husband hired Poe for $100 to edit her poems; Poe died before he could reach Philadelphia to do the job.

Lynch, Anne C.: See Botta, Mrs.

McIntosh, Maria J.: Of Providence, R.I.; friend of Sarah Helen Whitman; Poe presented a copy of *Eureka* to Miss McIntosh just after its publication in 1848.

Mahan, Milo (1819–1870): Of Suffolk, Va.; priest, Church of Holy Communion (Episcopal), New York City, 1846–1847.

Mr. G.: See Gill, William F.

Mr. H.: See Hopkins, John H.

Mr. R.: See Richmond, Charles B.

Mrs. S.: See Houghton, Marie Louise Shew

Mrs. W.: See Whitman, Sarah Helen

Morison, N. H.: Official at the Peabody Institute, Baltimore; friend of Neilson Poe's; copied several letters from Mrs. Clemm to Neilson Poe for Ingram.

Morris, George Pope (1802–1864): Journalist and minor poet; known as "General" Morris; coeditor, with N. P. Willis, of the New York *Mirror* and *Home Journal*; remembered for his sentimental and popular verse, "Woodman, Spare that Tree."

Mott, Valentine (1785–1865): Of New York; noted surgeon, pioneer in vein surgery; confirmed Mrs. Houghton's diagnosis that Poe suffered from a brain lesion.

Muddie: Marie Poe Clemm, Poe's aunt and mother-in-law.

Mulenberg, William Augustus (1796–1877): Rector of Church of the Holy Communion, New York City, in 1846; Poe attended services at least once with Mrs. Shew and a friend and spoke well of the minister.

Neal, John (1793–1876): Of Portland, Maine; novelist, editor of the *Yankee*; wrote encouraging review of Poe's early verses; Poe dedicated *Tamerlane* to him in 1827.

Nichols, Mary Sargeant Neal Gove (1810–1884): Of New York and London; author, reformer, water-cure physician; knew and visited the Poes at Fordham in 1847; introduced Marie Louise Shew into the Poe household just before Virginia Poe's death; in London, helped Ingram locate Marie Louise Shew Houghton in America.

Osgood, Frances Sargent Locke (1811–1850): Of Massachusetts and New York; lively, popular member of the New York literati; Poe admired and praised her and her verses extravagantly in print; Griswold wrote her obituary and quoted her last poem "Israfel" in it, but changing the masculine pronouns to feminine, since he admired her too, and was jealous of Poe's interest in her and her interest in Poe.

Osgood, Samuel Stillman (1808–1885): Artist; married Frances Sargent Locke; painted portrait of Poe about 1845, which now belongs to the New York Historical Society.

Ostrom, John Ward, ed. *The Letters of Edgar Allan Poe*. 2 vols.; Cambridge: Harvard University Press, 1948.

Pabodie, William J.: (d. 1870): Close friend of Sarah Helen Whitman in

Providence; Poe's host on occasions; did not wish Mrs. Whitman to marry Poe; wrote letters to the editor of the New York *Tribune* in June, 1852, in defense of Poe and challenging Griswold's statements about Poe.

Poe, Amelia Fitzgerald (1832–1913): Of Baltimore; cousin of Edgar Poe; daughter of Judge Neilson Poe; Ingram's "spy" on the Poe scholarship of J. H. Whitty, Killis Campbell, and Eugene Didier; sent fifty-five letters to Ingram in addition to family records and materials for his biography.

Poe, Josephine Emily (b. 1808): Of Baltimore; daughter of William and Harriet Clemm; Maria Poe Clemm's stepdaughter; wife of Neilson Poe.

Poe, Neilson (b. 1809): Of Baltimore; cousin of Edgar Poe; paid for Poe's burial in Westminster Churchyard in 1849; lawyer, later became Judge; "Neilson" was pronounced "Nelson" in Virginia, as well as Maryland.

Poe, Nelson: See Poe, Neilson.

Powell, George W.: A Baltimore minister who delivered lectures on Poe's works to raise funds for Rosalie Poe.

Quinn, Arthur Hobson: *Edgar Allan Poe: A Critical Biography.* New York: D. Appleton-Century Company, 1941.

Redfield, Justus Starr (1810–1888): Publisher, diplomat; published Griswold's four-volume edition of Poe's works between 1850 and 1856.

Richmond, Charles B. (d. 1873): Well-to-do paper manufacturer in Lowell, Mass.; husband of Nancy Locke Heywood, Poe's "Annie."

Richmond, Nancy Locke Heywood (1820–1898): Wife of Charles B. Richmond; probably Poe's greatest love; changed her name legally to "Annie," after her husband's death in 1873, because Poe had written one of his most celebrated poems to her under that name; copied for Ingram all of the letters Poe addressed to her, the only copies she ever made for anyone.

Robins, Sallie E.: Of Putnam, Ohio; a young Poe enthusiast who wrote articles and signed them "S.E.R.," obviously to disguise her sex; planned complete vindication of Poe's name and invited Mrs. Clemm to accompany her to Europe and then live as a permanent guest in her Ohio home to help her with the vindication; these plans were not carried out because shortly after Mrs. Clemm's arrival in Ohio in the early 1860s, Miss Robins was taken, hopelessly mad, to an asylum.

Rouse, William: Friend of Annie Richmond to whom she gave as a souvenir Poe's letter to William E. Burton, dated June 1, 1840, which proved that Poe wrote "The Journal of Julius Rodman"; Rouse made a perfect copy of this letter for Ingram in May 1877, allowing Ingram to score an important "find" in Poe's writings.

Royster, Sarah Elmira Shelton (d. 1888): Poe's boyhood sweetheart in Richmond; Poe proposed marriage to her in 1849, when she was a fairly wealthy widow.

Sarah: See Heywood, Sarah H.

Scharf, John Thomas (1843–1898): Historian; chronicler of Baltimore City.

S.E.R.: Pseudonym of Sallie E. Robins.

Shelton, Mrs.: See Royster, Sarah Elmira.

Shew, Mrs.: See Houghton, Marie Louise.

Snodgrass, Joseph Evans, Dr.: Editor, with Nathan C. Brooks, of the *American Museum of Science, Literature and the Arts*, in Baltimore; Poe contributed "Ligeia, " among other stories and articles; Joseph Walker called on Dr. Snodgrass to help when he found Poe dying in Baltimore.

Stanard, Jane Stith Craig (d. 1824): Mother of Poe's boyhood friend in Richmond, Robert Stanard; reported inspiration of Poe's great lyric poem, "To Helen."

"Stannard, Mrs.": See Stanard, Jane Stith Craig.

Star, Mary Jenning (d. 1887): Of Baltimore; perhaps the object of Poe's early admiration; see August Van Cleef's article, "Poe's Mary," in *Harper's Magazine*, LXXVII (March, 1889), 634–40, for a highly imaginative account of this romance.

Starr, Mary: See Star, Mary Jenning.

Stoddard, Richard Henry (1825–1903): Poet, editor, biographer; author of hostile biographical article, "Edgar Allan Poe," in *Harper's Magazine*, September, 1872.

Tabb, John Banister (1845–1909): As a seminarian, attended unveiling of Poe's monument in Baltimore in 1875; became Roman Catholic priest; wrote many poems in defense of Poe and attacking Poe's defamers.

Thompson, John Reuben (1823–1873): Lawyer, editor; owner of the *Southern Literary Messenger*, 1847–1853, and editor from 1853 to 1860; unreliable witness and reporter of Poe's actions.

Valentine, Edward Virginius (1838–1930): Richmond sculptor; friend of the second Mrs. John Allan; loyal ally and correspondent of Ingram's for thirty-five years.

Weiss, Mrs. John: See Weiss, Susan Archer Talley.

Weiss, Susan Archer Talley: Of Richmond; published a long and valuable article of her memories of Poe in *Scribner's Monthly*, March, 1878, pp. 707–716; later grew more loquacious and less dependable in her many accounts of her meetings with Poe.

White, Thomas Willis (1788–1843): Printer, publisher, founder and sometimes editor of the *Southern Literary Messenger* in 1834; gave Poe a job on the magazine in 1835; Poe became editor in December, 1835.

Whitman, Sarah Helen Power (1803–1878): Of Providence, R.I.; author, poetess, spiritualist; fiancée to Poe after Virginia Poe died; sent Ingram her recollections, newsclippings, copies of portions of her letters from Poe, copies of daguerreotypes of Poe; Ingram hailed her as his "Providence," and she was that, in many ways, in helping him build Poe biography.

Willis, Nathaniel Parker (1806–1867): Journalist, poet, editor; friend of Poe as well as his employer briefly.

Woodberry, George E.: *The Life of Edgar Allan Poe*. 2 vols.; Boston and New York: Houghton Mifflin Company, 1909.

Bibliography I
Annotated bibliography, in chronological order, of the works John H. Ingram published concerning Edgar Allan Poe

Books

The Works of Edgar Allan Poe. 4 vols. Edinburgh: Adam and Charles Black, 1874–75. New York: W. J. Widdleton, 1876. Black's was the first volume printing in which the type was set and the entire job was executed by women printers.

Edgar Allan Poe: His Life, Letters, and Opinions. With Portraits of Poe and his Mother. 2 vols. London: John Hogg, Paternoster Row, 1880. New York: Cassell, Petter, Galpin & Co., 1880.

Tales and Poems by Edgar Allan Poe; with Biographical Essay by John H. Ingram, and Fourteen Original Etchings, Three Photogravures, and a New Etched Portrait. 4 vols. London: John C. Nimmo, 1884.

Tales by Edgar Allan Poe. Edited by John H. Ingram. Tauchnitz Edition. Leipzig: Bernhard Tauchnitz, 1884. Paris: Librarie Gaulon & Fils, 1884.

Poems and Essays by Edgar Allan Poe. Edited by John H. Ingram. Tauchnitz Edition. Leipzig: Bernhard Tauchnitz, 1884. Paris: Librarie Gaulon & Fils, 1884.

The Raven of Edgar Poe. With Commentary by John H. Ingram. London: George Redway, 1885.

The Life and Letters of Edgar Allan Poe. London, New York, and Melbourne: Ward, Lock, Bowden & Co., 1886. The Minerva Library of Famous Books. This is a one-volume reprint of Ingram's 1880 *Edgar Allan Poe: His Life, Letters, and Opinions.* It is not a revised edition; only a few bibliographical items have been added.

The Complete Poetical Works and Essays on Poetry of Edgar Allan Poe, Together with His Narrative of Arthur Gordon Pym. Edited, annotated, and arranged, with Memoir, by John H. Ingram. London and New York: Frederick Warne & Co., 1888. Variorum edition.

Poems of Edgar Allan Poe, with a Sketch of the Author. London: George Routledge & Sons, Ltd., 1909. New York: E. P. Dutton & Company, 1909. Muses Library edition.

Letters Chiefly Concerning Edgar Allan Poe from Algernon Charles Swinburne to John Henry Ingram. Printed for Thomas J. Wise, 1910. Edition limited to twenty copies.

"The True Story of Edgar Allan Poe." Unpublished biography of Poe completed about 1916. Manuscript in Ingram Poe Papers, University of Virginia Library.

Magazine Articles and Newspaper Letters

1874

"New Facts About Edgar Allan Poe." London *Mirror*, January 24, 1874.

"More New Facts About Edgar Allan Poe." London *Mirror*, February 21, 1874, pp. 248–50.

"Edgar Allan Poe's Early Poems." *Gentleman's Magazine*, XII (May, 1874), 580–86. Reprinted in *Every Saturday*.

"Edgar Poe." *Temple Bar*, June, 1874. Reprinted in the *Eclectic Magazine*, XX (August, 1874), 203–210.

Letter to George W. Eveleth requesting information about Poe. Published in the *Southern Review*, XV (October, 1874), 428–30. Reproduced in Chapter I of this volume.

"Poe and Griswold's *Memoir*." Published in the *Eclectic Magazine* sometime in 1874. Unlocated.

1875

Ingram published a caustic review of R. H. Stoddard's memoir of Poe which prefaced Stoddard's edition of Poe's poems, issued in New York by W. J. Widdleton, on March 9, 1875. This review of Ingram's was printed in the *Civil Service Review*, April 13, 1875.

Review of Henry Curwen's *Sorrow and Song: Studies of Literary Struggle. Academy*, VII (March 13, 1875), 262–63. This review is principally concerned with Poe matters.

"Edgar Allan Poe." *International Review*, II (March–April, 1875), 145–72. Condensation of Ingram's memoir prefacing his edition of Poe's works.

An article on "The Philosophy of Handwriting" printed before April 14, 1875. Unlocated.

"Miss Rosalie Poe." Obituary printed in London *Mirror* (August 15, 1874), 231.
"Poe's Politian." First printed in the *London Magazine*. Reprinted in the
  Southern Magazine, XVII (November, 1875), 588–94.

1876

"The Guild of Literature." *Athenaeum*, January 1, 1876, No. 2514. Someone has protested R. H. Horne's receiving a pension awarded out of the
  Civil List. Ingram takes violent issue with the protester.
"A Disclaimer." *Athenaeum*, January 15, 1876, No. 2516, p. 89. Ingram violently attacks William F. Gill.
"Edgar Allan Poe a Plagiarist." *Notes and Queries*, V, 377, May 6, 1876. Ingram
  sharply questions someone signing himself "Uneda" as to how, when, and
  where it was proved that Poe stole his story "The Gold Bug." Ingram also
  denies Uneda's statement that Poe was "a most unprincipled man."
"Edgar Allan Poe." *Notes and Queries*, V, 455, June 3, 1876. Ingram replies to
  J. Brander Matthew's remarks in *Notes and Queries*, V, 386–87, May 13,
  1876, about Mrs. Clemm's being the mother of Poe's *first* wife, informing
  Poe's "English admirers" that Poe was but once married, and then to his
  cousin, Virginia Clemm.
"Poe's Suppressed Poetry." New York *Daily Graphic*, Thursday, June 8, 1876.
  Reprinted from the *Belgravia* for June. This is a reprint of most of the poems
  in Poe's *Tamerlane*. Ingram had just found the first known copy of the book
  in the British Museum Library.
"E. A. Poe a Plagiarist." *Notes and Queries*, V, 78, July 22, 1876. "Uneda" has
  answered Ingram's note of May 6th, saying that Miss Imogene Sherburne,
  author of *Imogene; or, the Pirate's Treasure*, has personally told his friend
  that Poe plagiarized the plot and the language of her story for his "The Gold
  Bug." Ingram asks "Uneda" in this note to state, in justice to the dead, and
  for the satisfaction of the living, how, when, and where, this charge of
  literary theft was *proved*. Shortly thereafter, again in *Notes and Queries*,
  "Uneda" surrendered, admitting that Miss Sherburne had imposed upon
  his friend, for he has found a copy of her tale, and Poe's "The Gold Bug"
  bears no resemblance to it whatsoever. Another public triumph for Ingram.
  "Uneda's" apology appeared in *Notes and Queries*, V, 175, August 11, 1877.
"The Bibliography of Edgar Poe." *Athenaeum*, July 29, 1876, pp. 145–46.
  Ingram has assembled all four volumes of Poe's poems, and in this long
  article he presents the first bibliographical study of the variants.
"Edgar Allan Poe's 'Raven'." *Notes and Queries*, VI, 108, August 5, 1876.
  Ingram wants information about Lewis Gidley's translation of "The Raven"
  into Latin, and will welcome copies of any other translations.
"The Lunar Hoax." *Athenaeum*, August 19, 1876, pp. 241–42. A Mr. Proctor
  has written a paper, "On the Lunar Hoax," in the *Belgravia Magazine* for

August, and Ingram sets him straight about the author being Richard *Adams* Locke and not Richard *Alton* Locke, and refers his readers to Volume IV of his edition of Poe's works for Poe's analysis and demolition of the absurdities of Locke's "Moon Story."

"The Bibliography of Edgar Poe." *Athenaeum*, August 19, 1876, p. 241. H. Buxton Foreman has questioned Ingram's statement about there being "earlier publications" of "The Raven" before 1845. In this brief article Ingram replies that he is without data and opportunity of reference while traveling as he is without access to his records, but on his return to London he will give Mr. Foreman a complete answer.

"John Neal." *Athenaeum*, October 14, 1876. An obituary for John Neal who had died on June 20, 1876.

1877

A review of *The Life and Poems of Edgar Allan Poe; and Additional Poems*. Edited by E. L. Didier. New York: Widdleton, 1877. *Athenaeum*, February 10, 1877. Unsigned, but written by Ingram.

"Recent Edgar Poe Literature." *Civil Service Review*, February 17, 1877, p. 161.

A review of *The Life of Edgar Allan Poe* by William F. Gill (New York: C. T. Dillingham). *Athenaeum*, October 6, 1877. Unsigned, but written by Ingram. In this review Ingram lets slip the fact that he wrote the unsigned review of Didier's book by saying "Could he have seen our recent review of Mr. Didier's volume. . . ."

"The Journal of Julius Rodman: A Newly-Discovered Work by the Late E. A. Poe." *Mirror of Literature*, November 3, 1877.

1878

"Unpublished Correspondence by Edgar A. Poe." *Appleton's Journal*, May, 1878, IV, 421–29.

Same article published as "Unknown Correspondence of Edgar Poe." *New Quarterly Magazine*, XIX (April, 1878), 1–30.

Same article translated into Italian and published as "Edgar Poe E il suo Carteggio Inidito." *Revista Europe*, May and June, 1878.

"Mrs. Sarah Helen Whitman." *Athenaeum*, July 20, 1878, p. 80. Obituary for Mrs. Whitman who had died in Providence on June 27, 1878.

"Edgar Poe's 'Raven'." *Athenaeum*, August 17, 1878. A very long article in which Ingram details the genesis of Poe's familiar poem.

"Edgar Allan Poe." Richmond *Standard*, October 16, 1878. A long letter to the editor in which Ingram denounces William F. Gill's *Life of Poe* as a theft of his own work on Poe.

"Poe and His English Schoolmaster." *Athenaeum*, October 26, 1878. A long article discussing Dr. Bransby, "William Wilson," and Gill's foolish reproduction of a portrait of a man named William Cook, purporting to be a portrait of Dr. Bransby.

1880

A letter to *Athenaeum* before June, 1880, in which Ingram accuses E. C. Stedman with crediting W. F. Gill with a matter of interest relative to Poe which Gill copied verbatim from Ingram's work. Ingram also writes that Stedman is simply repeating various exploded myths and libels on Poe. Unlocated.

"Edgar Poe's Life." *Academy*, July 31, 1880, p. 83. In this long article, Ingram refutes questioning of his statements in his two-volume *Life* about Poe's date of birth, school days at Stoke Newington, dimissal from West Point, and Poe's death. Moncure D. Conway had reviewed the two volumes and had raised these questions, in *Academy*, July 21, 1880, pp. 55–56.

An article in which Ingram challenges statements made by R. H. Stoddard in his article, "Some Myths in the Life of Poe." New York *Home Journal*, August 4, 1880. Unlocated.

"Stella (S. A. Lewis)." *Athenaeum*, December 4, 1880. Obituary, unsigned, but Ingram wrote it. Mrs. Lewis had died in London on November 24; her remains were brought back to America for burial.

1881

"Edgar Allan Poe." By Ingram H. János-tól. *Budapesti Szemle*, January, 1881, pp. 93–108. A condensation of Ingram's Memoir of Poe.

A letter to the editor of *Critic*, March 10, 1881. Ingram denies that Poe was fond of "mystifying his readers," as he is accused of being, in an article in *Scribner's Monthly* for February. Since Colonel Thomas W. Higginson has been unable to find, in a search of Tieck, that "Journey into the Blue Distance," to which Poe refers in "The Fall of the House of Usher," he should know that "Das alte Buch und die Reise ins Blaue hinein" is Tieck's *chef d'oeuvre*.

1883

."Edgar Poe and His Biographers." *Academy*, October 13, 1883, pp. 248–49. Ingram defends himself against charges brought by an anonymous writer in *Temple Bar* that he has tried to "whitewash" Poe.

1884

"Ein Dichterleben." Biographische Skizze von John H. Ingram, translated by Leopold Katscher. *Der Salon, fur Literatur, Kunst and Gesellschraft*, 26–40. A German translation of Ingram's memoir which was attached to the 1884 edition of Poe's *Tales and Poems*, published by John Nimmo.

A letter to the editor of the Richmond *Dispatch* in which Ingram denies that Poe wrote the poems "The Skeleton Hand" and "The Magician." Undated copy in the Ingram Poe Collection, Item 836.

post 1886

"Poe, the Cipher Wizard." Undated, unidentified newsclipping in the Ingram Poe Collection, Item 864. Ingram complains to the editor of this English newspaper that "your weekly" has printed this article which can be found in his own 1886 edition of Poe's life; he adds, "Our American cousins are very fond of extracts from my work; if they would only quote correctly, and without adornments, I should feel more gratified. As for Mr. R. H. Stoddard's refraining from getting too close to the poet, those who know the fact of their acquaintance will not be surprised. It was prudent. Poe was a hard hitter." Poe did threaten on one occasion to "kick Stoddard down the stairs."

1895

Review of Volumes I–IV of "The Chicago Poe," edited by G. E. Woodberry and E. C. Stedman (Chicago: Stone & Kimball, 1895). *Athenaeum*, December 21, 1895, pp. 865–66.

1896

Review of Volumes V–X of "The Chicago Poe." *Athenaeum*, March 28, 1896, pp. 406–407. In these two reviews, Ingram roundly condemns everything edited by Woodberry, faintly praises those parts edited by E. C. Stedman.

1899

Review of the Leonard Smithers & Co. edition of Poe's *The Raven and The Pit and the Pendulum*. Manuscript in Ingram's handwriting in the Ingram Poe Collection, Item 403.

1902

"New Glimpses of Poe." *Athenaeum*, March 1, 1902, p. 274. Ingram observes that there is no fresh material in Professor Harrison's article, noticed in *Athenaeum*'s last number, under the above title.

1904

"Edgar Poe's Poem of 'The Bells'." *Athenaeum*, December 3, 1904. A Mr. Waddington refers to the evolution of Poe's poem in his article on Tennyson's "The Death of the Old Year," and he made some errors which Ingram says were probably derived from an American source. Ingram sets the record straight.

1905

Ingram engages in a literary quarrel with R. G. T. Coventry and J. B. Wallis. In an article on lyrical poetry in *Academy*, November 4, 1905, Coventry offended Ingram by his remarks on Poe's adverse criticism of Wordsworth. Ingram engaged him in the same magazine on November 18; J. B. Wallis replied to Ingram on November 25; Ingram answered again on December 2; Coventry closed the argument on December 9.

1907

"Edgar Allan Poe and 'Stella.'" *Albany Review*, July, 1907, 417–23.
"Poet and Literary Women." *Evening Standard and St. James Gazette*, July 11, 1907. The first two-and-one-half pages of "Edgar Allan Poe and 'Stella'" are reprinted verbatim.

1909

"Edgar Allan Poe's Lost Poem 'The Beautiful Physician.'" *New York Bookman*, XXVIII (January, 1909), 452–54.
"Edgar Poe and Some of His Friends." *London Bookman*, Poe Centenary Number, January, 1909, pp. 167–73.
"Edgar Poe et Ses Amis." *Mercure de France*, January 16, 1909, pp. 208–219. Translated and reprinted with Ingram's permission.
Letter to the editor of the Bristol *Times and Mirror*, January 16, 1909. "C.W." has written a paragraph in this newspaper calling G. E. Woodberry "Poe's best biographer." Ingram informs the editor and "C.W." that Woodberry's volumes are so largely pirated from his own work on Poe that they may not be imported or sold in the British Empire, and he wants to know where "C.W." got the copy he refers to.

An article on W. C. Brownell, in the *Review of Reviews*, January, 1909. Unlocated.

"Poe and Mrs. Whitman." A letter to the editor of the New York *Tribune*, January 18, 1909.

"Variations in Edgar Poe's Poetry." *Bibliophile*, III (May, 1909), 128–36.

"The Poe Cult." *Athenaeum*, August 28, 1909, p. 238. Ingram informs British publishers and booksellers that E. L. Didier's book, *The Poe Cult*, infringes on his copyrights and contains gross libels on his integrity; he will, therefore, take legal proceedings against anyone circulating the book.

"The Poe Cult." *Athenaeum*, October 16, 1909, p. 462. Didier has answered in *Athenaeum* for September 22, 1909, pp. 425–26, saying that no one in America has been able to find what Ingram's "copyrights" are; that Ingram did steal valuable Poe items from the Houghton family, and he, Didier, can prove it; and, finally, that all of Ingram's threats of law suits are empty talk. Ingram replies in this issue of *Athenaeum* with words to the effect that Didier is a liar.

1916

"Edgar Allan Poe." *Notes and Queries*, I, January, 1916. Someone has written in a question about the location of Dr. Bransby's school in Stoke Newington, saying there is "confusion" about the matter. Ingram replies, tartly, in this which is probably his last publication, that there is no confusion in his mind about it.

Bibliography II
Annotated bibliography, in chronological order, of the works John H. Ingram published about subjects other than Edgar Allan Poe

Books

Poems by Dalton Stone. Ingram's first use of a pseudonym. Volume published in 1863, but quickly suppressed. Listed in *Lippincott's Pronouncing Biographical Dictionary*, but not listed in Library of Congress or British Museum Library catalogues of suppressed volumes. Walter Hamilton reproduced one of the poems from this volume, "Hope: An Allegory," saying its metre was adapted from Poe's "Ulalume," in *Parodies* (London: Reeves and Turner, 1885), II, 66.

Flora Symbolica: Or The Language and Sentiment of Flowers. Including Floral Poetry, Original and Selected. London: F. W. Warne & Co., 1868; New York: Scribner, Welford & Co., 1868.

The Philosophy of Handwriting, by Don Felix de Salmanca. London: Chatto & Windus, 1879. An imitation of Poe's *Autography*, and Ingram's second use of a pseudonym.

The Bird of Truth (translated from the Spanish of Fernan Cabellero). Introduction by John H. Ingram. London: Sonneschen & Allan, 1881. Part of the *Illustrated Library of Fairy Tales*.

Claimants to Royalty. London: David Bogue, 1882.

The Family of Chatterton. New Facts Relating to the Chatterton Family. Reprint of correspondence between J. Taylor and John H. Ingram. 1882 (?). (Information from the British Museum Library Catalogue.)

Oliver Madox-Brown: A Biographical Sketch. London: Elliot Stock, 1883.

Haunted Homes and Family Traditions of Great Britain. London: W. H. Allen, 1883. A *Second Series* was published in 1884.

Poetical Works of Elizabeth Barrett Browning, with a Memoir, edited by John H. Ingram. London, 1886.

Elizabeth Barrett Browning. Cambridge: John Wilson & Sons, University Press, 1888. Boston: Roberts Brothers, 1890. *Famous Women Series*. This was the first biography of Mrs. Browning. Ingram discovered in his research that Miss Barrett had concealed her real date of birth; the result was that Robert Browning broke off all relations with Ingram before the publication of the book.

The Life of Robert Burns, by John Gibson Lockhart. Revised Edition. With new notes, appendices, and literary illustrations, by John H. Ingram. London, New York, and Melbourne: Ward, Lock, & Bowden & Co., 1890.

The Poets and the Poetry of the Century, edited by A. H. Miles. John H. Ingram contributed biographical sketches and excerpts from the poetry of George Darley, William Motherwell, James Clarence Mangan, Walter Thornbury, Oliver Madox-Brown, and Eliza Cook. 10 vols. London: Hutchinson & Co., 1891/92.

Sylvia, or The May Queen, by George Darley. With a biographical sketch of the author by John H. Ingram. London: Lover's Library, 1892.

Christopher Marlowe and His Associates. London: Grant Richards, 1904.

The True Chatterton. A New Study from Original Documents. London: T. Fisher Unwin, 1910.

Marlowe and His Poetry. London: George C. Harrap & Co., 1914. *Poetry and Life Series*.

Chatterton and His Poetry. London: George G. Harrap & Co., 1916. *Poetry and Life Series*.

Articles

1876

Notes and Queries, VI (July 29, 1876), 95. Ingram quotes a letter of Byron's in which he denies that he wrote "The Vampire."

1877

Athenaeum, November 17, 1877, announces that a critical and biographical article, by Ingram, on James Clarence Mangan, the Irish poet, will appear in the December number of the *Dublin University Magazine*.

1880

"A Posthumous Work of Théophile Gautier." *Academy*, August 7, 1880, p. 100. Ingram corrects M. Paul Bourget's apparent misapprehension concerning a "so-called" posthumous work of Gautier's.

1882

"The Poetry of Oliver Wendell Holmes." *Academy*, January 7, 1882, pp. 4–5. A review of a new edition of Holmes' poetry.

1883

"Chatterton and His Associates." *Harper's Magazine*, July, 1883, p. 225.

1889

"A New View of Marlowe." *Universal Review*, July, 1889.

1913

"Call a Spade a Spade." *London Bookman*, April, 1913. A review of Patrick MacGill's *Songs of the Dead End*.

Index